STUDIES IN LANGUAGE AND REASON

STUDIES IN LANGUAGE AND REASON

İlham Dilman

BARNES & NOBLE BOOKS
TOTOWA, NEW JERSEY

First published in the U.S.A. 1981 by
BARNES & NOBLE BOOKS
81, Adams Drive, Totowa,
New Jersey, 07512
ISBN 0–06–491691–X
LCN 79–55527

Printed in Hong Kong

Contents

192
D588s

Preface

These studies were written in the last four years. In different ways they all explore the same question: whether the forms of our language and our most fundamental beliefs are responsible to reason.

Both Plato and Wittgenstein were concerned with this question. Accordingly the book opens with some reflections on Plato's contribution to it in the *Phaedo*. Plato developed his notion of the Forms at least partly in response to this two-sided question: to meet the challenge of philosophical scepticism and to understand how it is possible to acquire values without surrendering one's autonomy. A discussion of this latter issue is continued in the studies on Hume, Wisdom and 'Self-Knowledge and Identity'.

A person's individual identity depends on the language and culture in which he grows up and on the most fundamental beliefs he has made his own. These determine both what it is possible for him to understand or make sense of and what it is possible for him to decide to do. The way Hume separated the understanding and the will made it difficult for him to see how a consideration of reasons could play a part in determining the will. This question is examined in the second part of my discussion of Hume.

Professor Wisdom, who has been equally sensitive to the challenge of philosophical scepticism, has thought of Hume's concession to feeling to be a concession to scepticism in the sphere of moral and religious belief, one which needs to be resisted. He quotes Hume in his paper on 'Gods'—'... after every circumstance, every relation is known, the understanding has no further room to operate' (Wisdom, 1953, p. 156)—and argues that Hume's conception of reason is too restricted. While Wisdom is right on this point, emphasis on it leads him to ignore something equally important which Hume was straining after, what may be called 'the dimension

of the personal' in moral beliefs. Both Plato and Wittgenstein ⸱
stressed this in their different ways.

Does this threaten the place of reason in ethics and religion?
'How we judge an action morally does not only depend on
what the action is like, but also on what *we* are like. If it does
depend on what the action is like then it is amenable to
reasoning. But is what we are like, in the sense of where we
stand morally, also amenable to the scrutiny of reason? Can
one ask "Are the values that I accept the right values?", as one
can ask "Was that the right thing to do?"?' I argue for an
affirmative answer (Hume I and II—especially sections I and
VI). The same question comes up in relation to religious belief
in 'Wisdom I: Religion and Reason'. It is the role of belief here
as measure or criterion, and the reference which
characterising it as true makes to 'the dimension of the
personal', so that conviction and commitment are
inseparable, that poses this question in an acute form for me.

The role of belief as measure or criterion takes us to the
other side of the issue raised by Plato's Forms. Are the forms
of understanding that are embedded in our language
responsible to any reality independent of that language? If
they are not susceptible to any justification does that leave
them suspended in mid-air? Does it make them akin to what is
arbitrary? In 'Universals and Family Resemblances', section
IV, where I criticise Bambrough for the kind of 'realism' he
imputes to Wittgenstein, I discuss one aspect of this question. I
argue that what makes a particular classification genuine and,
therefore, non-arbitrary is not its grounding in certain facts—
namely the similarities and differences that exist
independently of any language—but the way it interlocks with
our use of language in other connections and connects with
ways of going on with the use of words which we find natural,
given the way we have been brought up. Where we have
objects to classify, we have already names for them and so a
whole range of similarities and differences from which we
choose in classifying them in the ways we do. We must already
have come a long way before we can classify things; we must
already have things to classify. So the similarities and
differences that hold between what we already call by a certain
name cannot give us the basis for our use of that name.
Realism, therefore, involves a vicious circle, and trying to give

an ultimate justification of our systems of classification with reference to 'objective similarities and differences' is like trying to lift yourself up by your boot-straps.

This question comes up for consideration also in 'Meaning and Circumstances'. There I consider Wittgenstein's treatment of the question: What is being able to speak and understand a language apart from knowing its vocabulary and how to form sentences? I discuss Wittgenstein's claim that well-formed sentences are not necessarily meaningful. As he pointed out, a mouth smiles in a smiling face and a smiling face is one we see under the aspect of a smile 'in the normal play of expressions'. Freeze the smile, so that it does not change with varying circumstances, and you no longer have a smile at all. Sentences too are used in the course of conversation and human intercourse, in the traffic of human life. Their significance, their identity as parts of a language we understand, the meanings of the words in them, depends on this.

In philosophy, especially in trying to meet scepticism or resist the tide of relativism, there is a strong temptation to try and state what is presupposed by the intelligibility of the language we use, to affirm background 'beliefs' (the inverted commas are essential here) that belong to the framework of our thought and language. We try to put into words what we take for granted, what remains unmentioned in our use of language and in our reasonings. We then come up with sentences which seem to state truths that are too obvious to need stating in normal circumstances. It seems that the threat of philosophical scepticism and relativism does provide perfectly legitimate circumstances for stating these truths: 'Human beings have consciousness; they are not automata' (Descartes). 'There are uniformities in nature' (Hume, Russell). 'There are recurrent characteristics in the world' (H. H. Price). 'There are objective similarities and differences' (Bambrough). Take the last—considered in my discussion of Bambrough's paper. Bambrough would add: 'These exist independently of language, just as planets and galaxies do. There were planets and galaxies before there were any human beings on earth and any language in which this could be stated.' I comment on a similar response in 'Meaning and Circumstances': 'Whether we say it or not, the fact remains that I am a human being.

This is independent of language—of whether or not I ever need to say it.'

Wittgenstein's treatment of the question of the meaning of sentences is obviously directly relevant to the question of whether we can intelligibly say what Professor Price or Bambrough wish to insist on, and also to the question of what sense we can make of the claim that there are uniformities of nature: 'Is there not some truth in the conviction that it is a *fact* that there is at least some order or uniformity in natural phenomena without which it would not be possible to investigate them, suggest explanations and make predictions at all?' I have already discussed this question at some length in *Induction and Deduction*, chapter 4, and in the present work I return to some of the issues which an inclination to give an affirmative answer raises.

The ultimate basis of our forms of thought and language; the ultimate basis of our most fundamental beliefs and identity: this, in brief, is the theme that runs through and links together the individual studies presented in this book.

The two studies on Wisdom have appeared in the *Canadian Journal of Philosophy* (vol. V, no. 4, December 1975). I would like to thank the Canadian Association for Publishing in Philosophy for permission to reprint them here.

I would also like to thank Mrs Drury for kindly giving me permission to quote a passage from an unpublished work by Dr Drury entitled *Letters to a Student of Philosophy*.

May 1979   İLHAM DİLMAN

1 *Phaedo* I: 'Learning as Recollection'

I A Problem for Plato

Socrates points out in the *Phaedo* that we could not possibly have derived the notion of absolute equality (the one signified in mathematical equations by the sign of equality) from the comparison of sensible objects. For to be able to carry out such comparisons we would have to understand what it means for two objects to be of equal length. Of course, we do learn or acquire concepts from experience, by comparison and abstraction. But such learning presupposes certain categories of thought and standards of comparison which cannot themselves be derived from experience by comparison and abstraction. Plato is right to point this out. But unable to think of an alternative way in which we may have acquired these concepts he concludes that we must have acquired them in a previous life when we were not dependent on the senses, that we must have been born with them, though they were not accessible to us at first. He describes the process of their becoming accessible as *recollection*. Thus just as we can be ignorant about something without recognising our ignorance (e.g. Meno on virtue—see Plato 1961, 80b), we can also know it without realising that we do (e.g. Meno's slave boy on how to double the area of a square whose sides are two feet long).

So we can come to formulate a truth by ourselves which, in one sense, we certainly do not know. We can do so without being given any new information. That is we can, in a sense, extend our knowledge by reflection on what we already know. But there is here another sense in which what we thus come to is already contained in what we know, so that coming to it is a form of 're-collection'. The philosophical problem is to elucidate the sense in which we do not know what we come to in this way and the sense in which it is contained in what we already know.

II Forms and Mathematical Discoveries

But how does someone extract a new mathematical truth from the knowledge he already possesses? There are two distinctions that need to be made here. The first one is between *proof* in mathematics and *calculation*, and the second is between discovering a truth that is new to mathematics and discovering one that is new only to the discoverer. In the *Meno* Plato gives us an example of a proof through which a slave boy with only a rudimentary knowledge of mathematics discovers a truth which is well known to Socrates but unknown to himself. I speak of proof here advisedly. For when one calculates one uses mathematics to draw conclusions that do not belong to mathematics. Thus one may calculate one's debts or one's expenses. A proof, on the other hand, establishes connections between mathematical concepts. It makes one see such a connection for the first time: 'I have never thought of this before.' Here the proof has brought one to something that is new to one even though it need not be new to others. And for this it is not even necessary that one should have discovered the proof oneself.

Because what one comes to here does not come from the senses, and because it is not conveyed to one by someone else either, one could say that it does not come to one from *outside*. Hence Socrates says that it must have been within one all along, though in a latent form. So what one grasps by the construction of the proof was 'within one', yet it is true whether one is convinced of it or not. It was there before one came to know it. That is one has come to a truth that is both *independent* of one's assent to it and also *contained* in one's thoughts. Unless it were thus independent we could not speak of its 'discovery'. Yet because it is contained in what one already knows the discovery is a form of recuperation. The truth which Meno's slave boy comes to is also something he recuperates, since nothing and nobody has put it in his mind. He comes to it himself. Yet it is not something that he makes up, since not anything that he says or thinks is acceptable. His thinking is subject to correction; it is answerable to public criteria.

'He comes to it on his own; what he comes to does not come to him from outside. Yet he is not the arbiter of its acceptability.' From this Plato concludes that he must have known it all along. Yet there is an obvious sense in which he did not know it, since he began by giving the wrong answers to Socrates: 'It's no use, Socrates, I just don't know.'

What Meno's boy has come to he has come to himself, and he has done so through reflection on what he already knows. This tells us something important about what it means to grasp a mathematical truth: to understand it, to know it is true, means seeing what makes it true, being able to prove it. It cannot simply be put into our minds by an outside source. Yet the possibility of seeing this, one's ability to prove it, to construct the proof oneself, or at least to follow it, presupposes a knowledge of mathematics in one, however elementary. And one cannot come to that knowledge oneself in the way that Meno's boy came to the knowledge elicited by Socrates' questions. One comes to it by instruction, and this involves learning things by rote—learning to count, to add, memorising the multiplication table and so on. This is essential to our ability to reason, to understand or prove anything in mathematics. Once this kind of *training* has built for us a firm piece of ground on which to stand, the process of furthering our understanding involves the kind of reasoning which Plato illustrates in the *Meno*.

Does Plato recognise this last point? In a way and to a certain extent he does. For he holds Meno's slave boy to have had an acquaintance with the Forms in a previous life; and this acquaintance, however acquired, is essential to the discovery he makes, essential to the possibility of his making such a discovery. But so is his ignorance of the truth he discovers. Yet it is sufficient for his ignorance to be confined to *this* truth. Plato does not have a clear recognition of this. He intends us to be impressed by the slave boy's ignorance, and this overshadows the knowledge he already possesses. For he can count, add lengths, compare areas and understand simple mathematical questions even if he doesn't always know the answers to them. So for Plato the knowledge or understanding which is essential to the possibility of engaging in the kind of reflection that leads to the grasp of a new mathematical truth remains something abstract and shadowy: it is something we are supposed to have acquired in a previous existence and then forgotten. He does not see that this knowledge finds expression in the life of the discoverer apart from and previous to the discovery he makes, that it consists in his ability to carry out various operations. If he had recognised that acquaintance with the requisite Forms consisted in this kind of ability he would have had little difficulty in appreciating the way it is acquired in *this* life and how it differs from the process of coming to new truths which, perceptively, he characterises as 'recollection'.

What one 'recollects' is in one's mind in the sense that it is contained in the mathematical knowledge or understanding which one already possesses. And one question is: In what way is that knowledge supposed to *contain* what one comes to through the kind of proof or reasoning illustrated in the *Meno*? The answer is that it is contained much in the way that the conclusion of a deductive argument is implicit in its premises. But how is it implicit or contained in the premises? One answer to this which applies at least to a restricted set of cases was provided by Wittgenstein in the *Tractatus*. I have discussed this and an aspect of Wittgenstein's later modification of it in *Induction and Deduction*. But putting this question aside, Plato seems to me to be right in this, namely that if a truth which one comes to is contained in the knowledge which one already possesses then its discovery is a form of recuperation or 're-collection'.

Still, unlike Plato, I do not think that all discoveries in mathematics are forms of recuperation. For although, of course, I agree with Plato that mathematical truths are timeless, I do not think that this means that mathematics itself is something that can properly be characterised as timeless. Thus, although I cannot argue this now, momentous discoveries in mathematics constitute *extensions* of mathematics. Here there is no distinction between mathematics and mathematical knowledge, so that an extension in our knowledge is an extension of mathematics. I am well aware of the distinction between a person's knowledge, which may be limited, and of what there is for him to know, which may be vast. But I am talking of 'mathematical knowledge' ('our knowledge of mathematics' or 'the early Greeks' knowledge of mathematics') in the sense of 'accepted opinion in mathematics at a given time in history', and not in the sense of the sum of what individuals know. Does that mean that there is no distinction between 'knowledge' and 'opinion' here? In reply let me ask another question: Can what is at the centre of what we regard as acceptable and beyond question in mathematics turn out to be false or mere opinion? Can we come to question it without our very conception of mathematics changing radically? Can we both question it and continue to talk of 'mathematics' as we did before? I admit that at its peripheries one can imagine discoveries that modify what is regarded as acceptable by the authorities so that it is no longer regarded as such. In these cases 'mathematical knowledge' and 'the accepted view' do not coincide. But by their very nature such cases are bound to be peripheral.

The questions that I raised in the above paragraph are very difficult questions which I cannot attempt to discuss in a brief space. I shall, therefore, content myself by pointing out that Plato's view that nothing that is new to us in mathematics can be new to mathematics itself, so that all mathematical discoveries are forms of recuperation, is at least questionable. It can be argued that developing a new proof in mathematics is more like 'saying something new', in the sense of an original contribution, than like 'making the implications of what has already been said clear and explicit'.

III   Forms and the Limits of Empiricism

What according to Plato we are supposed to learn in a previous life are the Forms and thus such mathematical concepts as number and equality as well as the particular numbers. He thinks that our knowledge of mathematical truths and of such operations as counting and adding flow from our knowledge of these Forms and so can be derived from it in a way that is best characterised as 'recollection'. I have suggested that if these truths may be said to be contained in the Forms, the reverse is just as true, namely that the Forms are an expression of what we accept as incontrovertibly true in mathematics and of what we regard as the correct way of carrying out mathematical operations. The Forms are not, as Plato thought, something over and above what we actually do in carrying out these operations. One could say that mathematical practice determines mathematical Forms rather than flow from them. This was my criticism of Plato's wider claim that all progress in mathematical knowledge is recollection. I have not denied that on an individual basis this is often true. On the contrary, I have tried to show how perceptive Plato's claim is in connection with the kind of example he discusses in the *Meno*.

In the *Phaedo* Socrates argues that since mathematical Forms are not exemplified in experience ('No two logs can be perfectly equal') they cannot be derived from what is exemplified in experience—by observation and abstraction. So far this view is sound. Socrates argues that we could not have acquired the idea of equality from a perception of sticks and stones of approximately equal length and size lying side by side. We would see them lying side by side, but we wouldn't think of them as equal unless we had the idea of equality. That idea cannot thus be derived from sense experience. Kant would have said that having this idea makes it possible for us to see the two sticks as equal in length. He would say that perception involves thought or judgment. Since there can be no perception, and more generally experience, without judgment, there must be some concepts in terms of which the judgments involved in experience are made. These concepts themselves, therefore, cannot be derived from experience. But this doesn't mean, as Kant points out, that we must have acquired these concepts *before* we had any experience: 'Though all our knowledge begins with experience, it does not follow that it all arises out of experience' (Kant, 1961, p. 41).

Wrongly thinking that it does follow, but rightly wanting to deny the above consequent, Plato wrongly ended by denying the above premise:

'It must have been *before* we began to see and hear and use the other senses that we got knowledge of the equal itself, of *what it is*' (75b).

'Now we were seeing and hearing, and were possessed of our other senses, weren't we, just as soon as we were born?'

'Certainly.'

'But we must, we're saying, have got our knowledge of the equal *before* these?'

'Yes.'

'Then it seems that we must have got it before we were born.'

'It seems so.'

'... And so we must have got pieces of knowledge of all those things before birth.' (75b–d).

This conclusion is unwarranted. Yet it is an important step in Socrates' arguments for the indestructibility and immorality of the soul. Still, it could be shown, I think, that what he wants to hold about the soul in this respect stands without this step. But with this I am not now concerned.

I said that Plato's view that we cannot derive our conception of what he calls Forms from what is given to us in sense experience is sound. What is sound in this view is expressed by Wittgenstein in the following remark: 'Do not believe that you have the concept of colour within you because you look at a coloured object—however you look' (Wittgenstein, 1967, §332). In other words, just because a creature can see coloured objects it doesn't mean that he knows what a colour is, that he has the concept of colour. In learning the meanings of words from ostensive definitions we are pointed at things which we can see, hear or otherwise experience. But can we learn or acquire all the concepts that enter our judgments in this way? Wittgenstein points out that 'we must already be master of a language in order to understand an ostensive definition', in order to understand what is pointed to, what we are supposed to abstract in forming a concept. Unless one can play chess, for instance, the words 'This is the king', accompanied by pointing to a chess-piece, will mean little to one—at least it will not mean what it is intended to mean. Thus the position a child is in when he learns to speak is very different from the one of an adult who learns a foreign language.

Does this mean, as Plato thinks, that if a young child is to be able to speak and judge, to acquire concepts, to learn new words, he must be in possession of certain concepts he could not have acquired in his life and which, therefore, he must have acquired in a previous existence? As I said, this does not follow in the least. Wittgenstein was speaking of the direct learning of new words, which is obviously part of learning to speak. But it is not the whole of it. So he emphasises another kind of learning, learning to act in certain ways, to respond to various situations, very much in the way in which a dog learns to do tricks. He calls the teaching from which such learning proceeds 'training', in contrast with 'giving explanations and definitions—including ostensive definitions'. It is this which makes it possible for the child to come to ask questions, among them questions about the meaning of words, and to understand explanations and definitions. Thus he learns some of the important concepts which belong with Plato's Forms *indirectly*. For instance, he acquires the concept of number, among other things, in learning to count. He acquires them in learning to act, to perform various operations—some elementary, and some (later) sophisticated: operations the learning of which presupposes familiarity with more elementary operations.

What is true and important in Plato's view here is that we cannot acquire all our concepts *directly*, through abstraction from experience and generalisation—since all abstraction and generalisation presuppose a grasp of certain concepts and operations.[1] But this doesn't mean that we cannot have acquired the grasp in question in this life. We acquire it *indirectly* in learning to act, in learning to do certain things.

So Kant and Wittgenstein agree with Plato that 'empiricism' cannot provide an adequate account of human knowledge and that there are concepts or ideas that are presupposed by forms of human thought and language. But these three philosophers take different views about the way these concepts are acquired and their relations to speech and action. Plato thinks of them as predating earthly human existence. Kant thinks of them as belonging to the structure of the human mind. He does not think that we learn them; he thinks of them as in some sense 'innate': we are born with them, they are innate dispositions which are realised with the development of our minds through physical growth and experience.

Wittgenstein does allow for something similar in the form of shared primitive reactions and propensities. But what propensities we actually develop depends on and so varies with the society into which we are born, the culture in which we grow up. He thus thinks of 'formal concepts' as embedded in the forms of our social life and the activities in which we learn to take part. We *learn* them as we learn to act and speak, learning these two in harness.

He would agree with Plato and Kant that much of what is first in the senses presupposes these categories of language. He would say that the reality of the language we speak is not something that is founded on the senses. The senses enter the foundations of human knowledge in a different way, namely through their peculiar role in the life of those who speak that language. Both the use of the senses and the use of language are part of our natural history. They are intertwined in the sense that the *ways* in which we use our senses and the activities in which the senses play their peculiar role—e.g. observation in scientific experiments—are inconceivable apart from the language we speak. Equally, the language we speak is one that has developed in the context of activities in all of which the use of the senses plays an important role. Wittgenstein, unlike Plato and Kant, does not regard those categories that belong to the form of our thought, speech and understanding as being immutable. With social life they are themselves subject to change. But this does not impugn the timelessness of the truths by which we judge sensible things, the changes in them and their relations.

IV   Forms and Philosophical Understanding

We have seen that Plato talks of 'recollection' in connection with mathematical discovery in the development of mathematical proofs. He also speaks of 'recollection' in connection with philosophical investigation and reflection— the kind on which we embark in response to such questions as 'What is knowledge?', 'What is virtue?'.

He says that we may think we know the answer to such questions, but we do not. So the first step in the quest for knowledge and understanding is to face up to our ignorance— allow ourselves to be perplexed, feel we have lost our way. Only then can we genuinely search for an answer. But in doing so where do we look? Plato wants to say: 'within our breast'. He sees a parallel between this kind of philosophical search and the search for an answer to the kind of mathematical problem which Socrates put to Meno's boy.

There are two different questions here between which Plato does not distinguish clearly.

(i) How do we acquire such concepts as knowledge, virtue, number, reason? Plato's answer is that since we cannot acquire them from experience, and since we could not have learnt anything from experience unless we possessed them, we must have acquired them in a previous life of disembodied existence. In this life we *recover* them by being reminded of them by their imperfect copies which present themselves to us in sense experience. This process of recovery he calls 'recollection'. We have seen that it is true that learning from experience presupposes a grasp of certain concepts, a grasp which finds expression in our mastery of certain operations and in our responses to various situations. But from this it does not follow that this grasp is acquired prior to experience, that the use of our senses is inessential to our acquiring these concepts. We learn them from experience, only in a different way, and this learning is much less like recollection than the process of coming to a mathematical truth for the first time.

(ii) The second question (in contrast with 'How do we acquire these concepts?') is: What enables us to answer such questions as 'what is knowledge?', 'what is virtue?', 'what is time?', 'what is number?'? Plato wants to say that we have the requisite knowledge and understanding already within us when we ask such questions, and so answering them is a form of recollection. Here I agree with Plato; the reflection which these questions prompt is more like recollection than the process of coming to a mathematical truth for the first time. My reason for saying this is that we already possess the concepts of knowledge or time when we ask 'what is knowledge?', 'what is time?'. But the fact that we possess them does not guarantee that we can meet ('answer') these questions. Nor does it mean that if and when we can meet ('answer') them we shall not have a better understanding of what is in question than we did when we asked them. St Augustine wrote: 'What then is time? If no one asks me I know. If I want to explain it to someone who asks I do not know.' One can add: If I succeed in satisfying someone who asks me, I give him an understanding he did not have when he asked—one which I lacked myself when I was stumped for an answer. This understanding is *new* to me in one sense, yet it did not come to me from *outside*. I acquired it by reflection; a reflection on what I already know in my mastery of the language I speak.[2] If what I know can be described as 'within my breast' then what I have to consider in attempting to meet such a question as 'what is time?' is within my breast. What I need to get clear about in the process of meeting the question is the mastery I exhibit in answering such questions as, '*when* did you meet your solicitor?', 'was that *before* you had lunch?', 'were you *long* with him? *Longer* than it took you to have lunch? *How long?*' Not having thought about it I do not have this clarity. What is more, I tend to look for it in the wrong place; once I begin to think I am constantly led astray—not the least, perhaps, by my idea that I have to grasp something neat and rounded: the essence that is hidden behind these coarser phenomena. So reflection at first makes me realise how little equipped I am for answering questions like this one, how difficult it is to answer them. Yet it is not in any other way that I arrive at the clarity and understanding I lack than by reflecting on something that I already possess.[3]

What I possess, in Plato's language, is acquaintance with the Forms in question. What I lack is clarity or clear-mindedness about them. In one sense, I have to become child-like in order to attain this clarity, to return to a frame of mind when my thinking was uncluttered by the knowledge which prevents me from asking the right questions today, or at any rate which constantly deflects me from doing so. This return too is a form of *recollection*. It is the recollection of a frame of mind which has since become sullied by a certain kind of sophistication. Purification may be a better description of it.

In summary, we have seen that Plato talked of learning as recollection in three different connections, connections between which there are various links: (i) the kind of learning we have in connection with the discovery or rediscovery of mathematical truths—truths that are new to mathematics, or truths that are new only to the discoverer; (ii) an important part of the kind of learning that takes place when as children we learn to speak and think for the first time; (iii) the kind of learning that takes place in later life when through philosophical reflection we come to an understanding we lacked before we embarked upon such reflection.

While Plato was sceptical about whether virtue can be taught, in the sense of 'acquired through training and instruction', he never thought that we already possess it or that we are born virtuous. Far from it, he thought that the love of the good which is virtue must be kindled in us and can only be kindled through contact with something *outside* which inspires us. He did believe, however, that the Forms could be the source of such inspiration. Hence he thought that Forms are a source both of virtue and philosophical understanding. But the kind of contemplation which makes the Forms its object is different in the two cases, even though there are important links between them—one of these consisting in the *wonder* involved in both.

2 *Phaedo* II: 'Forms and the World of the Senses'

I The Senses as an Obstacle to Knowledge

At the beginning of the *Phaedo* we are introduced to the theme of the kind of ideal that informs the philosopher's search for knowledge and understanding and the kind of detachment which it demands—a detachment which Socrates calls 'decent indifference' of the body:

> The true philosopher ... keeps his attention as much as he can away from the body and towards the soul ... [For] the soul can best reflect when it is free of all distractions such as hearing or sight or pain or pleasure of any kind—that is, when it ignores the body and becomes as far as possible independent, avoiding all physical contacts and associations as much as it can, in its search for reality (64B–65C).

> Don't you think that the person who is likely to succeed in this attempt most perfectly is the one who approaches each object, as far as possible, with the unaided intellect, without taking account of any sense of sight in his thinking, or dragging any other sense into his reckoning—the man who pursues the truth by applying his pure and unadulterated thought to the pure and unadulterated object, cutting himself off as much as possible from his eyes and ears and virtually all the rest of his body, as an impediment which by its presence prevents the soul from attaining to truth and clear thinking? Is not this the person, Simmias, who will reach the goal of reality, if anybody can? (65C–66E).

> If we are ever to have pure knowledge of anything, we must get rid of the body and contemplate things by themselves with the soul by itself. It seems ... that wisdom

... will be attainable only when we are dead, and not in our lifetime. If no pure knowledge is possible in the company of the body, then either it is totally impossible to acquire knowledge, or it is only possible after death, because it is only then that the soul will be separate and independent of the body. It seems that so long as we are alive, we shall continue closest to knowledge if we avoid as much as we can all contact and association with the body, except when they are absolutely necessary; and instead of allowing ourselves to become infected with its nature, purify ourselves from it until God himself gives us deliverance. In this way ... we shall ... gain direct knowledge of all that is pure and uncontaminated—that is, presumably, of Truth (65C–66E).

Here Socrates talks of a form of knowledge, of obstacles to it, and of a way of seeking it. He thinks of devotion to the pursuit of this knowledge as involving certain moral ideals and as constituting a way of life which he calls the philosophic life— the life of the man who loves wisdom. He characterises this knowledge as 'pure' and 'direct', and its object as 'unadulterated' and 'uncontaminated' and also, in other passages, as 'invisible' and 'transcendent'. He says, for instance, that absolute beauty and goodness cannot be seen with the eyes and that they are to be found outside the world of the senses. If one wishes to understand what goodness and beauty are 'in themselves' one has to approach them 'with the unaided intellect'. He speaks of this as 'contemplating things by themselves with the soul by itself'.

What does he mean by 'pure thought' and its 'pure and unadulterated objects'? What has this to do with the 'vision of the soul' and what it reveals?

It seems to me that he has two different things in mind: (i) Those logical categories which belong to the form of our thinking and which he calls Forms. These include the categories of moral thinking—moral and aesthetic values. (ii) Those among these values which may be characterised as 'spiritual values'—values not of this world. Both may be described as 'transcendental', 'outside or beyond the world', though two different senses of these words are involved here. In one sense what is transcendental is contrasted with what we use language to talk about.[1] There is also the sense in which what is transcendental is contrasted with what is worldly.[2] Socrates runs these together.

There are also two different forms of knowledge and understanding that are in question, though Socrates sees a close relation between them: (i) Philosophical understanding of the relation between the categories which belong to the form of our thinking and the things we think about and describe in terms of them. Hence Plato's distinction between sensible and purely intelligible objects. Here we have some of the big questions of philosophy about the viability and/or limitations of empiricism, the status of its limits and the relation between mathematics and physics. We have also questions about what it means to know something, what it means to draw an inference, what it means to have moral knowledge or virtue, which Socrates expressed in the form of 'What is knowledge?', 'What is virtue?', etc. He described what he was seeking in these questions as a knowledge of the Forms of knowledge and virtue, and said that most people who had knowledge of many things and also knew how to use the word 'know' correctly were nevertheless ignorant of 'what the thing itself—knowledge—is' (see Plato, 1957). (ii) Spiritual knowledge of life and death. Here too Socrates asked such questions as 'What is justice?' and said that many people who could talk about justice not only intelligibly but also impressively, nevertheless did not know what justice is (see Plato, 1961, 'Meno'). I submit that there are two different forms of 'ignorance' here. One is an inability to 'find one's way about' among the mazes one enters into when faced with the kind of philosophical question Plato raised about language, thought, knowledge and reality, an inability to obtain an over-all or synoptic view of these mazes. Or, better, not being able to take an investigation of these questions forward and make it yield some light. The knowledge in question is bound up with the critical response exemplified in Socrates' inquiries, one which cuts through certain preconceptions encouraged by abstract thinking, or simply opens up questions where none have been asked. The second kind of ignorance is a form of conceit or self-satisfaction; and the understanding which Socrates hoped for here is bound up with a spiritual response that cuts through indifference, habit, complacency and arrogance by turning its critical attention inwards, on one's own motives and character.

To distinguish between these, to resist running them together, is not, of course, to deny that they may be closely connected. The connection which Socrates saw between them lies in his belief that philosophy, and the development of the kind of criticism central to it, is itself a spiritual discipline, that the search for philosophical understanding involves a commitment to spiritual values.

II   The *a priori* and the Transcendent

It is clear that Plato wishes to make a connection between the world of Forms, i.e. the timeless world of logical and mathematical truths, and the eternal or everlasting world of religious faith. This is interesting. But he speaks of them in one and the same breath. I find this puzzling: Are they one and the same thing? When he speaks of (i) the world of the senses and the world of Forms or purely intelligible things, and (ii) this world and the other world which the myths at the end of the *Gorgias* and the *Phaedo* describe, is he making the same contrast?

My own suspicion is that in the dichotomy of 'the world of becoming and the world of being' Plato conflates a *philosophical* contrast with a *religious* one, and the fact that he characterises both contrasts in the same terms disguises this. Thus when Socrates tells us that 'the senses acquaint us with what is changing' he is thinking of two different things: On the one hand he is thinking of the objects of perception and the unchanging standards we employ in our perceptual judgments; the contrast between perceptual objects and mathematical norms. On the other hand he is thinking of pleasure and pain and the fickleness of a man who lives for pleasure and is over-influenced by a fear of pain. Thus by 'sense' he means both perception and sensuality in a broad sense which I shall clarify below. The objects of perception are changing in the sense that what qualities they have they may fail to have in contrast with the objects studied by the mathematician. The point in question is a purely logical one. But when he speaks of what the senses acquaint us with as being 'changing' he is also making a judgment about the goods of a life devoted to pleasure and self-interest. He is saying that these goods are ephemeral. By 'acquaintance' he means both sense perception and also contact with values that thrive in a life of sensuality. He thinks that the kind of justice that is possible in such a life is only an imperfect copy of the kind that can be found and known in a life where one is detached from considerations of pleasure and pain. It cannot be known by a man who lives for sensuality: 'we cannot see such things with our eyes'. Thus when he speaks of 'viewing objects themselves with the soul by itself' he means two very different things: *a priori* reasoning in mathematics and spiritual discernment in morality.

It is the same when he speaks of the senses as being deceptive and therefore not to be trusted. On the one hand he is inclined to say, wrongly, that we can have knowledge and are justified to be certain of mathematical propositions only. On the other hand he is thinking of the snares of the flesh, of the way sensuality is a hindrance to knowledge in the sphere of morality. 'The senses are deceptive': this is directly connected with what he says in the *Gorgias* about the man who does what he pleases in contrast with the man who does what he wills. The big question here is in what sense is such a man deceived. 'The senses are an impediment, the body a hindrance to knowledge': Socrates has in mind the way sensuality, a love of worldly things, responsiveness to praise and weakness in the face of pandering, turn one away from that love of the good which he identifies simultaneously with both virtue and knowledge. Here 'sense' or 'sensuality' is meant to include the pleasure of being thought well of by others, the enjoyment of the praise and prestige one can find in a life of conformity, the pain to be found in public shame. It is susceptibility to the attraction of pleasures of this kind and to the fear of such pains which constitutes an obstacle to moral action and vision.

If we are ambitious for advancement, greedy, lustful, vindictive, susceptible to the praise of others, envious of their possessions, in need of their support, Socrates would say that we are 'infected with' or 'contaminated by the nature of the body'.[3] While we are so infected, even if we do the right thing we will not have done it from the right motive. So, for example, he speaks of people who appear to be brave because they face death or danger of their own free will, but who in reality are cowards because they do so through fear of something they consider worse, namely losing the regard of their fellow men. Such men, he says, simply barter or exchange one kind of pleasure or pain or fear for another. The really brave man is the man whose action is not motivated by fear, one who does something which he knows to involve danger because he believes that doing so is right. He acts from moral conviction despite the danger with which doing so faces him. Thus the bravery of someone who faces danger in order to avoid disgrace or ridicule is only apparent bravery; not the real thing.

Socrates holds that true moral qualities cannot flourish in a life of the senses, nor can a man immersed in such a life know them. He puts this by saying that real justice cannot be known by the senses: 'Do we say that there is something *just* ... and something *beautiful*, and *good?* Now did you ever yet see any such things with your eyes?' He says that it is to be found in another world, a world that one can enter by turning away from a life of the senses. There is nothing very recondite or metaphysical about this claim, as one will appreciate if one cashes it in terms of examples. But talk about 'a world of forms beyond the reach of the senses' can obscure this. I have insisted that the sense in which real or perfect justice lies beyond the reach of the senses and the sense in which mathematical norms do so are quite different. Yet Socrates runs them together. He also runs together the sense in which a man immersed in a life of the senses does not know what justice is and the way a philosopher may be unable to respond adequately to the question, 'What is justice?' He speaks of both as being ignorant of the essence of justice.

But once more we should remember that 'essence' could mean different things. It could mean the 'spirit' of justice, the 'inner dimension'—I mean the kind of concern, love, motive, detachment from those influences which Socrates represents as belonging to the senses, without which, however a man acts, he can at best act only with apparent justice. Compare with the use of the word in such phrases as 'the essense of classical Greece', 'the essence of impressionist painting'. Here to search for the essence is to search for the spirit of an age or movement. To do so one has to distinguish its pure and unadulterated expressions from cases where other influences dilute these expressions. Obviously this involves judgments of worth. In this sense to know the spirit of justice is to have been touched by its oneself, its having entered one's life. Here the form of ignorance that is in question, for instance in the case of Meno, is complacency (Plato, 1961, 80b). It is, therefore, a moral defect of the will. The kind of orientation in which a man has vested all his interest excludes a whole mode of response to life and its contingencies. A man who is complacent will be satisfied with what he knows, and lack of thoughtfulness and criticism will mark his life. Socrates' 'philosophic life' is the antithesis of precisely such a life. What characterises it is the inability to remain content with appearances, the desire to look for a reality that lies beyond them. In connection with moral values this desire to go beyond appearances, to grasp the essence of justice, is a *religious* quest. For one is looking here not merely for an *account* of the way conduct must be related to morality before it can be characterised as moral, not just in appearance but *in reality*; one is also looking for that *reality* in one's life. That is, one is oneself trying to go beyond that life in which one's actions are so related to morality that one's morality is only an imitiation, a life in which considerations of self-interest, pleasure and pain are prominent. In the *Phaedo* Socrates describes such an attempt to transcend a life of the senses as a *purification*. My point is that such a purification can, without much strain, be described as a search for the *essence* of justice.

Yet Socrates also talks of the ignorance of the essence of justice in a totally different way, a way with which we are only too familiar today in philosophy. And here it is a different set of problems that come to the fore, problems with which Socrates is *not* concerned in the *Phaedo*. Philosophers often invoke a reference to 'essences' in connection with the problem about the basis of our classifications and the meaning of general terms. Thus where, for instance, one witnesses an act of justice, a man putting his life at stake to testify to a truth in a court of law, there is some inclination to say that what one witnesses is one thing and what makes it an act of justice is another thing. This other thing is not something that one witnesses. It is what the witnessed act shares with all other acts that can be properly described as acts of justice.

Here many philosophers have talked of grasping the one

universal in many particulars that constitute a kind. They thought, to change the example, that what makes red things red is the property of redness possessed by red things, much in the way that what makes telephone booths red is the red paint on them. Just as the booths are one thing and the red paint on them another thing, it seemed that the things we describe as red are one thing and their redness another thing. This thing which they all share is the universal which the word 'red' designates.

This way of thinking is confused, however; the two cases are by no means parallel. Of course telephone booths are one thing and their redness is something else, since they would still be telephone booths if they were a different colour. But it is a tautology that red things would not be what they are, namely red, if they were not red. Thus if we said that all red things have something in common, namely their red colour, we would not be referring to something additional to what they are, some common ingredient that could be distilled out of them and contemplated in isolation, something that makes them what they are and explains their being the same kind of thing, namely red objects.

Here the universal is thought of, wrongly, as something *distinct* from the particulars which are instances of the same kind, and therefore as something that can be contemplated apart from the individuals which share it. But it is still thought of as something *in* the many individuals which are of the same kind. Whereas Plato wanted to speak of justice and equality not only as things we can think of by themselves, but also as existing by themselves in separation from their instances: 'We say, don't we, that there is something *equal*—I don't mean a log to a log, or a stone to a stone, or anything else of that sort, but *some further thing beyond all those, the equal itself*' (74a, *italics mine*). He went further and said that they are not to be found in the particular acts we witness, among the particular objects we compare or measure. The objects of sense only *approximate* or *imitate* them:

> 'Then those equals (log to a log, stone to a stone) and the equal itself are not the same' (74c).

> 'Do they seem to us to be equal in the same way as *what it is itself*? Do they fall short of it at all in being equal, or not?'

Simmias replies: 'Very far short of it.'

Socrates goes on: 'Then whenever anyone, on seeing a thing, thinks to himself, "this thing that I now see seeks to be like another of the things that are, but falls short, and cannot be like that object: it is inferior" ...' (74d–e).

If we wish to understand why Socrates speaks like this what we have to turn to is not the problem of universals, but rather the relation between mathematics and physics—the relation between propositions of pure mathematics and descriptions of sensible things. In the above passage Socrates is thinking of mathematical equality, what the equality sign ($=$) signifies in mathematical equations, and there is something important in what he says. For if we think about the way a mathematical equation is solved or checked, the way a particular mathematical equality is verified, we shall see that it is indeed different from the way a physical equality is established or verified. If asked whether such and such a number is equal to the sum of this string of numbers we *calculate*. This is a purely reflective procedure. What is more, the equation is either correct or it is not. There are no degrees of accuracy here. If the equation is true then it is so absolutely and irrespective of time and place. With a physical equality this is not so. That this log here is equal in length to that one over there is something we establish or ascertain by *measurement*. This is an empirical procedure; it involves the use of the senses. Also a measurement can be more or less accurate. Its accuracy is a relative matter. One could say that there is no such thing as an absolutely accurate measurement, meaning that to speak of absolute accuracy here is a misunderstanding. One could only say that this measurement that one has carried out is accurate relative to one's purposes.

These are, I think, the kind of considerations that led Socrates to say: 'Then those equals, and the equal itself (that is physical and mathematical equality) are not the same.' And again that the logs seem to us to be equal in a different way from equality itself, that the equality of the logs is visible to the senses, but not the absolute equality of mathematics: 'Now did you ever yet see any such things with your eyes?' So far, I think, he is right, and he has his thoughts fixed on something important.

He goes wrong, however, in the way he compares the two forms of equality when he says that physical equality is inferior, that it falls short of mathematical equality. For this suggests that they are competitors in the same field. As I said: One could say that there is no such thing as an absolutely accurate measurement. But this does not mean that there is an ideal of accuracy, to be found in mathematics, which measures, compares, equates very different kinds of entity, ethereal and not coarse like sensible things, one which our physical measurements cannot emulate. It does not mean that our physical measurements are coarse and inaccurate. One could say that mathematics does give us an ideal of exactitude; but not for measuring things, rather for describing them (see Rhees, 1970, pp. 126–7).

I spoke of the way Plato *separates* mathematical and physical equality. (i) Mathematical equality, the geometrical circle, are not to be found among sensible things. (ii) They are known or apprehended by the intellect alone; what is true of any such Form is established by pure reasoning or reflection alone. (iii) Physical or sensible things at best resemble, imitate or approximate them; they can never possess or share the characteristics of geometrical lines or figures. So (iv) physical or sensible things fall short of these ideal objects, the Forms; they are inferior—viz. 'the imperfection of the world of the senses'. I suggested that it is not for nothing that Plato speaks like this, that there is something important that he is trying to focus on—though what he says is also misleading in certain ways. There is something important even in the idea of physical, sensible things falling short of these ideal objects of the world of pure thought—the description and comparison of physical figures with reference to a geometrical norm, ordering them in relation to a mathematical limit.

As for the idea of imitation and striving to be like ('this thing that I now see seeks to be like another of the things that are, but falls short, and cannot be like that object: it is inferior'— 74e), here Plato is thinking not only of the relation between physics and mathematics, but also of the relation between human conduct and moral ideals. Some human beings, at any rate, do really strive to be as nearly just, charitable and generous as possible, and they speak of weaknesses in their characters which keep them at a distance from these ideals.

While Socrates thought that such weaknesses can be remedied and the individual's relation to his ideals improved, he also thought of them as expressions of general tendencies in the human soul itself and thus as rooted in the very conditions of human existence.[4] He thought of them as transcending individual and cultural differences.[5] To overcome them you have to renounce life itself; perfect justice and real charity can, therefore, neither be attained nor contemplated in this life: 'The wisdom which we desire and upon which we profess to have set our hearts will be attainable only when we are dead, and not in our lifetime' (Plato, 1973, 65c–66e).

By 'death' Socrates means the severance of the soul from these general tendencies in which almost the whole of its life is rooted. Since he thinks of these tendencies as partaking of the nature of the body he described the death in question as the separation of the soul from the body, or as the purification of the soul from everything that partakes of the nature of the body. These are alternative descriptions of the same thing. Simone Weil, who is the only philosopher I know to have written with real penetration on what is in question here, speaks of this state of soul as spiritual death—'spiritual' as opposed to 'physical'. But it is a death in and through which the soul finds a new life. She compares the soul to a gas that tends to occupy all the space that is available to it and says that it finds it impossible to contract or to resist expanding. To do so means for a person to stop feeding on the nourishment which the bodily part of his soul or self[6] needs to keep alive. It means giving up the armour which protects it so that the individual person is exposed to the thought that he is *nothing*— that he has no privileges, nothing that he can be proud of, nothing on the support of which he can count, nothing he can look forward to or expect any solace from. It is bearing this void, resisting any thought or action which would tend to reduce it, that constitutes spiritual death, that is the death of the bodily part of the soul. She points out that this is more terrifying than physical death. The soul automatically protects itself from such a death and runs away from any threat of it faster than men run away from physical death.

How? For instance, when we are hurt or insulted we seek revenge. Wounded pride is a small instance of what Simone Weil calls the void. If we cannot fill it by revenge we turn on those who are weaker than ourselves. This too is a form of expansion. More generally, we return onto others the evil of which we have been the victim. This compensates for the sense of annihilation which goes with suffering evil. Again, if we have power, refraining from exercising it creates a void and we are sorely tempted to exercise our power. In doing so, in asserting ourselves, we expand and thrive. Nietzsche appreciated this well. But if we have to check ourselves we find it easier to do so by exchanging one form of expansion for another—that is to do so from a 'base' motive. The really difficult thing is to do it without any compensation. Normally we expect to be rewarded for our good deeds. When we put ourselves out or make sacrifices we need some replenishment in the form of appreciation, and the mere thought of having done something good can provide this replenishment. Generally we feed on the identifications we establish in our associations, our beliefs and loves. We find no interest in any relation or activity which does not provide such food, and we turn away from those that threaten to deplete us. That is why Simone Weil speaks of compassion, as opposed to ordinary benevolence, pity and sympathy, as a supernatural virtue.

Thus there can be no compassion without contraction and, therefore, self-abdication. Therefore if one aspires to perfect justice one will have to resist this natural propensity of the soul to expand and to bear the void which resisting it creates. This is the meaning of Socrates' claim that perfect justice cannot be found in this world, the life rooted in the general tendencies which all human's beings share—those tendencies he describes as carnal or belonging to the flesh. So besides the words that 'no two logs are perfectly equal' we can set those that say that 'no human being who has not embraced spiritual death is perfectly just'. Socrates puts these together in the thought that perfect equality and perfect justice (the Forms) can only be found in an ideal world. I have suggested that what this ideal world amounts to is something very different in the two cases.

We see that the relation of human justice to perfect justice, of human virtues to saintliness, is not the same as the relation between physical and mathematical equality. The former has to do with the relation between human conduct and certain moral ideals and with the distinction between reality and appearance in spiritual life. Here, at least within certain limits, it makes sense to speak of 'aspiration'; but this makes no sense in connection with the behaviour of physical things. We describe physical things and their behaviour with reference to mathematical norms. Certainly we do so in physics. These norms enter our descriptions, they determine how we talk about the behaviour of physical things. But they do not influence the behaviour itself. To put it differently: nature does not conform to mathematics, though there is a sense in which it conforms to the laws of physics expressed in mathematical terms. In contrast, moral ideals enter into and inform human conduct. What moral ideals a man aspires to makes a difference to his conduct, not just to how we talk about it.

As for the senses as an obstacle, we have seen that it makes good sense to talk like this in connection with moral life—the senses as an obstacle to the attainment of virtue and wisdom. But I don't see what sense this makes in connection with mathematics. Certainly our senses may deceive us at times so that, as Socrates puts it, 'the very same stones and logs seem equal to one, but not to another' (74b). When this is the case, however, we do not turn away from the senses to detect and redress the error. On the contrary, we look again, consult others and, where appropriate, we use instruments. From the fact that our senses sometimes deceive us it would be wrong to conclude that they are unreliable, like lying witnesses. Yet this is a misunderstanding we find in the writings of many philosophers. Hence Socrates' thought that what sense perception reveals and the kind of certainty it justifies is inferior to the objects of mathematical reasoning and the knowledge we attain by means of such reasoning.

To summarise. When Socrates speaks of the essence of justice or perfect justice he is thinking of certain moral *ideals*. When he speaks of 'the equal itself' or perfect equality he is thinking of mathematical *norms*. Is it any wonder that he separates these from human actions and sensible objects in the way he does? What is in question is, in neither case, a doctrine of universals *outside* things.

I have argued that there is something important in what he says about each, though there is something confused in the way he characterises the relation between mathematics and physics, statements in pure mathematics and their application.

In particular, what it means to have knowledge in the context of moral ideals—vision of what is real or true there—is very different from what is means to have knowledge and understanding in mathematics. Perhaps the most important difference is that in spiritual life there is no distinction between vision or knowledge and the possession of what one has vision or knowledge of, so that one cannot gain knowledge without changing in oneself. Is it any wonder that very often here ignorance is a form of self-deception? Again, is it any wonder that what constitutes resistance to the kind of change necessary to the attainment of knowledge ('the body', 'the self', 'the senses') constitutes an obstacle to such knowledge? There is no counterpart to such obstacles in the sphere of mathematics.

More generally it has been my contention that in his characterisation of the relation between timeless Forms and changing things Socrates is concerned with two very different sets of relation, though the fact that he can and does use the same terms in characterising them disguises this. Thus when he speaks of Forms as separate from the world of experience and as having a reality independent from it, he runs together the *philosophical* distinction between measures, including moral norms, and objects measured, including human conduct, and the *religious* distinction between the worldly and the super-natural. We have seen that there is something important about the former distinction, though it is not without danger. The danger lies in thinking that the world of experience is un-related to the world of Forms. Plato does not fall into this danger; he thought of human experience and its concepts as logically dependent on the Forms. This is his critique of empiricism. But he thought of this dependence as being a one-way dependence; he thought that we could and must have come to know Forms in separation from experience: 'Before we began to use our senses we must somewhere have acquired the knowledge that there is such a thing as absolute equality' (74d). Thus he made the mistake of thinking that if we cannot derive our conception of Forms from experience, we must have acquired it apart from experience.

My main point, however, is that there are two different sides to the Platonic *separation* between the Forms and the objects of sense, a philosophical and a religious one. I say 'philosophical' in that Plato developed his 'Theory of Forms', of which this separation is a distinctive feature, in the course of a struggle with big philosophical questions: (i) the question of whether all human knowledge arises out of sense experience, (ii) the question of the relation between propositions of physics and those of mathematics, and (iii) the question of the relation between human conduct and moral ideals. In connection with the first question he held that there are certain ideas and truths which are essential to human knowledge and which cannot themselves be acquired by means of sense experience. In connection with the second question he held that although we use such words as 'equality', 'circle', 'point' and 'line', both inside and outside mathematics, we are not speaking in the same way in the two cases: 'Two logs are not equal in the same sense that two numbers may be equal.' In connection with the third question he held that moral ideals cannot be realised in a life of the senses. On the other hand when he talked of 'the imperfection of the world of the senses' and of 'the body as a hindrance to knowledge' he was using notions that belong to a religious morality, . even though their elucidation clearly belongs to philosophy. In the *Phaedo* Socrates is not merely concerned to elucidate them; he actually uses them and does so to talk about the nature of philosophy itself. I was puzzled by this and asked: How can this be? I now turn to this question.

III   Philosophy and Religion

How can one elucidate the nature of what one is engaged in when one does philosophy in religious terms? I noted above that Plato saw in the Forms a source of inspiration that could lead one both to virtue and philosophical understanding. For at the centre of both philosophical inquiry and a spiritual quest there is an attempt to go beyond what we are familiar with in our lives, an attempt to glimpse at or understand a reality that transcends what we know. Of course, what this amounts to is different in the two cases, but there is an affinity in the kind of wonder, dissatisfaction, rigour and dedication that drives one on in the two cases.

One of the questions I mentioned which Plato raises

concerns the relation between human conduct and moral ideals. I do not hesitate in characterising this as a purely philosophical question. To discuss it adequately one has to give due attention to the *variety* of moral ideals that have informed human life and the *difference* in the demands these make on people who give their hearts to them. Within this variety are to be found some ideals which have been described as impossible to attain in a life of worldliness. In relation to them the philosopher's task is to elucidate the meaning of such descriptions.

Let me put it differently: Where there are ideals, there are also obstacles to their realisation. What these obstacles are differs with the nature of the moral ideal in question, the kind of demand it makes on those who attach importance to it. There are ideals to the realisation of which some of the very features of human existence are seen as an obstacle, though they still demand from their believers that they should struggle with these obstacles. Thus while there is no question of surmounting these obstacles altogether and so of attaining the object of these ideals in this life, it is important that they should will these objects and not submit to these features—not in the sense of rejecting them, since that is impossible, but of not letting these obstacles turn them away from their ideals.[7] It is this *inward*, spiritual state that counts where these ideals are concerned. Loyalty to them is not measured so much in terms of what their believers do as in terms of what they endure. Think here of Plato's conception of virtue and happiness as a *state of soul*. Thus the object of the demand made by these ideals is represented as incapable of attainment in this life where we are inevitably attracted and influenced by human praise, the prestige of social position and the power vested in us by status, possessions, intelligence and physical force. Hence what they demand is spoken of as a turning away from all this, setting our face against what is part of our very humanity, transcending this life of the senses.

It is in this way that at least one conception of a *transcendent reality* belongs to the discourse of a religious morality in which these ideals are framed. One can call them 'spiritual ideals' or 'ideals of the spirit'. Thus the contrast between 'the world of the senses' and 'a reality which transcends it' is certainly a *religious* contrast. It arises in the development of the language of spiritual ideals. The philosopher's task is to elucidate the contrast, to clarify the language in which it is made. This task belongs to philosophy just because the clarity in question calls for conceptual analysis and can only be won against difficulties which spring from tendencies within that language to look in the wrong direction.

The point I am making is that when Plato spoke of Being or Reality in contrast with Becoming or Appearance he spoke at once both as a philosopher, whose philosophical problems I have indicated, and also as a religious teacher who contributed to the development of a religious language which is still with us—a language in which men have asked questions about the world, tried to size up their lives, and formulated ideals which inspired them in the way they lived. Yet I do not think that the interest which inspired him in his philosophical quest, in his struggle with big philosophical questions, what led him to take the line he took in these struggles, what left him dissatisfied with the solution of these problems by the Sophists of his day, his dissatisfaction with their empiricist, pragmatic and sceptical orientations, are irrelevant to the contribution he made as a religious teacher. As Dr Drury puts it at the end of a series of unpublished *Letters to a Student of Philosophy*:

> The God of religion means a great deal more than the absolute of philosophy because life demands a great deal more than speculative thinking. Nevertheless, what I have written about the desire for the absolute, the desire for a satisfying object of contemplative knowledge, the desire to know things as they really are, all this is not a matter indifferent to religion.

'The desire for a satisfying object of contemplative knowledge.' For Plato the Forms constituted this object. It was a 'satisfying object' in that it lacked all those features which made what it contrasted with—namely 'the world of sensible objects'—unsatisfactory. We have seen that the search for something that was not tainted by such features is a struggle with philosophical difficulties. It is interesting, however, that Plato's response took the particular form and direction it did. He was suggesting, paradoxically, that the most 'satisfying object of contemplative knowledge' is something that we cannot touch, something that cannot be found where we are most inclined to look for it.

Thus the *desire* that made Plato receptive to philosophical difficulties and kept him struggling with them and his *response* to those difficulties may be characterised as 'religious'. For it was a desire to find something pure; it linked knowledge with purity and distrusted our natural inclinations, emphasising that the road to knowledge is uphill and requires devotion and integrity. I should like now to comment on the way Plato identified the object of real knowledge with what we cannot touch.

Simone Weil makes some striking remarks in *La Pesanteur et la Grâce* which throw some light on this question. She speaks of putting one's life and heart in what one cannot touch at all and says that what one touches prevents one from finding access to the truth. She is speaking of a truth which one can only pursue in a spirit of truthfulness, that is by a wholehearted dedication from which any detraction would constitute a betrayal. One cannot hit it by accident, for instance, since what one comes to here is not independent of how one comes to it. The character of what one comes to in one's search cannot be assessed independently of what part of oneself one gives to it. If what one pursues is something that one cannot touch, it will draw from one very different qualities of soul than if it is something touchable.

Simone Weil speaks of beauty very much in these terms. She speaks of it as 'a fruit one looks at without stretching out one's hand towards it' (Weil, 1948, p. 151). Obviously where we are concerned with physical beauty—the beauty of a painting or statue, for instance—looking at it means using one's eyes, namely one of the senses. But the point is that one looks at what is at a certain distance from one, and stretching out one's hand, touching, are attempts to abolish this distance, to possess or incorporate the object. The most primitive form of this desire is the desire to eat, to take the object inside one and to feed on it. Psycho-analysts, especially Freud and Melanie Klein, have pointed out how much this tendency persists, in different forms, in many of an adult's relations to things other than food. Simone Weil writes: 'One wants to eat all the other objects of desire. Beauty is what one desires without wanting to eat it. We desire that it should simply be' (ibid., p. 150). The contrast is between what we desire to incorporate and feed on and what we are happy to see existing, what we are happy to contemplate. Feeding on something is using it, subordinating it to the self; whereas contemplating it is accepting the distance between it and oneself, its otherness, its independent existence. Often people who want nothing from a thing or person are indifferent to it. In relation to beauty, forms of corrupted attraction apart, we are the opposite of indifferent, yet we do not want anything out of it for ourselves. So Simone Weil says that beauty implies renunciation. It is for just this reason that it is elevating, why it develops a generosity of spirit both in action and in thought.

Regard for the truth means a recognition that it is something that we cannot alter to suit ourselves, something that we ought not to want to tamper with. There is a certain parallel here between the way in which truth is independent of our thoughts, and the autonomy of other people. Both can be an obstacle to our desires and constitute a threat to a natural propensity in us to expand. That is why a devotion to truth, as well as to justice, involves an abdication of this propensity. It implies a willingness to accept the distance between ourselves and things outside us, to renounce subordinating them to the consolidation of our identity, to give up attaching importance to those trappings that regulate other people's relations to us and make a kind of mirror image of ourselves in the improvement of which we find safety. Simone Weil speaks of accepting that distance and of refraining from expanding as 'bearing the void'. She speaks of giving up the protection we derive from our social position, achievements and relations as the shedding of our garments. To fill in the void by giving in to the natural propensity of our soul to expand, to take refuge behind our garments, metaphorically speaking, is to lie to ourselves, to turn away from the truth. Very much like Plato she says:

To be just, one must be naked and dead (ibid., p. 92).

One must be dead in order to see things in their nakedness (ibid., p. 71).

There is in the soul something like a phagocite. Everything that is threatened by time secretes a lie in order not to die. That is why there is no love of truth without an unreserved consent to die (ibid., p. 64).

Complete detachment is the only thing that allows us to see things in their nakedness, outside the mist of deceptive values (ibid., p. 59).

And in the chapter 'Renunciation of Time' she says, after Socrates, that 'to philosophize is learning to die' (p. 30).

Part, at least, of the point here is this. You cannot be dedicated to the pursuit of truth, in the way that a philosopher ought to be, and lie to yourself. The truth in your contribution as a philosopher is not independent of the spirit you bring into your philosophy. When I speak of the truth in a philosopher's contribution, this is inseparable from the depth of his penetration—for instance, in the questions he opens up. One of the questions that has always been central to philosophy is the question of 'Appearance and Reality': where does reality end and appearance begin, or vice versa? This is a many-sided distinction; I mean it comes to different things in different areas of the language we speak. Obviously unless we speak the language we could have no grasp of it to be able to elucidate it. The criteria of reality and appearance in spiritual life are notoriously difficult to grasp. Here a person who was prone to self-deception, prone to be taken in by appearances, would be particularly disqualified from making a philosophical contribution to a discussion of the question that was of any worth.

There is, then, the philosopher's dedication to truth and the way this affects the character of his contribution. It is this dedication which Plato characterises in religious terms—the very same terms in which he discusses what the difference between appearance and reality amounts to in the realm of the spirit. It is in terms of this same dedication that he distinguishes real virtue in spiritual life from its illusory or merely apparent varieties. Hence the expression 'philosophic virtue'. He thought of the contemplation of the Forms as supremely important for the development of the spirit and dedication common to what is best both in philosophy and in moral life. Here by 'contemplation of the Forms' we should not understand the kind of pursuit in which he engages when he asks for a definition of, say, 'knowledge', but rather the kind of quest he describes in the *Symposium* as 'the ascent to absolute beauty'. Thus the way in which Plato thought of the contemplation of the Forms as central to philosophical inquiry cannot be separated from his conception of the pursuit of truth in philosophy as a religious quest—that is, a quest which is religious in character.

3 *Phaedo* III: Note on the Immortality of the Soul

The *Phaedo* is a conversation which Socrates has with his friends before his death. In it Socrates attempts to convey the way he thinks about life and death, his vision of life and what he considers important. What is distinctive of his vision is that in it death does not appear as a threat and so as something to be feared. The notion of the soul's immortality is the notion of something in one's life which death cannot destroy.

The dialogue is concerned with both of the following questions: (i) How is one to live so that death will not constitute a threat to one's well being? What is the kind of well-being which death cannot destroy and how is it to be found? (ii) In what sense can a man's well-being be immune to his own destruction? This notion of immortality in the *Phaedo* is thus very closely connected with what Socrates says in the *Gorgias* about the impossibility of harming a good man, one who has devoted his life to the service of the good:

> CALLICLES: You seem to me, Socrates, as confident that none of these things will happen to you as if you were living in another world and were not liable to be dragged into court, possibly by some scoundrel of the vilest character.
>
> SOCRATES: I should be a fool, Callicles, if I didn't realise that in this state anything may happen to anybody ...
>
> CALLICLES: Do you really think, Socrates, that all is well with a man in such a position who cannot defend himself before his country?
>
> SOCRATES: I do think so, Callicles, provided that he has at his disposal the form of self-defence ... which consists in never having committed an offence against God or man in word or deed (521–522).

To have achieved such immunity, such an independence from the vagaries of fate, is to have found immortality. In the *Phaedo* Socrates describes how it is to be found.

The soul, he says in the *Crito*, is that part of us which is improved by right action, and is scarred and ultimately ruined by wrong action (47c). In the *Phaedo* he explains that there is much in life which interferes with the soul's relation to the good. For instance, a man's desire for praise and approval may, on occasions, conflict with his desire to do the right thing, or it may replace or corrupt this desire so that he does the right thing from the wrong motive. Similarly, his fear of punishment may corrupt the otherwise creditable things he does. Or, again, the self-centredness that flaws his character may poison his moral passion. His extreme moral zeal may itself be suspect, just as in the case of another person it is his half-heartedness, his reservations, his lack of complete commitment which mars his relation to the good, which corrupts the way he serves it. These are examples of what in *Purity of Heart* Kierkegaard talks of as 'barriers to willing the good'. Such 'purity of heart' is what Socrates has in mind when in the *Phaedo* he speaks of 'purification of the soul'. Since the only thing that harms the soul is wrong-doing and injustice, it follows that a man whose soul is completely at one with the good is one whose soul is immune to harm. Thus the soul flourishes in a life of dedication to the good. In wickedness its life ebbs. And where a man turns completely away from the good, he is said to lose his soul. Such a man is at the opposite extreme from eternal life. Here the indestructibility of his soul is the possibility of his being saved through repentance. Where he dies unrepentant the indestructibility of his soul is the same thing as its eternal damnation.

Now this is a way of talking, a language with which men have been familiar for centuries. When Socrates says that the only thing that harms the soul is wrong-doing, if one were to ask how he knows this one would be speaking nonsense. There is no such thing as finding out whether wrong-doing always harms the soul, or whether anything else may harm it as well. To say that the only thing that harms the soul is wrong-doing is to say something about what it *means* to talk of the soul, the role which reference to the soul plays in talking about a man's conduct and in sizing up his life. There is no question either about whether or not the soul really exists. The existence of the soul is the meaningfulness of a certain way of talking about men and their lives. For a man who finds no sense in this language the soul does not exist. But, as I have explained elsewhere, this does not make the soul's existence into a 'subjective' matter.[1]

In the *Phaedo* Socrates does not try to demonstrate the existence of the soul. He takes for granted the kind of language in which reference to the soul has sense. What he is concerned to do, in part at least, is to *elucidate* the meaning of that language. I take his arguments for the indestructibility of the soul to be part of that. If we did not think of the soul as indestructible we would not be speaking about men and their lives in the way we do when we refer to their souls. The idea of the soul's eternal destiny is an important part of the way people speak about their lives in many religions.

I said that Socrates' arguments for the indestructibility of the soul are elucidations of the meaning of a religious language he himself uses. The indestructibility of the soul is the possibility of a man finding eternal life or damnation. Thus the soul is necessarily indestructible, while immortality or eternal life is something that has to be won.[2] It is only the latter that removes the sting of death. In describing how a man can find immortality and so fearlessness in the face of death Socrates actually uses the language which he is concerned to elucidate. If we can follow what he says by means of this language we shall be in a better position to understand his elucidations of its meaning. Thus in the *Phaedo* Socrates' *use* and *elucidations* of the language in terms of which we talk about human life and death by referring to what happens to the soul are interwoven and they supplement each other's purpose.

In his Third Argument Socrates speaks of the affinity between the soul and the Forms—by which he does *not* mean that the soul is itself a Form. He says that contact with the Forms can transform the soul's vision and so the soul itself. Here there is no distinction between a man's spiritual vision and the state of his soul.[3] Contact with the Forms, with perfect justice for instance, the kind of justice that cannot be found in the world of the senses, means a complete reorientation of the soul, a reorientation in its love. Thus contact with perfect justice means that the love of perfect justice enters into a man's soul. This is how Socrates describes it:

> When it [the soul] investigates by itself [in other words, when it is no longer a victim to the snares of the flesh], it passes into the realm of the pure and everlasting and immortal and changeless; and being of a kindred nature, when it is once independent and free from interference, consorts with it always and strays no longer, but remains, in that realm of the absolute, constant and invariable, through contact with beings of a similar nature (78E–80A).

Compare this with what Diotima says in the *Symposium* about the soul's ascent to 'absolute beauty' which Simone Weil describes as 'the beauty of the world'—not of this or that thing, but of the world as an unlimited whole. The way followed, the 'ladder' used, may differ from one case to another. But what the initiate rises to in each case is the same, whether what enters into his soul is a love of perfect justice or a love of the beauty of the world. Simone Weil brings out well the sense in which these are all descriptions of the same thing.[4] A soul which has ascended to what Diotima describes in the *Symposium*, one which has come out of the cave of the *Republic*, has found what Socrates describes as 'immortality' in the *Phaedo*. I repeat, this is a state and vision of the soul at once. Some philosophers have said that such a soul sees things under the aspect of eternity, or *sub specia aeternitatis*—for instance, Spinoza. Kierkegaard spoke of it as hearing the voice of eternity. It is, of course, not easy to say what 'detachment from time' amounts to and what sort of temporal considerations a person becomes indifferent to when the love of perfect justice enters his soul. Certainly the desire for revenge, for consolation, for reward, for compensation, which Simone Weil has written about so perceptively, are examples of what such a person becomes indifferent to. The object of the desire in each of these cases necessarily involves a temporal reference.

Finding 'eternal life' or 'immortality' is finding a new love, the object of which Plato describes as 'perfect justice', 'absolute beauty' and places 'outside this world'. Of course, it finds expression and can best be seen in a person's attitude towards things of this world.[5] It is finding a new perspective on life, a new way of looking at things of this world, a reorientation in one's concern, so that what happens to one, the way one's fortunes may change one way or another, is no longer felt to matter. It is a transformation in the scale of importance one attaches to things. Although a man whose scale of values has undergone such a transformation has, obviously, still to act and, therefore, to plan for the future, to think of the consequences which acting one way rather than another would have, nevertheless he no longer feels the way time presses on the man who is anxious to get on, to achieve an ambition or one who is prudent in a worldly way. As I said, there is a sense in which time is bound up with worldly concerns, not easy to elucidate, from which he gains freedom. Obviously, such a man cares what he does, passionately. But he doesn't care about the consequences this would have for him, as we do most of the time. His compassion may drive him to stand up and speak for a poor oppressed person, knowing well that by doing so he puts in jeopardy what he has been working for all his life. If, as a result, all that he has been working for is undone, he may say that compared with standing by and doing nothing in the face of injustice what he suffers is a minor misfortune. With such a transformation of his perspective on life the centre of his own identity shifts, so that when what he has built is destroyed it does not destroy him; it does not knock the bottom out of his world.

The self is destructible. It can be crushed by illness, by misfortune and it will inevitably be destroyed by death. But through compassion, or what Plato calls a love of perfect justice, a man may find a new life and a new identity. The only thing that can destroy that is doing wrong, being sucked into evil. In that life none of the things we call misfortunes are seen by him as such. Remember Dmitry Karamazov's words: 'What do I care if I spend twenty years in the mines? I am not a bit afraid of that—it's something else I am afraid of now: that that new man may leave me.' The new man is the new identity he has found in his concern for the good as this finds expression in the compassion he feels for others who live as he lived, in the remorse he feels for his previous life. In that identity he has come nearer to gaining access to immortality. What separates him from it is the work of repentance.

4 Hume I: Reason and Feeling in Moral Judgment

I Reason and Moral Judgment

Hume held that when we make a moral judgment we need to be properly acquainted with the action and situation we are concerned to judge. This involves the apprehension of *facts* and in this apprehension we are guided by *reason*. But after having done so when we pass a moral judgment and say that the action we have been concerned with was 'despicable' or 'noble', when we blame or praise its agent, the blameworthiness or nobility of the action is not a further fact. The wickedness or merit of the action which we put into words in our moral judgments is not to be found in any of the features of the action and its relations, but in the judge's mind. Since it is not to be found among what Hume described as the facts of the situation, the judgment which attributes moral value or wickedness to the action cannot be accountable to reason; it arises from the sentiments. It is not an expression of 'the cool assent of the understanding' but 'the work of the heart'.

So for Hume the morality or immorality of an action lies in its being the object of a certain feeling in us—e.g. the detestation we feel for Nero for the murder of his mother. He notes that Nero himself, who did not condemn his own action, was not ignorant of any of the relations we see when we condemn it. This is part of his argument that our moral judgment is an expression of the detestation we feel. There is no reason why we detest what we thus judge adversely. It is a brute fact about most uf us that we are horrified by wilful murder and feel revulsion particularly for the murder of those who have brought us into life, fed and raised us. Hume speaks here of 'the particular fabric and constitution of the human species'.

Yet he does allow that reasoning plays a role in directing our sentiments: 'In order to pave the way for such a sentiment and give a proper discernment of its object, it is often necessary, we find, that much reasoning should precede, that nice distinctions be made, just conclusions drawn, distant comparisons formed, complicated relations examined, and general facts fixed and ascertained' (Hume, 1957, p. 6). Thus reasoning helps us to distinguish between Oedipus' killing of his father and Nero's killing of his mother and so to sift out our affective, moral reactions to the two killings. Without such reflection the former case might have evoked the same sentiments in us as the latter one. All the same it takes for granted an unreasoned affective response in us—e.g. horror and revulsion inspired by parricide. There is something right in what Hume says here. From the fact that a change in our apprehension, brought about by reasoning, can bring about a change in our sentiments it does not follow that reasoning can give our sentiments new objects or beget new affective responses in us. Whether or not it can do so is a question which needs to be considered on its own merits (see section VI below). So Hume does not wish to deny that reasoning can direct our sentiments and moral judgments in particular cases: 'No man reasons concerning another's beauty, but frequently concerning the justice or injustice of his actions' (ibid., p. 5). He allows that reasoning can change our apprehension of the objects of our moral responses, but he holds that it can do so only around fixed points determined by our sentiments and not responsible to reason:

In moral deliberation we must be acquainted, beforehand, with all the objects and all their relations to each other; and from a comparison of the whole fix our choice or approbation. No new fact to be ascertained, no new relations to be discovered. All the circumstances of the case are supposed to be laid before us ere we can fix any sentence of blame or approbation. If any material circumstance be yet unknown or doubtful, we must first employ our inquiry or intellectual faculties to assure us of it, and must suspend for a time all moral decision and sentiment. While we are ignorant whether a man were aggressor or not, how can we determine whether the person who killed him be criminal or innocent? But after every circumstance, every relation is known, the understanding has no further room to operate, nor any object on which it could employ itself. The approbation or blame which then ensues cannot be the work of the judgment but of the heart; and it is not a speculative proposition or affirmation, but an active feeling or sentiment (ibid., p. 108).

Professor Wisdom quotes part of this passage in 'Gods' (Wisdom, 1953, p. 156) where he asks whether the manifestations of an attitude or sentiment in the application of an evaluative word has a 'logic'. He argues that it does and he thinks that Hume's philosophy is defective because it does not allow this. Hume, in the above passage, claims that the facts of a situation, grasped by reason and the understanding, cannot justify the judgment of value we make. Wisdom thinks that this is a mistake and that Hume fell into it because he did not see that there are forms of reasoning and justification other than those with which we are familiar in inductive and deductive reasoning.

Wisdom compares the making of a moral judgment to a ruling by a judge: 'It is not an arbitrary decision though the rational connections are neither quite like those in vertical deductions nor like those in inductions in which from many signs we guess at what is to come ... With the judge's choice of a name for the facts goes an attitude, and the declaration, the ruling, is an exclamation evincing that attitude. But it is an exclamation which not only has a purpose but also a logic, a logic surprisingly like that of "futile", "deplorable", "graceful", "grand", "divine" ' (ibid., p. 158). He agrees with Hume that when we consider the facts and then make a moral judgment we are not like the doctor who on the basis of the patient's symptoms diagnoses an inflamed appendix, nor like the accountant who on the basis of the entries in the ledger concludes that the firm is solvent. He further agrees that a moral judgment expresses an attitude and evinces feelings. But he disagrees that this is all there is to it, that it is a matter merely of how we feel towards the object of our moral judgment. He thinks that such a judgment also embodies, and so evinces, a certain apprehension of the facts.

So far Wisdom seems to me to be right, though more needs to be said about how a moral judgment or sentiment involves an apprehension of the facts (see section II below). When in a court of law opposing counsel are agreed as to the facts they may still disagree about whether or not the defendant had been negligent. Wisdom describes well how argument, reasoning, comparing the case at hand with others may bring about agreement and, even when it does not, how it increases apprehension and brings opposing counsel closer together. He thinks that the situation is the same in moral disputes. This is, I think, true of many moral disputes. People who are equally well acquainted with the details and circumstances of a man's actions may nevertheless disagree in their moral characterisation of it and in the moral judgment they make. It may happen here that when one of the parties can bring out its affinities to actions the characterisation of which they agree on, the others will come round to his characterisation. Reflection of this sort which alters their moral apprehension of the action may also alter their judgment and the way they feel towards it.

How does such reflection alter their moral apprehension of the action? By comparing it with actions not in dispute with regard to certain specific *moral* features. This is moral reasoning and it guides one in one's moral apprehension of what one is concerned to judge fairly. Hume did not recognise that once all the facts are in there may still be scope for reasoning, that one may misapprehend what lies open to view, and that such reasoning can guide one in one's apprehension of these facts. However, not only is there scope for reasoning here, but the reasoning in question is *moral* reasoning. It compares an action with others which we unhesitatingly characterise in certain moral terms. If the comparison shows it to be like those others in the moral respects in question then we shall be justified in using the relevant moral terms to describe it. The difference between thinking of it as unlike these familiar actions and thinking of it as like them is a difference in moral *apprehension*. How we apprehend an action in this way, and so the way we describe it in moral terms, is obviously relevant to the moral judgments we make about it. There is no logical gap here, as Hume thought, since the transition, though not deductive, is nevertheless from moral descriptions to moral judgments.

How we judge an action morally, however, does not only depend on what the action is like and whether we apprehend this properly, but also on what *we* are like, in the sense of where we stand morally. This means what we value, the kinds of thing we consider important, and how they are ordered for us in their scale of importance. What is in question is our conception of what is good and noble, and what is wicked and base; the ideals we have given our hearts to and so the things that give us hope and those that fill us with shame. To reason and argue in the way that Wisdom describes, people must agree in their use of moral terms in a large number of cases: 'When one calls a man a sinner or declares him a saint one may be said hardly to mean what one says unless one ... grasps his affirmity to a paradigm, as when one calls a spade a spade' (Wisdom, 1965, p. 80). But people who speak the same language and agree in their use of many specific moral terms may yet stand morally in different places. What kind of moral interchange there can be between them and whether they can learn from each other depends on how they are separated. Often part of the difference between them consists in their having different *measures* of what is good and right (what Hume calls 'rules of right') and in their having given their hearts to different things. But is this something about which reasoning can legislate?

Hume may not have recognised that the facts we must be acquainted with before we can arrive at a fair moral judgment have already a moral significance for us which we mark in the moral terms we use in describing them. But he was right in thinking that the framework of values within which we see these facts as having moral significance cannot themselves be based on any facts. This was one reason why he said that 'the rules of morality are not conclusions of our reason'. He argued as follows:

A moral action, a crime, such as ingratitude, is a complicated object. Does the morality consist in the relation of its parts to each other?

No, say you, the morality consists in the relation of actions to the rule of right; and they are denominated good or ill, according as they agree or disagree with it. What then is this rule of right? How is it determined? By reason, you say, which examines the moral relations of actions. So that moral relations are determined by the comparison of actions to a rule. And the rule is determined by considering the moral relations of objects. Is not this fine reasoning? (Hume, 1957, p. 107).

In other words, if the moral significance you find in actions presupposes your recognition of a 'rule of right', you cannot without circularity base that rule on anything that already possesses moral significance. This is both right and important, but it does not follow from it that our moral beliefs (those that we take for granted in our moral judgments and reasonings) are beyond the reach of reason and criticism.

A discussion of whether there was negligence in this case, to return to Wisdom's example, can turn into a discussion of what counts as negligence, which may itself be conducted in terms of 'reasoning by parallel cases'. For just as people may have the same facts before them and still differ in their apprehension of them, they may attach the same meaning to a word like 'negligence' and still disagree in what they say counts as negligence. A discussion of the latter question may guide them in their understanding of what the word they themselves use means, and consequently also in their appreciation of what they describe by means of it. Similarly, a discussion of whether generosity is more important than prudence may be conducted in terms of 'reasoning by parallel cases'. For a consideration of instances where these virtues find expression may guide one in one's apprehension of what these virtues amount to and, as a result, one may come to see them in a new light. This may alter the importance one attaches to one relative to the other.

There is a sense in which one may be uncritical of the values to which one gives one's heart. A reflection which clarifies what is in them, a comparison with other values, may alter one's allegiances. This too is moral reasoning for which there is scope where people have not been sufficiently critical about the values they accept or sufficiently thoughtful about those they reject. But people who are thoughtful and critical may still differ in their values and, therefore, in their value judgments about the same actions and situations. Beyond this point reasoning turns into 'persuasion'. Its aim is no longer to show the other what he doesn't see or fails to appreciate, but to win his allegiance: 'At the end of reasons comes *persuasion*' (Wittgenstein, 1969b §612).

Hume did not recognise the kind of logical relation there is between value judgments and what is judged. This is something that Wisdom points out. But he showed some recognition of the logical relation there is between value judgments and the moral place where the judge stands as a person. In so far as he recognised this he appreciated the possibility of irreconcilable moral conflicts between people. We could say, in short, that moral judgments logically link both outwards, as Wisdom pointed out, and inwards, as Hume insisted.

I have characterised the two kinds of reasoning I mentioned as *moral* reasoning. The person who engages in such reasoning recognises the force of the considerations advanced because he already thinks in terms of moral concepts which embody certain norms of reason. These enable him to appreciate the relevance of the cases considered on the question discussed—a relevance that turns on their moral features. But the norms which enable him to do so are themselves exempted from reflective scrutiny in these considerations: 'If I want the door to turn, the hinges must stay put' (ibid., §343). This is not to say that in a different context they may not themselves become the object of reasoning and scrutiny; but when they do, it will be in the light of others that we shall be able to question them. For the very possibility of our asking and considering moral questions presupposes our willingness to adhere to some moral norms without question. This is, I think, what Hume had in mind when he argued that to think of 'rules of right' as determined by reason is to put the cart before the horse. The horse for Hume is feeling or sentiment, but the priority which he rightly gives to feeling over reason at this level does not justify the subordinate role he assigned to reason in our moral appraisals.

II   Feeling and Moral Appraisal

Hume does not only claim that reason alone cannot help us in our assessment of the moral worth of an action; he does not simply emphasize the importance of sentiment in moral appraisal. He goes further and claims that the worth of actions which we express in our moral judgments is 'the object of feeling'. On Hume's view reasoning is essential, but only at a pre-moral stage of the inquiry. The transition from what is established by reasoning to a moral judgment is not governed by any logic; it is 'the work of the heart'. I argued that this is a defective view of the role of reason here without implying that Hume is wrong in his emphasis on the sentiments.

I want to ask now what this emphasis amounts to: What does Hume mean when he says that the worth or demerit of an action is 'the object of feeling'? In a famous passage he writes:

> Examine the crime of *ingratitude*, for instance, which has place wherever we observe good will, expressed and known, together with good offices performed on the one side, and a return of ill will or indifference, with ill offices or neglect, on the other; anatomize all these circumstances and examine, by your reason alone, in what consists the demerit or blame: you never will come to any issue or conclusion ... Twist and turn this matter as much as you will, you can never rest the morality on relation, but must have recourse to the decisions of sentiment (Hume, 1957, pp. 106–7).

Is Hume saying that sentiment judges the blameworthiness of ingratitude? Is he saying that a man devoid of moral sentiments would not *see* here what someone not so devoid of sentiment *sees*? This would mean that the moral character of an act of ingratitude 'consists in the relation of its parts to each other', that it 'arises from a complication of circumstances which excites the sentiment of blame', and that in this sentiment we grasp the relations which constitute its character and give it the particular aspect under which we see it. That is in our feelings we apprehend something which our reason is too coarse-grained to grasp. But Hume does not allow this; it is not what he means when he says that 'morality is more properly felt than judged of' (Hume, 1967, p. 470). For him the morality of an action does not lie in any of its features. Besides, he does not think that a feeling can stand to its object in the kind of relation in which a thought or judgment of fact does: 'When I am angry … in that emotion I have no more a reference to any other object than when I am thirsty, or sick, or more than five foot high. 'Tis impossible, therefore, that this passion can be opposed or be contradictory to truth and reason' (ibid., p. 415).

His view is that the morality or immorality of an action does not lie in any facts or relations which can be the object of the understanding, but arises entirely from our sentiments. Thus if we did not feel any disapprobation when we contemplate ingratitude, barbarity or treachery, there would be nothing immoral about these acts. Our moral judgment is no more than an expression of this feeling. That is these actions have the moral character we attribute to them because we disapprove of them or condemn them, and not the other way around as we are wont to think: Nothing is good or bad, but feeling makes it so.

Yet our moral judgment is not just an expression of what we feel. Rather our feelings show what moral view we take of the matter as this is expressed in the judgments we make. They can do so because our feelings involve judgment and apprehension. It is in that sense that our judgment finds expression in what we feel. But Hume's conception of the passions did not permit him to recognise this. For he thought that a judgment can at best 'accompany' a passion or feeling, these two being distinct and identifiable independently of each other (see ibid., pp. 415–16).

We may find Hume's view plausible if we confuse it with the view that since the intellect is detached, it is the heart which, possessed by the sentiment of humanity, does the discrimination: 'What is honourable, what is fair, what is becoming, what is noble, what is generous takes possession of the heart and animates us to embrace and maintain it. What is intelligible, what is evident, what is probable, what is true procures only the cool assent of the understanding, and, gratifying a speculative curiosity, puts an end to our researches' (Hume, 1957, pp. 5–6). When the head and the heart are identified with the man who is morally indifferent

and the man who is morally concerned, it becomes true that
no moral motive can come from the head, and also no first-
hand moral perception. Yet Hume's view is not that the heart
discerns moral character, but that its response *constitutes* it.

However, even Hume is not always consistent with this
view: 'No qualities are more *entitled* to the general good will
and approbation of mankind than beneficence and humanity'
(Hume, 1957, p. 10—italics mine). He slips from:

(i) What is generous is estimable because it takes possession
of the heart,

to

(ii) What is generous takes possession of the heart because it
is estimable. It is entitled to the good will and
approbation of mankind. It is what entitles it to such
approbation that makes it estimable, not the
approbation itself.

But what is it that entitles it to such approbation? The kind of
thing that generosity is, characterised in moral terms, *and*
what values we believe in and are moved by. This presupposes
an understanding of moral language, a life in the context of
which its terms have sense, a culture in which certain values
have developed and for which people have come to have
regard. Understanding what it means to use moral terms and
so appreciating that these terms are the right ones to use in
certain situations: this involves the use of reason. Concern or
regard for certain values: this involves the heart and brings in
feeling or sentiment. Thus moral judgment expresses both
feeling and apprehension; it is the work of both the heart and
the intellect.

For Hume, however, reason and feeling were exclusive
categories. Assimilating feeling to something like sensation he
did not recognise how feelings can involve thought and
apprehension. Yet if I approve of something it must be at
least because I think of it as good. Its goodness must be
independent of my approval, as the truth of what I believe
must be independent of my belief. A belief may be false, but it
involves the idea of truth. Likewise the notion of approval
involves the idea of something valued. You cannot explain
what 'approval' means without referring to the idea of
goodness. Someone who had no idea of goodness could

neither understand what 'approval' means, nor could he approve of anything. If I approve of something, I must have certain thoughts about it, think of it in certain terms. In the case of moral approval these terms must be moral terms.

Hume wrote:

> Take an action allowed to be vicious ... Examine it in all lights ... The vice entirely escapes you, as long as you consider the object. You never can find it, till you turn your reflection in your own breast, and find a sentiment of disapprobation, which arises in you, towards this action (Hume, 1967, p. 469).

But how did he think of this disapprobation? How did he think of approval? He said: 'To approve of a character is to feel an original delight upon its appearance. To disapprove of it is to be sensible of an uneasiness' (ibid., p. 296). He meant: an uneasiness *within you*. Hence his claim that the moral character which you attribute to an action 'lies in yourself, not in the object'—just as the pain which you feel on touching a hot stove lies in yourself, not in the object.

This, however, is the opposite of how it is. *What* you disapprove of lies in the object, not in yourself, and your disapproval is the form which your apprehension of it takes. How is this different from disliking ice cream? Presumably both the child who likes ice cream and the one who dislikes it taste the same thing when they eat ice cream. But the terms in which a man who disapproves an action thinks of it cannot be the same as those in which one who approves of the same action thinks of it. It makes sense to ask, 'Why do you approve or disapprove of what he did?' Two men who disagree would say different things about the action. Perhaps one would see in it an expression of humility, while the other man finds it cringing. He may say that it is dishonourable to take an insult lying down. They may agree that the action shows a lack of pride and it may be just this which one admires and the other condemns. But then each will have more to say about what he sees in pride or in the lack of it. The different connections which this has for the two men give it two different aspects. Under one aspect it is an object of admiration, under the other it is an object of contempt. Thus the two men's different thoughts, their different terms of reference, are an integral part of their approval and disapproval, of their admiration and contempt, not merely an accompaniment. Without them no amount of delight or uneasiness can add up to approval or disapproval.

This is true of all moral feelings or emotions. In each case the aspect under which a person, action or situation is seen and the feeling are internally related. Thus unless I think of what I have done as base, shabby or low, the feeling which contemplating it evokes in me cannot be *shame*. Unless I see what someone has done as evil I cannot *detest* it morally. If I *admire* someone for what he did it means that I think highly of him for doing it; and if I am *grateful* to him for what he gave me then I think of it as something good and I think well of him.

If I feel *remorse* for something I have done it means that I think of it as something terrible, and I might be able to go on to say what it is I find so terrible in it. The remorse I feel is my pained apprehension of this. I could appreciate all this, of course, and not care. I may speak the language in which the words used to describe what I did have meaning. I may recognise the trust which the person on whom I have turned my back had put in me; I may know well that I have let him down. Yet I may be morally indifferent. In that case I do not see the terribleness of what I did for myself; at best I know that people would say that what I have done is something terrible. But given that I am not indifferent, the remorse I feel is the form which my apprehension takes—my apprehension of the terribleness of what I did.

The epithets 'terrible', 'despicable', 'base', 'shameful', 'admirable' are often used to indicate the moral character of actions and their agents. A man who is morally indifferent cannot see for himself what is being said in these words. He could say, 'I know that what he did was terrible, but I cannot in all honesty say that I find it so.' He means that he knows that this is what people would say, that this is how they would respond to the particular action. Or take: 'I know that was an admirable thing to do, but I don't admire it.' He doesn't mean that he doesn't have certain feelings in him now in the sense that Hume understood this. If he feels no admiration then this will be seen not only in what he says and does or cannot bring himself to say and do now, but also in the future. This is something he understands when he says 'I know it was admirable' and means no more than 'I know that others find it so'.

It is tempting to say that here the defect belongs to the heart and not to the understanding. This may be perfectly correct, for he may add sincerely: 'I don't admire it and blame myself for not doing so.' Compare with: 'I know this novel is good. I can tell you what makes it a first-rate novel. All the same I did not enjoy reading it. It may be my taste that is at fault.'

Still, it is not always possible to draw a line in this way between the understanding and the emotions. For there are cases where what our use of language means to indicate in the way we characterise things belongs to the emotions they evoke in us. The vision we wish to communicate in these cases, the mode of awareness, the aspect we are interested in describing, comes from the emotions, and we may be unable to share it with someone who lacks these emotions. I am thinking, for instance, of the way terror changes the aspect under which we see the things that frighten us. This aspect is something which one can only grasp or imagine through having experienced the emotion. The experience makes accessible a new form of awareness. Words like 'sinister' and 'menacing' are used to mark such aspects. There is no way of describing features of things which one sees under one of these aspects save by comparing them with those of other things people find sinister or menacing. A person who lacks the emotion and hasn't had the experience can only have a second-hand understanding of what these words mean. There are many other such words—'horrible', 'haunting', 'tantalising', 'oppressive', 'eerie', 'comical', 'grotesque', 'shameful', 'despicable', 'wonderful'.

These terms are certainly descriptive, and they are not used to describe our feelings but their objects. However, since what they describe is what comes into focus when we feel certain emotions their sense cannot be fully understood by someone to whom the perspective of these emotions is closed. In the case of moral emotions what this perspective brings into focus can only be described in moral terms. Someone who does not speak the language to which these terms belong cannot have the emotions in question, just as someone who speaks it but lacks the emotions cannot mean or understand the terms at first-hand. But a person may possess the concepts and be capable of having the feelings in question, although nothing evokes them in him. In that case his understanding of some of these moral terms will be second-hand. I spoke of remorse as a person's pained apprehension of having done something terrible and argued that the pain is part of the apprehension. It follows that just as the pain would not be the same without the particular aspect or apprehension (e.g. the pain of regret), so also the apprehension would not be the same without the pain (e.g. the apprehension of a morally educated but indifferent man who has done something bad).

Earlier I quoted part of a sentence by Wisdom in 'The Metamorphosis of Metaphysics'. The part I omitted reads: 'When one calls a man a sinner or declares him to be a saint one may be said hardly to mean what one says unless one … also feels towards him in a certain way' (Wisdom, 1965, p. 80). I do not think that this follows from what I said—not without qualification. 'One may be said hardly to mean what one says'—Wisdom means: 'one may be said hardly to speak sincerely'. But one may say with sincerity: 'I know that what I have done is wrong, and yet I feel no shame.' One may then add: 'I know that I ought to feel ashamed.' Here there need be no defect in one's understanding unless one knows no shame at all. This would be the case of a man who is morally indifferent, one whose heart is closed to all feelings of decency. Only here would Wisdom's words be true; only when such a man makes a moral judgment may he be said hardly to mean what he says. Otherwise, although he feels no shame for what he has done, he may still show in other ways that he does mean what he says. Compare this with someone who finds something funny but does not laugh. This does not mean that he does not really find it funny. It would mean that only if, taken with other things, it showed that he has no sense of humour. Only perhaps where a judgment is concerned with great good or extreme evil will a lack of feeling show moral indifference and so reflect on the sincerity of the person who makes the judgment.

What is fatal to moral understanding is not the lack of appropriate feelings on a particular occasion, but moral indifference. Such a person may not be blind to many of the moral features which others see and express in a language he understands well. But he will be blind to *some*, namely those that come into focus with the emotions he lacks. Similarly, I think that a decline in the moral sentiments that were alive in a community also constitutes a decline in their sense of good and evil, and so in the moral understanding that was once alive there. The moral terms that continue to form part of the current vocabulary of its language will inevitably lose part of their sense as the surroundings in which they are used change, as the affective moral reactions in the weave of which they are used drop out of these surroundings. It is in this sense that the reactions which exhibit people's moral sentiments are essential to the sense of their moral terms. If we want to understand the kind of conceptual tie there is between moral judgments and moral sentiments this is where we have to turn our attention.

Earlier I had indicated how our moral feelings contain our thoughts about the situations that evoke them in us, thoughts which presuppose an understanding of moral terms. We now see how the possibility of moral judgment presupposes moral sentiments which find expression in particular cases. The forms of life and behaviour apart from which such sentiments could not have developed carry criteria of intelligibility and categories of reason. Moral sentiments thus presuppose the recognition of certain norms and values that are embedded in ways of living that underlie their possibility. We could say that the possibilities of reason and feeling are interdependent in the sense that what each requires largely overlap. This is something that Hume did not appreciate.

Yet with regard to his question 'concerning the general foundation of morals' Hume is right in the priority he gives to feeling over reason. His view is that to think that 'rules of right' are determined by reason is to put the cart before the horse—the horse being feeling or sentiment. I now turn to this question.

III Moral Values and Sentiments

As children we learn to use moral terms and to respond to other people's use of them in conjunction with learning how to behave. We learn, for instance, what to call a 'lie' and also that a lie is something that is normally condemned. We learn not to lie and also to feel ashamed when we do. We learn not only to say 'That is a lie' in appropriate circumstances but also to condemn what we so describe. We thus come to use these words to express our condemnation; and when we confess that we have lied we do so with contrition. At first the connection between our use of the word and what we feel stands isolated. But as we learn to use new words and to say new things, the aspect under which we see what a person said or did when we describe it as a 'lie' acquires new dimensions. We see it as breaking someone's trust, for instance, or as showing disregard for him. These new words and the affective attitudes which come to be linked with their use give support to our reactions to dishonesty. The isolated connections begin to form a network and this makes it possible for us now to give content to our condemnation of lying.

We learn moral language and acquire moral values in harness. The circumstances in which we learn the language, what we learn it in conjunction with, the situations in which we learn to put it to work, give it a special role in our lives. In this role the aspects which the use of moral terms brings into focus and the sentiments which these aspects evoke in us are internally connected. These are 'connections of meaning' since learning them is part of learning the meaning of the terms in question. But it is possible for a child to learn the use or meaning of these terms without acquiring the values implicit in the language. He may learn what it is to lie and that it is something that is generally condemned, without coming to care for honesty or condemn lying himself.

Still what interests me now is the way in which learning moral language and acquiring moral values go together and are part of the same training. This training, in the form of praise and blame, reward, rebuke and punishment, takes place in the course of the development of relationships in which the child meets love, anger, sorrow and gratitude, learns to care for, consider and help others, to give up things for them, to co-operate and, in certain cases, to look up to and emulate them. He develops expectations with regard to others and learns to respond to their expectations with regard to him. He learns to make promises and to rely on those made by others, to trust and be trusted. He develops a sense of responsibility and begins to act on his own behalf in the light of concerns which are now his.

Acquiring values, learning standards of behaviour and criticism, is a central part of the formation of a child's identity and the development of his emotions and character. The child does not learn rules of conduct which are backed by emotions that come to attach themselves to these by reward and rebuke. The emotions are already *moral* emotions which themselves develop in the course of early personal interactions—love and the desire to be worthy of it, gratitude for what he receives and guilt at damaging it, the wish to make amends for such damage, the desire for the approval of those he loves. The rules make sense in relation to these emotions. Certainly praise and blame, reward and admonishment, play a role in his learning to observe rules of conduct. But the praise and blame that play this role are already endowed with moral significance for him. His response cannot be detached from his feelings for those who praise and blame him and for those in whose presence he is praised and rebuked. They are expressions of acceptance and rejection. They mean that he is worthy of those he looks up to or unworthy of their regard. Accordingly he responds with pride and gratitude or with dejection.

If the child were not responsive to praise and blame, if he were devoid of love and pity, incapable of gratitude, sorrow and shame, I doubt that he would learn any rules of conduct or come to see any moral sense in them. Further, unless these sentiments are shared and reciprocal it is hard to imagine how a people could have moral beliefs. For the child to develop such sentiments there must be situations capable of evoking them. This presupposes forms of thought and appraisal which he becomes capable of through acquiring language and other skills. Since these sentiments and the responses in which they find expression presuppose some intellectual appreciation they are already susceptible to criticism. Thus criticism and reasoning may well have a role to play in early moral teaching.

To what extent parents make use of it depends on their moral outlook. Thus some parents will encourage and others will discourage any early search for reasons in their children: 'Why should I share my toys with other children?', 'Why should I not laugh at him when he makes a fool of himself?', 'Why is it naughty to pull the cat's tail?' But the answers given already take much for granted; and if they could not do so the questions themselves would hardly make sense. Perhaps the mother says: 'If someone else did that to you, you wouldn't like it'—hoping to get the child to accept that others are entitled to the consideration he takes for granted for himself. If the lesson he learns is to be more than a prudential one, his mother will try to get him to connect what he is doing to the cat, or a friend of whom he is jealous, with someone doing something similar to someone he cares for: 'If someone did that to your mother, she wouldn't like it. Now you wouldn't like that to happen, would you?' Or: 'You wouldn't do that to your mother, would you?' This presupposes that the child is not indifferent to his mother, that he would respond to her pain with sorrow, that he would be dejected if he hurt her, that he is capable of pity. Otherwise his mother's reply to his questions would have no moral force.

So even if we grant, as I do, that reasoning and criticism can play a part in early moral teaching, we must admit that at the bottom of these reasons are the child's primitive affective reactions. It is these that are extended, built on and modified in the course of his moral development. This is made possible by other forms of learning. As the child learns to participate in new forms of thought and activity the foundation is laid for new responses and new sentiments. What direction this development takes depends on the forms of thought and activity with which the child comes into contact. What is built up in the earlier part of the child's moral development is thus what makes it possible for him to have a place on which to stand morally. His acquiring moral beliefs depends on that. It is because he has such a place to stand on that he can question what his parents tell him. Coming to have such a place is at the same time acquiring a certain measure of autonomy and independence. The child no longer merely complies; he sees some sense or point in what he is asked to do and so wants to do it on his own behalf. As he develops other moral influences begin to impinge on his life, influences which he embraces and is modified by, or criticises and rejects. These are influences he meets in becoming a member of new groups, in forming new friendships, in coming to be involved in new activities, in entering new movements. He may be critical or uncritical; but where he is critical it is the place on which he already stands that enables him to weigh and appreciate what he meets.

Thus while there is room for reason in a child's moral learning and development, the possibility of its operation presupposes the existence of something to which the child is not morally indifferent—people for whom he cares, relationships in which there is room for give and take, trust and gratitude, guilt and grief. Coming to a conception of other people is largely possible in surroundings where the child can form such relationships. So in the beginning is the affective response, shared and reciprocated, which is neither reasonable nor unreasonable. This is what I take to lie behind Hume's view that to think of 'rules of right' (or values) as ultimately based on reason is to put the cart before the horse.

The point is not merely a temporal one. The possibility of moral judgment presupposes the reality of some moral norm or value. Such values exist independently of whether or not individual people show recognition of their reality. What constitutes this reality is the place they have in the life of a community. The kind of response its people exhibit in particular situations that arise in this life is an important part of what determines this place. These affective responses are an expression of the reality of these values and underlie the *possibility* of moral judgment. Someone asks: 'Why is that a reprehensible thing to do?' We may, in response, compare it with other things he finds reprehensible, things about the moral character of which he is in no doubt. There must be such things, though—acts, motives, persons—to the moral character of which he responds without reflection. Or we may give him descriptions of the act which will make clear the moral character we see in it. We may say that it was a reprehensible thing to do because it involved cheating, or letting someone down, or making money out of his distress. Once this is granted there should be no doubt about the original moral claim. But if he doesn't see that cheating is wrong, or that capitalising on someone's distress is reprehensible, then either his moral beliefs are radically at variance with ours, or his moral development has suffered an early arrest or undergone a decline.

These individual judgments we make in particular cases are interconnected and they give each other mutual support. The fact that we can always refer from one to others in supporting it may disguise their 'ground level' character. But the truth remains that such a judgment is as much a verbal expression as our affective response to the particular situation as is the feeling it evokes an expression of our apprehension. As I said, the possibility of moral judgment, reasoning and discussion presupposes some measure of agreement between people in their use of moral language and in their affective reactions. It is in such 'ground level' judgments that these two forms of agreement interlock—even though they may come apart in individual cases. By 'ground level' I mean that there is nothing more fundamental to which we could appeal to justify them, that the affective reactions of which these judgments are the verbal expression are 'unreasoned'. I have in mind such reactions as pity for someone in his suffering, anger for those who have brought it about, indignation with those who are indifferent to it, gratitude for those who come to his assistance, guilt at turning away from him, horror and revulsion at cold-blooded murder. Why are we horrified by such murder? Because we find something horrifying about it. But this is not an answer and there is something important in Hume's rejection of the question. We are the kind of creatures who are horrified by cold-blooded murder.

If I go along with Hume in thinking that the use of moral language has grown out of certain unreasoned affective reactions, I am not saying that this is all there is to the use of moral language. Here I part company with him. To speak as Wittgenstein does, one could say that moral words are connected with the primitive, natural expression of certain feelings. A child, for instance, recoils before a brutal act, and then adults talk to him and teach him exclamations and, later, sentences. They teach the child new moral behaviour (see Wittgenstein, 1963, §244). 'But this is not the *end* of the language-game: it is the beginning' (ibid., §290). Pretty early in the course of this development words or sentences like 'Good for you' and 'That was a naughty thing to do' begin to express more than feelings, pro-and-con attitudes. They become a vehicle of apprehension and, as such, contestable. The child can then ask why his parents say that what he did was naughty or why they praise his little sister for what she did. But he must already have learnt a fair amount before he can ask such questions.

What he will have learnt will depend on the kind of activities that go on around him, the language that is used in connection with them and the ideas that belong to this language. How his questions will be met and even whether he will be encouraged to ask them; how he will develop and what values he will come to accept—all this is not something that is fixed by what he begins with or determined by 'the particular fabric and constitution of the human species'.

If belief in moral values engages the will through the emotions, this is not to deny that they provide the believer with a certain way of looking at things, a perspective which finds expression in a moral vocabulary that belongs to a language that goes all through his life. It is not to deny that these values and the kind of life which they make accessible to the believer can enable him to transform and transcend old sentiments and to develop new ones. Nor is it to deny that there is room for reasoning and reflection at different stages of his moral development. If the possibility of moral reasoning presupposes a moral basis which one accepts without reason this does not imply that moral learning excludes all reasoning. Nor does it imply that reasoning and reflection have no role to play where a person deepens his regard for the values he holds and develops new sentiments, or gives his heart to new values. Reasoning can guide a man in his moral decisions as well as in the moral commitments which delimit the choices and decisions that are open to him in particular situations. I turn now to these two topics.

5 Hume II: Reason and Feeling in Moral Decision

IV Reason and Moral Decision

Hume's difficulty with moral decisions arose out of the notion of *decision* in contrast with belief and, in part, overlaps with his difficulties about moral judgments as expressions of sentiment. How can reason engage the will? It seemed to him that there is nothing problematic about the idea of reasons engaging the understanding and guiding a man in his assessment of what interests him. By 'the understanding' he meant 'the faculty of knowledge'. There was no doubt in his mind that the capacity to know anything is bound up with the capacity to consider reasons. His sceptical doubts were concerned with the extent and scope of this faculty or capacity. It was not the connection between the notions of reason, truth and knowledge that he found problematic.

However the connection between the notions of reason and action did present him with problems. He saw reason, thought and the intellect as belonging with the understanding, that is the capacity to ascertain facts, the ability to distinguish between truth and falsity. He thought of the will as a separate faculty from the understanding; for it is the ability to act. The understanding is what grasps truths or facts; the will is what moves a man to action. The terms in which he thought of their relation were responsible for Hume's problems; but this is not to say that there are not genuine philosophical problems here. Hume must be given credit for raising them. For there is, indeed, something important in Hume's dichotomy between the understanding and the will; and one can present it without recourse to the language of faculties. One could put it in terms of assessment and decision: What I assess is independent of my wishes and desires. If a proposition I am considering is true, it is true whether I like it or not. If I am seriously concerned to know whether or not it is true, I have to put aside my wishes and hopes on this matter, to detach myself from my likes and dislikes. Thus Hume characterises reason as 'cool'; whereas with decisions, what I decide are my own proposed actions to which I stand in a special relation. I determine what they are to be. The personal pronoun is, therefore, an integral part of the characterisation of human actions.

Hume did not doubt that we do consider reasons for acting—as he did not doubt that we consider reasons before making moral judgments. One could put it more strongly than Hume and say that decisions that are not responsible to reasons would be arbitrary and hence not decisions at all. Still it seemed to Hume that the consideration of reasons alone, or by itself, could not determine the will and so move a man to action. I think that he has an important point here, even though it needs to be distilled from what is erroneous in his thinking. When in the *Treatise*, Book II, he said that 'reason alone can never be a motive to any action of the will' he was thinking, rightly, that if a man is indifferent to what he assesses he will not have a motive for action. Thus if, for instance, I come to believe that there will be a severe shortage of potatoes in the winter, this will not in itself give me a reason for growing potatoes unless I want to eat potatoes in the winter. And I may want to do so because I like potatoes, or because I believe they are essential to a healthy diet and I care to keep healthy. Hume thought that it is through their connection with my likes and dislikes, desires and aversions, concerns, interests and fears that reasons and considerations get a grip on my will—of which my decisions are an exercise. He spoke of these as 'passions' and 'affections'. But the question is: How do reasons get a grip on my will through these? Here, I think, Hume's account was defective, and it led him to assign a subordinate role to reason. He claimed that reason is 'inert' and that what moves a man to action, what engages the will, are his passions. But since the passions themselves are not subject to reason, there is an unbridgeable gulf between reason and the will. 'Reason is, and ought to be, the slave of the passions, and can never pretend to any other office than to serve and obey them' (Hume, 1967, p. 417). This was one of the main reasons—though, as we have seen, not the only one—why Hume held that moral principles are not 'conclusions of our reason'. For what moves a man to action, he claimed, cannot be derived from reason, and moral principles do move those who accept them to action in particular situations, or move them to refrain from acting as they are inclined to do.

There is much that needs disentangling here. In acting, Hume thought men do things for the sake of certain ends. These are determined by their passions and the desires implicit in them. But the passions and, consequently, the ends which they determine, are not amenable to reason: 'It appears evident that the ultimate ends of human actions can never, in any case, be accounted for by *reason*, but recommend themselves entirely to the sentiments and affections of mankind without any dependence on the intellectual faculties. Ask a man why he uses exercise; he will answer, because he desires to keep his health. If you then inquire why he desires health, he will rapidly reply, because sickness is painful. If you push your inquiries further and desire a reason why he hates pain, it is impossible he can ever give any. This is an ultimate end, and is never referred to any other object' (Hume, 1957, p. 111). In other words, I can have a reason for wanting to take exercise and, therefore, for actually doing so, because I want to keep healthy. What reason discovers is that if one wants to keep healthy one should take exercise. But this would not move one to action unless one does want to keep healthy. Reason, here, points the way or means to something one wants independently of reason. Hume is right that reason does *sometimes* play this kind of role. He is also right to point out that the reasons we give for what we do come to an end and that we cannot go on indefinitely giving further reasons for our actions. But it does not follow that we are related to the reasons for which we cannot give further reasons always in the same way, nor that the ends for which we act are always determined in the way Hume thinks they are.

He thinks that reason can have an influence on our conduct through the passions only in two ways. First, it can give rise to a passion or desire by informing a person of the existence of something which is a proper object of that passion or desire.

Take Hume's example: 'I may desire any fruit as of an excellent relish; but whenever you convince me of my mistake, my longing ceases' (Hume, 1967, p. 417). It is reason that points out my mistake; but it is not for any reason that I like fruit of a certain relish. What makes me partial to the relish which this fruit lacks is not reason but taste. It is because of this partiality that I was going to reach for it; but upon discovering my mistake I lose the inclination I had to do so. For I discover that, contrary to what I had supposed, the fruit before me is not of the kind to which I am partial.

The second way in which Hume thought that reason can influence conduct is by pointing out the connections of cause and effect so as to afford us a means of exerting any passion or obtaining satisfaction of an objective. Hence the previous example of the man who takes exercise as a means of keeping fit and healthy.

Hume's view, then, is that reason may be 'the *mediate* cause of an action by prompting or directing passion'. It is passion and the desire connected with it that are the *immediate* or *final* cause of action. Speaking of moral judgments which also move a man to action—such judgments as 'That was a despicable thing to do, so I shan't speak to him again', or 'That would be an unjust thing to do, so I won't do it'—he says: 'This final sentence depends on some feeling which nature has made universal in the whole species. For what else can have an influence of this nature? But in order to pave the way for such a sentiment and give a proper discernment of its object, it is often necessary, we find, that much reasoning should precede ...' (Hume, 1957, p. 6). So, according to Hume, reason does not enter into the relation between a sentiment of disapprobation, horror or pity and what we disapprove of, find horrible or pitiable. What reason establishes is that what, for instance, this man did is the kind of thing we find horrible, or that the state which that man is in is the kind of state which inspires pity in us. If we are indifferent to the kind of state which reason discovers, we shall not pity him and we shall not do what we would have done were we to pity him. There is something right about this, but also something wrong. What is right is that a man may be hard-hearted or devoid of pity, and there is nothing unreasonable about his hard-heartedness. If this is a defect, then it is a defect of the heart, not of the understanding. But to talk of it as a 'defect' is to make a moral judgment, and that, according to Hume, is itself a response of the heart. So a man may not pity someone whom he sees to be in a state of misery and suffering. He cannot, on the other hand, pity someone in any state whatsoever. In so far as Hume thought so he was wrong.

We call a man hard-hearted just because what he himself sees as pitiful does not move him to pity. That is, the connection between what he apprehends and the affective response which is not forthcoming in his case is not purely accidental. If someone told you he pities a common acquaintance whom you think to be reasonably well off and happy, you would ask: 'Why do you pity him?' or 'What do you pity him for?' You would expect to be told something about him you didn't know which changes your picture of him. Perhaps he is suffering from an incurable disease. Or perhaps, while he has what others envy him for, he nevertheless is not able to enjoy it. You would expect to be told that he lacks something important, or something he himself wants, or that he is suffering, or that what he does now will bring about his suffering in the future. You would expect to be told something like this just because of what the words 'I pity him' mean or imply. Thus while Hume is correct in thinking that within certain limits men differ in their affective responses, he is wrong to think that there is no intelligible connection between how they *see* a situation, the *terms* in which they think about it, and their *affective response* to it. Hume is right in thinking that reason has a grip on the will through the emotions, but wrong to think that there is a gap between the life of reason and the life of the sentiments. So we have to ask: (i) How do the emotions themselves have a grip on the will? How is the will related to the emotions? (ii) Though there may be discrepancies between reason and the emotions in individual cases, what kind of unity is there normally between the two? Hume failed to answer these questions adequately.

Take Hume's claim that reason is 'impotent', 'inert', 'inactive', 'cool' or 'detached', that it shows us things but does not move, and that what does move us cannot be derived from reason. Obviously men greatly differ from each other in what they care for or are interested in, in what they attach importance to, like and dislike, in what moves them and in what they want and enjoy. But these differences are not all of the same kind and they do not all have the same source. Of course one man may be indifferent to what reason discovers in a particular case while another man may not be. Consequently they may choose to act differently. Each will have some reason for doing what he does, though they will be different reasons. Hume puts this by saying that what reason discovers in this case moves one man to action because he is not indifferent to it, and it fails to move the other man to action because he is indifferent. But here 'indifference' may cover a wide variety of things. For Hume the model is provided by the man who is not horrified by wilful murder, or the man in whose heart there is no pity. If such a man is plotting to kill somebody, the only way you have of prevailing upon him not to do so is to convince him that he will not benefit from it, or that if he does things will turn out to his detriment. If you succeed, you will have given him reason for not doing what he plans to do. This is how you have to proceed in this case just because certain considerations do not weigh with him or engage his will—because he is indifferent to other people's lives, to their sorrow, to doing them harm. This is an extreme case where a man is cut off from certain aspects of reason, and in this respect he is separated from contact with other people—although he speaks and understands their language nearly perfectly.

Hume is right to think that such a person is not 'unreasonable' in the sense that he can think, reason and calculate as well as anyone what he should do, given what he wants to obtain or achieve. But he is wrong to think that you can go on extending the scope or limits of his indifference indefinitely without curtailing his powers of reasoning. For in so far as speaking and reasoning necessarily involve acting and are, in fact, themselves modes of action, they must presuppose a lack of indifference in men, a concern for or an interest in aspects of their environment. Take this away and you will not have left man even with a detached intellect; you will have taken from him his powers of understanding, his capacity to engage in normal conversation with ordinary men. Sentiments, in the broad sense that Hume used the term, are an integral part of the life of speech and reason.

The reverse is equally true; reason and speech are just as

much an integral part of the life of the sentiments. Hume said that 'passions can be contrary to reason only so far as they are *accompanied* with some judgment or opinion' (Hume, ·1967, p. 416). He thought of the passion as one thing and the judgment or belief as another. He did not recognise that the judgment is one with the passion, a part of it. Take the case of pity again. As I said, I cannot pity just anyone. If I pity someone I must think of him and see him as in a sorry state. If you can show me that I am wrong you will have also removed my pity for him. If we both know the man well this may take much subtle reasoning on your part. But if my vision of him is more sensitive than yours things may go the other way. You may come to appreciate why I pity him and so see something in or about him which had eluded you. As a result you may come to pity him yourself. It is well known that reason can guide us in what we feel, just as our feelings can guide us in what we see.

Iago, through the hints he dropped, aroused Othello's jealousy. But only by getting him to believe that Desdemona was unfaithful to him. Othello's weakness was his gullibility— not that he was easy to convince through weakness of judgment. He had a readiness to believe certain things and, his jealousy once aroused, he was not disposed to consider dispassionately the facts relevant to Iago's allegation. This made him immune to reason. One should be clear that it is not the emotion as such, jealousy, that can have no transaction with reason. For unless Othello really believed Desdemona to be unfaithful, however falsely, he could not be jealous. The truth is rather that once jealous Othello's ability to consider reasons was impaired. Having come to feel the way he did, he became unable or unwilling to consider reasons. He jumped to a conclusion and, his jealousy once aroused, he was unwilling to question it. One could say (*vide* Sartre, 1939) that here the belief and the emotion give each other mutual support and perpetuate each other.

Hume contrasted such violent emotions as jealousy with what he called 'calm passions' which, he claimed, are often confused with reason. But these are what I should wish to characterise as *affective reasons*, of which moral reasons are a good example. Thus a friend asks me to give a message to an acquaintance to let him off a promise he has made. I want to help but know the message to be false. I say: 'But that would be telling a lie.' This is my reason for not doing what my friend asks me to do. It is because I see lying as something bad and, therefore, as something to be avoided that I refuse to comply. To see it as something bad is to have certain thoughts about it, thoughts about matters to which I am not indifferent. I could express this by saying that honesty matters to me, that it is important or that I care about it. What this caring amounts to can be unpacked in some detail. It would involve going into what I would feel, how I would respond to various eventualities—for instance the way I would feel about betraying someone's trust. If I did not feel for people, if I were incapable of entering into certain kinds of relationships with them, if I were devoid of any feeling of shame, how could I be said to care for honesty or to think of lying as a bad thing? Seeing it as something bad involves being affectively disposed in certain ways or having certain sentiments—sentiments that belong to a form of moral life and which cannot exist independently of its concepts. It is in this sense that 'it would be a lie' is an affective reason. My point is that the judgments which have the role of reasons for doing or not doing something and the feelings in question are not merely coincident or contingently connected, the one then being confused with the other—as Hume believed. They form a whole and could not exist apart. In fact moral life is a dimension of life in which concepts, the judgments which these permit and moral emotions, such as guilt, shame and remorse, love, pity and gratitude, are mutually dependent on one another—logically dependent.

It is true that the consideration of reasons demands that one should be fair and objective, that one should not let wishful thinking bias one's appreciation. This is characterised as being 'dispassionate' and 'disinterested'. The idea is that one should be free from the bias of one's interests and the confining focus of one's emotions. For emotions can transform one's awareness and bias one's appreciation. But it is not true that their perspective always impairs one's contact with what is going on around one. On the contrary, if one did not feel for people and care for things, if one had no interests, one would be an outsider to so much of what goes on around one that one would be hardly aware of anything. When Hume characterised reason as 'cool' and 'inactive' he was identifying it with *indifference*. But we have seen that being dispassionate is not the same thing as indifference.

If reasons for action did not weigh with people they would not be reasons at all. Their doing so is not some additional feature of them which is external to their being reasons for action. People must, of course, find them intelligible as reasons; and some reasons may not weigh with some people. But if they are to be intelligible as reasons they must be capable of carrying weight with some people, of engaging their will. This they do through their emotions and affective dispositions. It is through these that people find identity with norms of reason; it is these that give such norms a special place in their lives: 'Extinguish all the warm feelings and prepossessions in favour of virtue, and all disgust and aversion to vice; render men totally indifferent towards these distinctions; and morality is no longer a practical study, nor has any tendency to regulate our lives and actions' (Hume, 1957, p. 6). Except that Hume misunderstood the way they bear on our moral actions and decisions.

V   Mrs Foot on Moral Reasons

Mrs Foot quotes the passage from Hume which I quoted earlier: 'Ask a man why he uses exercise ...' She comments: 'Hume might just as well have ended this series with boredom: sickness often brings boredom, and no one is required to give a reason why he does not want to be bored, any more than he has to give a reason why he does not want to pursue what interests him. In general, anyone is given a reason for acting when he is shown the way to something he wants; but for some the question "Why do you want that?" will make sense, and for others it will not' (Foot, 1958). She then continues: 'It seems clear that in this division justice falls on the opposite side from pleasure and interest and such things. "Why shouldn't I do that?" is not answered by the words "because it is unjust" as it is answered by showing that the action will bring boredom, loneliness, pain, discomfort or certain kinds of incapacity' (p. 101).

Her claim is this: If you show or get a man to believe that a novel he has picked up is thoroughly dull and boring, you will have given him a reason why he should put it down and not read it. The connection is intelligible: nobody wants to be bored. Whereas if you persuade a man that what he intends to do is unjust, you have not *so far* given him a reason for not doing it. For he can ask: 'Why should I not do what is unjust?'—as he cannot ask: 'Why should I not do what bores me?' The assumption is that no one would want to do what is boring—except as a means to some further end. So it is not enough to persuade a man that what he proposes to do is unjust; you have *further* to persuade him that an unjust action leads to something that he wants to avoid—like boredom, pain, injury or discomfort: ' "It's unjust" gives a reason only if the nature of justice can be shown to be such that it is necessarily connected with what a man wants.' In other words, 'it is boring' is a reason for avoiding doing something *in its own right*. In contrast, a man must have a reason for wishing to avoid doing what is unjust.

Mrs Foot presupposes, in contrast with Hume, that men are indifferent to justice, that they don't care for justice except in so far as it is a means to something they want—as opposed to enjoyment, for instance. In this she is wrong; one does not need any inducement to act justly if one cares for justice.[1] But does this mean that justice is something that men want in the way they want enjoyment, comfort or excitement? Does it mean that when a man says, 'I shall give him what he asks for; it is only just that he should have it', 'it is just' provides a reason for what he intends to do in the way that 'it is enjoyable' does? The answer is No. That far Mrs Foot is right. But justice does not fall on *either* side of her dividing line—ends or means. She is wrong to think that everything that counts as a reason for doing something must have a place on one side or the other of this dividing line. This is an assumption she shares with Hume.

Take the case of a man who witnesses an action he characterises as 'unjust' and who tries to stop it. Obviously he is not indifferent. What moves him to action is the *moral significance* of what he witnesses. The aspect under which he sees it gives him reason for doing something about it. He wants to prevent the intended victim from being the recipient of injustice. Why? This is not intelligible in the same way as someone's wanting to do what he enjoys or finds interesting is. Nor is it intelligible in the way that actions done as a means to something one wants are intelligible.

He sees what he does as a requirement or demand of justice. What moves him to action is the sight of injustice. But he can only see what he sees if he possesses certain moral concepts. And that moves him to action because justice does matter to him. Let us grant that there is a conceptual tie between intentional action and wanting, so that if a man acts intentionally he must want to do what he does—if only as a means to something else that he wants. According to Mrs Foot a want that is not intelligible as a means, is intelligible as an end for which no further reason can be given—e.g. a man wanting to sit here and not there because it is more comfortable, not wanting to go on with the novel he has been reading because he finds it boring. In such cases the agent's reasons for doing or not doing something are relative to what he wants, and what he wants is intelligible in itself because it is the kind of thing that men normally want or are averse to. In the example of the man who acts out of a concern for justice this is not so. He wants to do what he does; but his reasons are not relative to what he wants. Rather what he wants is relative to the reasons that weigh with him.

In so far as certain reasons weigh with him he will want to do certain things in particular situations. But he will not want to do these things as a means to some end that lies beyond what he is doing. To say that certain reasons weigh with him (the content of which can be specified in such moral terms as 'desert', 'equity', 'rights', etc.) *is* to say that he has regard for justice. Justice is not an end as a means to which he wants what he wants. The relation of justice to what he wants in the particular circumstances is not that of ends to means. We could say that justice is a *norm* in terms of which he apprehends and weighs certain situations and actions that he considers. A norm, but not a goal. What is *ultimate* here is that certain sorts of considerations weigh with him. This is a measure of the kind of person he is.

The kind of reasons that weigh with him: this fact cannot be understood apart from their moral significance. To understand this we have to consider *what he sees* in what for him constitutes a reason for acting or for refraining from acting. What he sees in the facts that constitute a reason for him is determined by the terms in which he looks at them, the concepts in terms of which he considers them. Norms of behaviour and judgment are implicit in these concepts.

In the passage quoted by Mrs Foot, Hume points out the way in which the chain of reasons for acting comes to an end in such descriptions as 'because I find it enjoyable', 'because I am thirsty', 'because I am interested in it', 'because it is painful'. These are intelligible as reasons for action because of their place among what men are naturally attracted by and averse to. But there are other descriptions in which the chain of our reasons for acting comes to an end, whose intelligibility cannot be accounted in this way—e.g. 'because it is unjust', 'because that would be dishonest', 'because I promised him'. Their intelligibility lies in their being descriptions in terms of concepts we understand, concepts which embody norms of action.

VI Reason and Moral Commitment

Deliberation before acting is a common and familiar phenomenon. People find themselves in situations in which they do not know what to do. They deliberate, consider reasons, and as a result they come to know what to do. Deliberation leads to the formation of an intention which they execute or put into practice. We could say that here reason guides the will. We have seen that Hume found a difficulty in this idea: 'Demonstration [which is the exercise of reason] and volition are totally removed from each other' (Hume, 1967, p. 413). He did not deny that reasons do guide the will; he denied that they can do so *directly* and *on their own*. The will, he held, can only be moved by passion, and although reason cannot initiate or oppose any passion, it can direct it. That is reason can guide the will only by directing the passions. It does so by informing us of objects and characteristics towards which we are not indifferent, and by pointing out the means to what we want: 'Were what is discovered indifferent and beget no desire or aversion, it could have no influence on conduct and behaviour' (Hume, 1957, p. 6). It is as if reason said to us: 'The situation that confronts you is a dangerous one. The man in front of you is in a sorry state. That would be a useful thing to have. If you do so-and-so it will have such-and-such consequences. Now it is up to you what you do.' Here the jurisdiction of reason ends, and passion takes over. If you are afraid of the danger and you have no reason for wanting to stand up to it, you retreat. If you feel sorry for the man, you try to help him. Whether or not you act and what you do depends on how you *feel* about what reason tells you and on what you *want*. But neither of these is determined by reason. Here Hume speaks of nature and of the way we are constituted.

We can summarise Hume's position as follows:

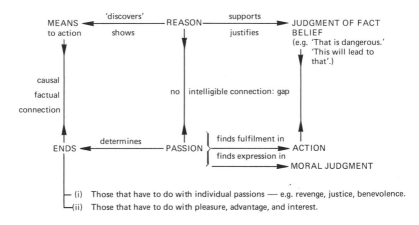

We consider the two kinds of judgment arrived at or supported by reason to be relevant to what we do because of their relation to our ends or goals which are ultimately determined by our passions. These ends, according to Hume, are of two kinds. So he speaks of two principles that operate on the will (Hume, 1967, p. 418). He means that there are two kinds of end for the sake of which we act. The first are *particular* ends of 'certain instincts originally implanted in our natures'

(p. 417). The second are the ends of 'the *general* appetite to good and aversion to evil, considered merely as such' (ibid.). By 'good' here he means 'pleasure', 'advantage' and 'self-interest'; and by 'evil' he means 'pain', 'harm' and 'injury'. Thus he writes:

> When I receive any injury from another, I often feel a violent passion of resentment, which makes me desire his evil and punishment, independent of all considerations of pleasure and advantage to myself ...
> The common error of metaphysicians has been in ascribing the direction of the will entirely to one of these principles, and supposing the other to have no influence. Men often act knowingly against their interest. For which reason the view of the greatest possible good does not always influence him (ibid., p. 418).

He then goes on:

> In general we may observe that both these principles operate on the will; and where they are contrary, that either of them prevails, according to the *general* character or *present* disposition of the person. What we call strength of mind, implies the prevalence of the calm passions above the violent (ibid.).

Note that Hume distinguishes between 'the *general* character' of a person and his '*present* disposition'. Presumably by the former he means a man's character traits, his settled dispositions, the kinds of consideration that weigh with him generally. For instance, he may be a man who always puts his own interest first and who never loses sight of it when he is tempted by particular passions, such as the desire to get his own back on someone who has upset him. By 'present disposition' he means what a man is disposed to do on a particular occasion though he has not yet formed an intention to do so. The present disposition would be an expression of a *passion*, given his view of his present circumstances. When, as a result, he forms an intention or makes up his mind to act in accordance with his inclination, this would be an expression of his *will* in those circumstances.

Disposition and intention, passion and will are not the same thing. For a man who is presently disposed to act a certain way may, on reflection, make up his mind not to do so. His disposition is a *passivity*, it is not subject to the will; whereas what he actually does is so. In doing it he is *active*. But how are reason and passion related to the will? How does reason guide the will? How does passion determine it? By 'the will' here I mean its particular exercise, such as in the making of decisions, the formation of intentions, in particular situations. In the above passage Hume also speaks of 'the direction of the will'. I believe that it is important to recognise the distinction between the *exercise* of the will in particular situations and its general *direction*.

However 'the direction of the will' is not the same thing as 'the general character of a person'. Hume does not seem to recognise this. I think that when Kierkegaard spoke of 'willing the good' and when Wittgenstein said that ' "to love one's neighbour" means to will' (Wittgenstein, 1961a) they were both speaking of 'the direction of the will' and not of particular decisions. Yet they did not mean anything like what is normally meant by 'traits and dispositions'. They were not referring to a man's settled dispositions, but to his commitments. Kant's distinction between inclination and duty is partly connected with this, and so is his distinction between a love seated in the propensities of sense and one seated in the will. Thus true courage as opposed to mere daring, for instance, is an expression of will.

There is a big difference in the way a man's will is determined in these two cases. The daring man identifies his will with his inclinations, whereas in the case of true courage, charity or honesty a man identifies his will with ideals which give him new inclinations. This is part of what Simone Weil has in mind when she says that 'one does not fall into the good' (Weil, 1948, p. 82). If one said that no one is charitable, honest, just or brave *by nature*, this would not be to deny that people do have natural reactions of kindness, etc. But it would be to say that these in themselves do not make a man charitable, just or honest—even though it is true that he could not have these virtues without such propensities. Where they are absent they will have to be awakened before a man can turn towards such virtues. But this is not enough. They will have to be turned into a principle of organisation around which his actions are centred before we can speak of something more than a mere spontaneous gesture of kindness or expression of honesty. For an honest man or a compassionate person does not merely act or react spontaneously in certain ways. He also checks many of his natural inclinations in particular situations, forgoes pleasure and faces dangers and difficulties for the sake of people for whom he feels and has regard. He has a centre other than his inclinations from which he acts. Compare with the contrast between a man who is attracted by a woman and one who loves her deeply.

Thus when kindness is no longer merely an expression of what a person is inclined to do, but an expression of will, it does not become something less spontaneous. But it does become something for the sake of which a man is willing to forgo pursuing conflicting inclinations. We can speak of *commitment* or dedication, of what he has given his heart to. Here the question, 'How does reason guide the will? How does passion determine it?' asks for the roles of reason and passion in the formation of this centre from which a man acts: Can reason guide a man in what he gives his heart to? In what way are his passions or sentiments redirected and transformed when he comes to a new moral belief? What we are now concerned with is not the exercise of the will in the decisions that he takes, but its formation, reformation or transformation.

Hume, we saw, distinguished sharply between assessment and decision. The former is the exercise of the understanding and finds expression in a man's judgments. These are arrived at and so supported and justifiable by reasons. In that sense we could say that a person is guided in his particular assessments by reason. But for him to be able to appreciate reasons on particular occasions and in specific fields of knowledge he must already know a great deal. He must have an understanding he can thus exercise. This he acquires through training and intellectual education. Decision, on the other hand, is the exercise of the will. This Hume severs from the understanding, as if it were possible to exercise the will blindly and in the dark. He holds that decisions are initiated by the passions; the will can only be moved by the passions, for reason is 'inert'. But if decision is the exercise of the will, the agent must be capable of assessment and know what he is about. This is his capacity to act for reasons. For this, however, he must have a will he can exercise, and this he could only have acquired and developed through 'moral education' and the experience of life—through human intercourse and engagement in the various activities that go on around him.

Because moral judgment is intimately connected with human action Hume thought of moral judgment as the expression of passion. So he classified it with decision rather than assessment: both issue from the passions. Thus we have a man's moral beliefs and commitments which are expressions of the will, and we have his decisions which are exercises of his will on particular occasions. As for his moral judgments, these are certainly expressions of his moral sentiments. But, contrary to what Hume thought, they are equally forms of his assessments. Their relation to the will lies in the fact that the sentiments to which these assessments belong are themselves moral sentiments and so presuppose his relation to certain moral norms or values. This relation constitutes the disposition of his will. This is not true of what Hume calls 'judgments of fact'. A man's relation to the logical norms and principles which are presupposed in these judgments constitutes his intellect or understanding, not his will. Thus although in representing moral judgments as less like beliefs than we imagine Hume made their relation to reason tenuous, he nevertheless showed some recognition of the way they are bound up with where the man who makes them stands as a person.

A man may approach a situation that calls for action with an open mind, that is with his mind not made up in advance. But this does not mean that he does not bring to it a particular disposition of will. His mind may be open about what he is to do, but his will is committed. There are certain things which he would not consider doing, certain actions that would be ruled out for him by his moral beliefs. Hume takes this commitment to issue wholly from the passions; he does not think that there is any logical room for the exercise of reason here. This is partly connected with his view that reason can only direct or redirect the passions to particular objects without being able to beget new passions or play a role in what a man gives his heart to. It is connected with his view of men's ultimate ends, the way they are determined, and their role in human action. When he speaks of 'ultimate ends' he has in mind such 'natural appetites' as hunger and sexual attraction, and such 'natural reactions' as we find in fear, anger and pity. He shows little recognition of the way a man's affective reactions are extended and transformed in the course of his development as a child and of how they acquire new objects. Much of the child's emotional life and sentiments are logically dependent on the culture in which he develops. The idea that his 'ultimate ends' are fixed by his passions which are determined by nature, therefore, needs severe revision.

There are a great many ends that human beings pursue which cannot be related to more basic ends. Yet they are not determined by nature, but by culture. They become ends for human beings in the development of common activities and institutions. We could not pursue these ends, nor could they mean anything to us, in separation from the life and activities to which they belong.

Especially in a complex culture like ours there is a great variety of ends, interests, ideals and loyalties that a man can have. Acquiring new interests, forming new allegiances, making new values and ideals his own, give a man new ends in particular situations and beget new sentiments in him. In this process of developing an identity a man brings his affections and sentiments to bear on new objects. He comes to love new things, to have respect for new ideals. He gives his heart to new causes, develops new interests, acquires new things to love, fight and die for. But if he can be described as giving his love to new ideals, it is equally true that the ideals transform his love. His capacity for love thus enables him to form new loyalties, to come into contact with new objects and so to widen his horizons. These new objects and loyalties, in turn, modify the love that enabled him to give himself to them. He comes into contact with new ideas, considerations to which he was previously indifferent now come to move him. In so far as these are internal to his sentiments, we can say that in coming to be moved by new kinds of consideration he acquires new sentiments.

This is a possibility which Hume could not have envisaged. He knew that our sentiments can be directed and redirected to particular objects by means of reasoning that changes our apprehension of these objects. In this way we may come to pity a man we did not pity before by coming to see that he is in a sorry state. But Hume denies that a hard-hearted man could be led by reason to feel pity for those he already knows to be in a pitiful condition. He denies that such a man can come to be moved by considerations which did not move him before. The difference I have in mind may be likened to the difference between coming to care for a person to whom one was indifferent and coming to care for a new value or ideal. The latter is a change in the direction of one's will. It means that new considerations come to weigh with one, many situations that previously left one cold now move one. One comes to care for new things, to want new things, one acquires new ends and objectives.[2]

Here what one wants, the ends or objectives one pursues in one's actions, are determined by one's allegiances, by what one attaches importance to, and not the other way around. What one considers important is something on which one can reflect; one's allegiances can be subject to appraisal and criticism. There are different forms of reflection, appraisal and criticism that are open to one here. One may ask oneself what it is that one sees in some of the values by which one has been living. The mere attempt to articulate this honestly may deepen or weaken the regard one feels for them. One may come to see that there is more in these values than one realised, or that one's regard for them had been superficial and, perhaps, not very genuine. This may trouble one; or it may cut one loose from something for which, without realising it, one had stopped caring. Or, again, new values which one comes into contact with and which win one's allegiance may give one a new point of view from which to consider one's old allegiances.

I am arguing that values which give one a perspective on things and enable one to see them in a new light, have themselves a sense or significance on which one can reflect: What does this significance amount to? What do I see in them? What is there to be seen in them? What do the people whom I admire and think wise see in them? What do they make of these values? What significance have these values assumed in their lives? Can I learn from these lives? I may come to ask such questions for various reasons—certain dissatisfactions I feel with my life, disappointments perhaps with my parents, or fearing that I have failed them. Reflection on these questions may bring me to give up pursuing certain ends and objectives, and to come to want new things in life. Here reflection and reasoning does not merely show me the way to what I want, the means to the ends I seek, as Hume thought; it gives me new wants, new purposes and new sentiments.

I spoke of allegiance, identification and loyalty. It is here, I believe, that the difference between will and passion, between commitment and mere inclination is to be found. For I may desire things and have inclinations that I find unacceptable and of which I feel ashamed. This is different from being afraid to seek their satisfaction. In the former case the desire or inclination is *mine*, but it is *external to my will*. It does not determine the direction of my will. When it is active it constitutes a 'temptation' for me, one which I would try to resist. Not because of any anxiety it provokes, but because of what the values that I believe in mean to me. The desire is mine, but I do not endorse it. It is not simply in conflict with other desires I have; it is incompatible with my moral beliefs. This is what makes it unacceptable to me. There is a condemnation here which no conflicting desire can provide.

We saw earlier that Hume did not recognise *how passions and sentiments involve judgment and apprehension*. We now see that he did not recognise *how the will involves endorsement and commitment*. Hume pointed out that if we were indifferent to what reasoning reveals in particular situations these considerations would not move us to action. I pointed out that this is important and that one could say that reason engages the will through our sentiments. Hume thought that the connection between what we apprehend and what we feel is purely contingent. I considered the example where someone refuses to comply with a request because doing so involves telling a lie. I described his reason for refusing as an 'affective reason' and pointed out that what we feel about telling a lie logically depends on the significance we attach to it and so on what honesty means to us.

We see now that the form which my reluctance takes here is different from the case where I am averse to doing something because I know by experience that it would upset me. I could say: 'I don't want to be upset. Who does?' But here there is no moral belief, no commitment, nothing that is endorsed or condemned. That I don't want to do something that would upset me is understandable; but not in the same way as my aversion to lying. Yet for Hume it seems to provide the model for the way the will is moved by passion.

Suppose that I am the kind of man who is averse to being upset and would do anything 'for a bit of peace'. You could say that 'peace' is an end that I pursue in many of my actions. In this respect I act consistently, and you could predict that in an argument I would say what I think the other person would like to hear me say. I would be doing so in order to avoid conflict. This is a feature of my *character*. Perhaps I am so intent always on avoiding conflict that I have never experienced mutual trust and the give and take which it makes possible. As a result I may find little that I feel worth defending and putting myself out for; little for which I am prepared to face danger and discomfort. Here my character is constituted largely by defences against threats and dangers which I have learned to imagine perhaps as a result of childhood experiences. The tightness of these defences stands in my way, prevents me from entering the life of others and sharing their interests, their joys and sorrows. Consequently I remain a man with no deep convictions, loyalties and commitments. It is true that I pursue certain ends; but I have no standards of criticism— except in Hume's sense of being able to evaluate means relative to fixed ends. I have not become an autonomous person, do not have a will of my own.

For Hume a man's will are the settled ends for which he acts. These are fixed ultimately by the passions with which nature has endowed him. The role of reason is confined to pointing the way or the means to these ends and to directing the man's passions in particular situations. But it cannot transform his passions or influence the ends determined by them: 'It appears evident that the ultimate ends of human actions can never be accounted for by *reason*, but recommend themselves entirely to the sentiments and affections of mankind without any dependence on the intellectual faculties.' I have argued that the ends which constitute a man's will are those ends which he endorses and which, therefore, presuppose his having made his own certain values and standards of criticism. So it is not true that what a man gives his heart to he does 'without any dependence on the intellectual faculties'.

Hume is wrong about the way our ultimate ends are fixed where the will is concerned. Furthermore it is misleading to characterise many of them as 'ultimate', since they are surrounded by thoughts, subject to question and criticism, and so amenable to reason. Here the role of reason is not to point the way to what we want in particular cases, but to examine what there is to be found in the kind of thing to which we attach importance, whether what *we* find in it falls short of that, how it fits in with other things we value and fares in their light—as well as *vice versa*. The kind of reasoning in question may be called 'self-reflection' or 'soul searching'. I have argued that such reflection may lead to a change in one's values and, therefore, in a transformation of what one wants out of life and a redirection of one's will.

VII   Summing Up

Hume asks and wishes to be clear about the way '*reason* and *sentiment* concur in almost all moral determinations and conclusions'. Instead of moral conclusions I spoke of moral judgments; how they can be arrived at and also supported or criticised by the consideration of reasons, the way they express the feelings of the person who makes them, and how this bears on his sincerity and moral understanding.

I think that although Hume had got certain things wrong here, he was nevertheless raising important questions and was right in the emphasis he put on the sentiments. He was wrong in thinking that moral judgments cannot evince a man's grasp or apprehension of how things stand morally, but right to think that they are expressions of his moral sentiments and thus show where he stands morally as a person. How we judge an action morally does not only depend on what the action is like, but also on what *we* are like. If it does depend on what the action is like then it is amenable to reasoning (see section I). But is what we are like, in the sense of where we stand morally, also amenable to the scrutiny of reason? Can one ask 'Are the values that I accept the right values?' as one can ask 'Was that the right thing to do?' I argued for an affirmative answer to these questions (see especially sections I and VI).

If a moral judgment can evince the moral apprehension of the person who makes it, this apprehension is not something external to the feelings which find expression in the judgment. Thus I spoke of the person's moral feelings, his affective responses to particular actions or situations, as the form which his apprehension takes, given the values for which he cares (see section II).

Hume's conception of the passions and his philosophy of language did not permit him to appreciate this. He thought of feelings as 'inner occurrences' that are only accidentally connected with their objects. Unable to find any characteristic or relation apprehended by their subject, Hume claimed that these feelings *constitute* the merit or demerit on which he pronounces: 'Nothing is good or bad, but feeling makes it so.' The morality or immorality of an action arises entirely from our sentiments; if we did not feel what we normally feel when we contemplate ingratitude, barbarity or treachery there would be nothing immoral about these acts. I did not examine Hume's unsuccessful attempt to escape the relativism of this view, but I did criticise it for the way it puts things upside down. However Hume runs this view into a very different one for which I have great sympathy. If we did not feel what we normally feel when we contemplate ingratitude, barbarity or treachery we would not come to talk of these acts as immoral and pass adverse judgment on them. In other words, certain affective reactions which, to some extent, we share, reactions in which common sentiments find expression, underlie the *possibility* of moral distinctions which many of us take for granted in our moral judgments. Here Hume is right in thinking that moral values are not based on ratiocination. They grow out of certain common primitive affective reactions in the context of a communal life (see section III).

It is important to emphasise that the sentiments which are presupposed by the possibility of moral distinctions and judgments are *moral* sentiments and they are themselves, in turn, embedded in a life in which people use moral concepts and make moral judgments. They are an integral part of such a life. This does not mean that with each moral judgment that a person makes he must have the appropriate moral feelings.

There is a world of difference between such a lack of feeling on particular occasions and moral indifference. I argued that it is only in the case of indifference, where a man is devoid of certain feelings or sentiments, that he cannot appreciate the moral significance of certain situations which belong to the perspective of these feelings.

Where Hume spoke of 'moral determinations' I spoke of *moral decisions*—in other words the moral determination of our actions. What does deliberation amount to here? How can it engage the will? How are our feelings related to what reason considers when we are trying to make up our minds? I argued that what has the force of moral reasons for action or for refraining from action are considerations to which we are affectively disposed. I examined how the link between reason and feeling here is an *internal* one. Hence I talked of 'affective reasons' (see section IV). This is the counterpart of what in connection with reasons for moral judgments I might have called 'affective apprehension'—*viz.* remorse as 'pained apprehension' of the enormity of one's own deeds.

When discussing moral judgment I had distinguished between the judgments that a man makes and the values in which he believes or to which he gives his heart. I made a parallel distinction between a man's moral decisions and the disposition of his will or his moral commitments. I argued that the disposition of a man's will is not determined by his passions through the ends or objectives which these give him, in the way Hume imagined, but through his *endorsement* of his passions and inclinations and through the determination of these by his moral beliefs. I thus distinguished between the way a man is moved by his loyalties and allegiances and the way he is moved by his desires and fears. The former has to do with his *identity* as an agent and individual, the latter with his *character* (see section VI). I argued that where a man's moral commitments are concerned his will is not unamenable to the guidance of reason as Hume imagined, that it is not immune from moral criticism. Reason can guide one in one's affective responses to particular situations, one's inclinations with regard to specific objects, as Hume acknowledged. But it can also guide a man in what he gives his heart to. This is what Hume did not allow.

There is room for reflection on the values to which one has

given one's heart and which determine the disposition of one's will. One may reflect on what these values come to and on the significance they have for one. As a result of attempting to spell this out honestly one may grow dissatisfied with oneself in the light of one's renewed appreciation of their claims. This may deepen one's regard for these values and this may amount to a change in one, a change in the disposition of one's will. Here one may learn from the lives of other people where these values play an active role; these lives—in the case of the exceptional individual—may become a mirror in which one sees the significance of these values. But it is also possible that one should grow dissatisfied with the values themselves. This dissatisfaction would be articulated in terms which give content to rival values which may be winning one's allegiance. Reflection here is sifting out one's moral reactions, not to a particular situation but to a whole spectrum of situations. Again the result may be a change in one's perspective on things, in what one wants in life, in the direction of one's will. One may describe this as 'moral conversion'. The more extreme case which combines features of both these cases is the one where a man is hit by certain aspects of life and human relationships to which he has hitherto been totally indifferent. Here too the process of opening his eyes to them and of integrating their emotional impact into his life is akin to a religious conversion and may involve self-criticism and moral reflection on life.

There is no incompatibility between my emphasis on the possibility of such moral reflection and my insistence that our reasoning about the moral judgments we make and the decisions we take is made possible by our allegiance to moral values which we take for granted in these reasonings. For these values become the object of moral scrutiny on the basis of others which draw our allegiance. It is even possible that these values themselves suggest new possibilities which provide the basis for the criticism of moral attitudes which have stemmed from them. The possibilities of moral scrutiny and self-criticism are richer than is normally allowed by philosophical theories in ethics.

6 Wisdom I: Religion and Reason*

I Wisdom's Position: Belief and Truth in Religion

Professor Wisdom holds that religions speak about the world we all know even when they seem to refer to what lies outside the sphere of our senses or beyond this life. He insists that even when there is little or no difference between the believer and the non-believer in what they expect in a future life, the difference between them is not confined to how they live their life and face death. They also differ in how they *see* life—though these two differences are logically dependent. So it makes sense to ask whether what they say about life is *true*; religious beliefs are amenable to *reasons* which ultimately rest on how things stand here and now. A belief in the God of the scriptures is no exception to this.

I want to argue that in what Wisdom claims on these questions truth and falsity are intermingled. In this paper I shall be concerned to sort these out. Let me say at once that I agree with Wisdom on three points: The believer and non-believer do differ in how they see life and this difference is crucial to religious belief. Believers do speak of their beliefs as true and this makes perfectly good sense. Thirdly, in some circumstances reasoning or reflection which starts from certain features of the world, as experienced by a man in the grip of religious doubt, may clear his doubt and lead him to belief. These I take to be obvious points and no philosophy that denies them can, therefore, be sound. But in view of the fact that they have been denied by philosophers their reassertion does make sense. This is the philosophical background against which Wisdom has written about

* Originally published in the *Canadian Journal of Philosophy*, vol. V, no. 4 (December 1975).

religion.[1] He did not think that there is nothing in these denials and he set out to provide an account of religious belief, truth and reason which met the objections which forced his opponents to deny what is both obvious and also important. It is with some aspects of this account that I want to take issue in this paper.

II Religious Belief and Apprehension of Facts

We are tempted to think of God as an invisible being, beyond the reach of our senses, yet influencing everything we know by means of them. Therefore we can either not know that such a being exists at all, or we can at best know that He exists by an inference. Wisdom has encountered this line of thinking elsewhere in philosophy and has exposed its weaknesses. He has, therefore, to clear the way for an alternative. He insists that if there is a God it must be possible for us to know there is and to know this without an inference.

The disagreement between those who say there is a God and those who deny this, he argues, is like the disagreement between someone who says that the world is a garden and one who thinks it is a wilderness. It is not like the one between someone who says that it is all taken care of by an invisible gardener and someone who thinks that no such gardener exists. That there is a gardener, unseen, behind the scenes, if there is one, is an additional fact to the appearance of the garden; whereas that the world is a garden or the garden not a wilderness is not something over and above the world's or the garden's appearance. Still those who are familiar with that appearance may find it difficult to know what to make of it, to appreciate what it all adds up to, and while some may see nothing there but a wilderness, others may discern an order and arrangement reminiscent of one to be found in a well-cared-for garden. So the dispute between them is like disputes about whether someone has been kind or cruel, generous or mean, *after* one knows exactly what he has done, what led up to it, and the circumstances surrounding his actions. It is like disputes about whether or not there is beauty in the picture before us. It is like disputes about whether or not the defendant has been negligent *after* the witnesses have been heard and the beer examined. In all these cases one of the disputants fails to see or appreciate something even though it is in front of his nose and 'visible' in the appropriate sense, and argument guides his apprehension and changes his vision of what is so.

Wisdom has a great deal to say about this kind of argument and appreciation and its relation to other forms of argument and knowledge. He has much to say about why we tend to denigrate it and the harm this does both within and outside philosophy. What he has said is illuminating in a great many ways and in surprising directions. The rewards he has reaped in following this line of thinking have been so rich that it is understandable that he should have high hopes from it here too. I think, however, that these hopes divert his attention and he fails to make a distinction which is crucial here. Let me illustrate it in terms of two examples he gives himself.

A loves B and we feel that he is a fool to love her so. We consider and argue with A what sort of person B is like. In the course of this discussion we realise that A recognises everything we tell him and still continues to love B. 'We then feel that perhaps it is we who are blind and cannot see what he can see' (Wisdom, 1953, p. 161). Perhaps now A takes the initiative in the discussion and continuing with the kind of procedure we adopted earlier he shows us the charm and qualities of B which we have failed to see because we thought they are not compatible with what we saw in B. In this way we come to see something to which we have been blind though it was before our eyes all the time.

There is, however, another possibility which Wisdom does not consider, although it throws greater light on religious conversion. As before we may feel that we have been blind. On further reflection we realise that what we have been blind to is *not* what B is like, but what love is like. We had been blind not to the nature of B, but to the nature of love—to a kind of love, instances of which we may have come across before. We realise that it is *possible* after all to love someone who has all the defects that B has. We realise that 'love' can mean other things than what we had our minds fixed on. Our conception of love changes and this makes a difference to our apprehension of what is so—to our apprehension of A, his relation with B and what he responds to in her. Given such a change of conception, our apprehension in a variety of instances is bound to be different.

Wisdom is well aware of this possibility elsewhere, though it is a pity that he does not consider it here. In his paper 'Freewill' he considers a man who starts by noting affinities between a wheel turning in air and a wheel turning in water, milk or oil, and develops a new concept or method of representation, a new geometry of motion (Wisdom, 1965, pp. 28–9). A body moving freely becomes an ideal which can only be realised in thought, a norm used in describing how bodies actually move—where the deviation from the norm is what is considered important for our calculations. The words 'Nothing really moves freely' now express a statement of grammar, a timeless truth. They do not convey anything about what is the case in contrast with what might have been. Yet, given this new conception or geometry of motion, we are able to see in particular cases of motion something which could have been otherwise.

The other example is this: 'Someone now looks back on what has happened and asks, "But *was* it all so right, so admirable?" Isn't he wondering whether he hasn't been mistaken, blind?' (ibid., p. 46). Perhaps he decides that he had been mistaken or blind. But this may mean two different things. He may have been mistaken about what happened— though not because he was ignorant of some incidents which since then have come to light. As a result of such a misapprehension he may have thought that what happened was admirable. Now that he recognises features which he had not previously appreciated he sees that it was not so admirable after all. On the other hand, time, experience, even reflection on what happened on this particular occasion, may change his *conception* of what is admirable, so he may no longer see what happened in the same light as he did before; his apprehension of it may change—change not only in this case, but in the case of a wide range of actions and relations.

In 'Religious Belief' Wisdom mentions the case of a woman whose son was killed in the 1914 war. From then on she cannot believe in God. He comments: 'One must not forget how a single incident may suddenly throw a light on ten thousand others which one had managed to forget or never seen for what they were' (ibid., p. 50). But again there is more than one possibility here. She may, indeed, see that she had been rash and over-optimistic. She may say that her hopes had not been well founded. Her belief may crumble in a way that an hypothesis does, or a judgment of some generality: 'I thought that these people, among whom I have spent more than half of my life, are a proud and noble people, incapable of an act of self-interest. I now see how much I had idealised them and deceived myself.' I may come to revise my view of them as a result of some isolated disappointment which opens my eyes. This is analogous to what Wisdom thinks has happened in the case of the woman who lost her son in the war.

Her belief, however, could have been different in kind and so crumbled in a very different way. For as a result of her tragedy, the belief that she had so far cherished and derived sustenance from may cease to have *sense* for her. She may find she can no longer look at life from its perspective. Here it is her *conception* of life, her geometry of the world, that has changed—not because it has been falsified, but because she can no longer find in it what she did before. One could say that she can no longer sing the praise of God with any expression, she cannot 'fill it with personal content'. Her thinking no longer flows along the lines which constitute her former conception of the world. She can no longer look at and see a thousand things in life as she did before.

In *this* sense 'some belief as to what the world is like is of the essence of religion'—and that means some perspective on life. Some of the examples which Wisdom gives are precisely examples of beliefs about life or the world as a whole, beliefs that amount to subscribing to a particular 'geometry of life'. To see this we must contrast two differences: (i) The difference between someone who sees a pleasing order in the way a garden has been designed and someone who finds that same garden 'a wilderness'. (ii) The difference between someone who says that the *world* is a garden and someone who says it is a wilderness. Wisdom recognises this difference when he contrasts two questions: 'What is the meaning of this?' and 'What is the meaning of it all?' He compares the difference between these two questions with the difference between a question 'What does this mean?' asked about a particular incident in a play and a question in which we wish to grasp the character, the significance of the whole play: 'What does it all

mean?', 'Is it a tragedy, a comedy or a tale told by an idiot?'
(Wisdom, 1965, p. 40.) This last question is to be answered by
comparing and contrasting this play with others which will
throw a light on its character, change our bewilderment to
comprehension. But when someone says, 'Life is a tale told by
an idiot', or 'It is all in the hands of sòmeone who made it all
and then fell asleep', or 'It's all in the hands of someone who
arranges the little ironies of fate' (ibid., p. 14) it isn't like that.

There is a difference between talking about 'the whole play'
and saying something about 'life as a whole'. What disguises
this difference is that there is such a thing as 'commenting on
life' and this is, in some ways, like commenting on a play.
Thus novelists, dramatists and painters are sometimes said to
'show us life', and we say that there is a great deal of 'truth' in
what they write or paint. A writer like Proust or Dostoyevsky
may even give someone who really enters into, savours and is
influenced by his work a new perspective on certain things. I
agree that here we are on our way towards something that is
of the essence of religion, namely a view of the world as a
whole.[2] When a work of art develops what may be called a
world-view, then the instances in terms of which it does this
are not so much used to support it as to give it content, to
exhibit what the artist sees in it and what it means to him. The
more this is the case the less will it be possible to find anything
that would count as evidence against it. For subscribing to it as
he does, the artist will be less inclined to describe incidents in
which others may see counter-examples to his view in the way
they describe these. It is only here that what we find in some
works of art provides an analogy to the kind of belief about the
world which Wisdom says 'is of the essence of religion'. Proust's
work constitutes a good example of what I have in mind.

However much of what we may call 'comments on life' in
works of art does not have this kind of invulnerability. What
the artist illustrates is more confined in character. He may lead
us to see, for instance, that there is more to people than we
realise, some good in them where we least expect to find it.
But this is still not something to which an exception is
inconceivable, still not a claim about 'all things', about the
nature of the world.

A person who often sees the good which most others do not
see because it is overgrown with avarice, ambition, envy and

hatred, will have expectations, or at least a hope, which others may not have. Having these expectations he may live his life differently from someone who does not have them. He may also find in what he sees a source of strength. It may give him courage in situations where others despair, even though he is not blind to what they see. But still such a man may be wrong in particular situations, his optimism may be misplaced, his hope unfounded. In Wisdom's words, it is not 'unamenable to reason', 'insensitive to what is so' (Wisdom, 1965, p. 50). When he sees how things really stand perhaps he will lose hope and heart. This is how Wisdom thinks the woman who lost her son in the 1914 war lost her faith.

This may well have been true in her case, though we can imagine her later to find a new faith, not the old one. In such a case some will say that she will have found 'a new life', that she was 'born again'. Wisdom knows this. He knows too that many 'teachers of humanity' 'teach that it is necessary for a man to die in order to live' (ibid., p. 34). Here 'to die' means to die to her old expectations, not to need to rely on them. This is part of the condition of 'rebirth'. She had expected that God would save her son and spare her the pain of losing him. She came to see that there was no reason to expect this here or anywhere. This meant for her that there is no benevolent power she or anyone else can depend on. Later she may come to see that she had been under an illusion about life, that the world is devoid of finality, that the rain and the light of the sun fall without discrimination on the just and the unjust alike. But out of this kind of 'realism' can spring a hope more nearly like the one preached by Christ, a love nearer the one He practised—a hope that is independent of the vagaries of fate, a love that does not bargain with the person to whom it turns its face. For her to find such a hope in her heart—as we are told Job found—is to attain a kind of spirituality which she had not possessed before.

In his anxiety to represent Christ's love as reasonable and well-founded Wisdom turned it into a worldly love. He argued that Christ could forgive, pray for and love the soldiers who took him to the cross, Pilate, Judas who betrayed him, and Peter who would deny him, because 'they knew no better', or because he could find excuses for what they did, or because he could see the good that was hidden in them (ibid., p. 141). But if, in a given case, there were no excuses, and no hidden good either—what then? Would Christ not pray for such a man's soul, and would he not love him still?

Sonia saw the good in Raskolnikov. But had she not seen it, had there been no good in him to see, could she not, would she not have felt just as sorry for him, and perhaps even more so? When Raskolnikov said to her, 'But I only killed a louse, Sonia. A useless, nasty, harmful louse', she replied: 'A human being—a louse?' She did not mean that there is some good in every human being—even in Alyona Ivanova. Her point was: You should not have done what you did to her, however nasty she may have been. Not because there was some good in her, but because she was a *human being*. She would have felt sorry for Raskolnikov for the same reason, even if she had seen no good in him—for the violence he had done to himself in killing Alyona Ivanovna whatever he may have been like.

'Oh, what have you done to yourself?' she cried in despair and, jumping up, she flung herself on his neck, and held him tightly in her arms (Dostoyevski, 1956, p. 425).

Such a love is neither reasonable nor unreasonable. It is a mistake to apply these categories to it. If one does, it will appear as foolish. From the world's point of view it *is* foolish.

Sonia's love[3] is the expression of an attitude to the world as a whole. At the centre of it is a vision of life that is logically inseparable from the content of such selfless love. One who possesses it will see all men as equal with respect to their claim to justice and compassion, irrespective of their merits and achievements. He will think of the goods of this world as of no great moment and he will see the good things in life and the bad ones as gratuitous. But is such a man right to think of the world is these terms? Are there any features of the world which justify him to think so? Can the kind of reasoning which Wisdom has so well portrayed establish that he is right or mistaken?

I do not think that a perspective on life as a whole is in this way vulnerable to any facts, since it determines its possessor's assessment of the facts. This does not mean that 'it loads the dice for him' any more than a particular concept-formation such as we find in mathematics can be said to shackle or distort one's assessment of facts about physical nature. The invulnerability of the perspective is the result of one's determination to stick to certain concepts, to adhere to a particular measure of life. In this respect it has a fixity akin to the fixity of a system of geometrical axioms. Like a fixed star the believer takes his bearing from it—in his judgments and decisions.

An example which Wisdom gives throws some light on what I mean. In 'Gods' he considers a child whose father dies. At first he no longer expects punishment or help from his father as he did when the father was alive. Then someone tells the child 'that nevertheless his father can see him and hear all he says. When he has been told this the child will still fear no punishment, nor expect any sign of his father, but now, even more than he did when his father was alive, he will feel that his father sees him all the time and will dread distressing him and when he has done something wrong he will feel separated from his father until he has felt sorry for what he has done' (Wisdom, 1953, p. 150). This is a good example. The child's belief that his father can see everything he does is *like* the religious believer's 'confidence in the everlasting arms, unease beneath the all-seeing eye'. It has the same kind of fixity and plays a similar role in the child's life. The child does not refrain from doing certain things because his father will punish him now or in the future. Perhaps he does not believe that his father can make this sort of difference to him, now or later, since he is dead. He refrains just because it would distress his father who sees everything he does. If the child still speaks of punishment, he may mean no more than this: believing himself to have done something that distresses his father *is* his punishment. If he does something bad there is no possibility of evading or escaping this kind of punishment, since his father sees everything he does. The possibility of hiding from his father's gaze is not part of the child's belief.

The child can depend on it—his father will see him whatever he does or thinks; the father will be distressed if he does something bad, pleased if he does something good, forgive him if he repents no matter how bad he has been. In what sense can he depend on it? Not in the sense that he can depend on a person he knows. The latter dependence is based on experience. For that very reason it is at least conceivable that a person we know well, however well we know him, may let us down. We may take him a gift, and though we have every reason to expect that he will be pleased, he may throw it in our face. But the child we are imagining finds it inconceivable that he should do something which his dead father does not know, that he should do something bad which does not distress his father in heaven. That is because he has made his father's gaze into a mirror of his life. He has frozen his father's reactions into a yardstick of the character and moral significance of his actions. He has come to judge his actions by them; and he depends on them in the way that one depends on a measure or criterion.

It is true that he can judge his actions in this way. The framework of these judgments makes sense to him, because he knows what it was like to hurt his living father, to ask for his forgiveness, to make amends and to be forgiven. Unless he had known and experienced this earlier, when his father was alive, belief in an all-seeing father could play no role in his life. This is a logical point. But that this belief has sense for him in a setting that can be seen as a development of an earlier relation with his father should not obscure the fact that it may now have a logical status different from any beliefs the child had about his living father. Nor should what made the child receptive to such a belief in the first place—such as his desire to keep his father, the dread of being separated from him— blind us to the fact that it may have become something more than just a means of perpetuating an old situation in which he found security and emotional sustenance. In fact, in its new role, his belief that his father still sees him cannot altogether meet this need, since the father can no longer help, punish or reward him as when he was alive. More than this, in its new role, this belief may help him transcend such a need, help him to grow out of it.

It is the same with the religious believer's 'confidence in the everlasting arms'. That is why, I think, this example of the child is a good one. Wisdom gives it to illustrate what happens to a religious belief when the believer's expectations about what is to come are so reduced that in *this* respect there is little difference between him and one who rejects his belief. He insists, rightly, that there would still be a difference between them, not only in how they live their lives and face death, but also in how they *see* life. He insists too, again rightly, that how the believer lives his life and faces death cannot be logically separated from how he sees the world. But it seems to me he is not clear about what seeing the world in this or that way comes to in this connection. I have suggested that what is in question where religions like Christianity are concerned is the perspective of certain beliefs which may be characterised as 'concept forming' and which give those who subscribe to them a fixed framework for their judgments and decisions.

III   Religious Belief and Truth

Certainly these beliefs guide the believer's apprehension in many situations, and those who adhere to them will call them 'true'. But this is not to say that they can be supported by considerations about what is so, in the way that judgments about a person's negligence or nobility can be. I understand and respect Wisdom's anxiety to argue that they can be so supported, that there is a process of reasoning and reflection which, if we can go through with it, will show these beliefs to be either well- or ill-founded. For he thinks that it would make no sense for anyone to call them true if there wasn't such a process of reasoning and reflection; they could not be said to guide the believer's apprehension if this was not so. Besides there *is* a form of reflection about life and people which religious believers engage in, and its outcome is relevant to whether or not they continue to believe when their faith is in trial. These two points have to be taken separately.

Can one intelligibly characterise a belief to which one adheres as 'true' if it cannot be supported by reasons or considerations of one kind or another? If one is inclined to think not, then he should be reminded of contexts where 'true' carries no such implication. We all speak of logical truths and we do not hesitate to acknowledge an arithmetical proposition such as '$2 + 2 = 4$' as true although we have no idea how we should go about proving or supporting it. Such propositions *need* no proof. If someone insists that still they *can* be proved, I would reply that the conviction we express when we call them true cannot be increased by such a proof were someone clever to devise one. As far as our conviction goes such a proof is an idle wheel, a false support. Worse than this, it obscures the real source of our conviction which lies elsewhere, in the service which what we are convinced is true gives us in so much of our life and thinking, in the way it is interlocked with so much of what we accept and judge by. Its truth then lies in the kind of understanding it makes possible for us in connection with so much that is of interest to us.[4]

My point simply is that there are contexts in which the notion of truth is not tied up with that of proof or verification. Take now the belief which Socrates attempts to convey to Callicles at the end of the *Gorgias*. The story he tells there about Judgment Day expresses the content of his belief. Socrates says that he believes this story to be *true*: 'You may despise what I have told you as no more than an old wives' tale. Personally I put my faith in this story, and make it my aim to present my soul to its judge in the soundest possible state.' The story is in the future tense since it refers to the time of the believer's death. Yet Socrates' faith in its truth does not rest on the kind of evidence with which one would support an ordinary prophecy. His desire to live a good life, his preference to suffer rather than to inflict wrong on others, is not conditional to what will happen to him in the future in the hands of his judges. These two points go together; they are logically connected. Let me explain.

If Socrates' desire to live a good life were conditional on what would happen to him in a future life, then the question of evidence for his belief concerning such a time would be pertinent. Where such a question is in place, the desire to live and act in a certain way is conditional on whether or not what we want to find evidence for will turn out to be the case. But then the object of our desire is not to live that way; it is what living that way will secure for us if we are right in our belief about the future. In that case any evidence which undermines our confidence in this belief will also weaken our reason for wanting to live that way. So, whether or not we have evidence and conform to that way of life will make little difference to what we are like.

Imagine a man who has or believes he has evidence which supports Socrates' story as he understands it. Given his desire to have things go well for him in this life and after death, he will do his best to live a life which resembles the one praised by

Socrates. But this will hardly make him like Socrates. For the very desire which makes him emulate Socrates is the one which separates him from Socrates and which Socrates' story condemns. All that his real or imaginary evidence does for him is to change his expectations; it does not touch his desires. So he alters or adjusts his life to obtain the object of his unchanged desire in the light of his changed expectations. No spiritual concern can enter his life this way, through a belief that is supported or undermined by evidence. That is why Wittgenstein insists that the question of evidence is irrelevant to religious belief: 'If there were evidence, this would destroy the whole business' (Wittgenstein, 1966, p. 56).

The parallel with Wisdom's example of the child is clear. The idea that he could get away with doing something bad does not enter the child's mind. Not because he has evidence that his father in heaven would not miss any of his actions and would be distressed if he did something bad, but rather because he has made his father's distress into a measure of the badness of his action and because that distress is the punishment he dreads most. This is the way he assesses his actions; the picture of his father in heaven is the fixed star by which he lives. It embodies what he cares for and values; it is both a vehicle of his devotion to the living, his capacity to trust them, and also what gives his devotions, fears and hopes their peculiar content and character.

It is the same with Socrates' belief about the judges who will judge his life infallibly when it is over. It makes a difference to his life *not* in the way that a man's belief that he could not get away with cheating keeps him on the straight path, but in the sense that it gives a crooked life the kind of significance which makes him want to avoid it at any cost, repent what he has done when he fails, and pity others who do so even when they escape justice. There is a great difference between the lives of two such men even if outwardly they are similar. And neither do they believe in the same thing even if what they believe can be expressed in the same words. The difference lies in their spiritual orientation. There is no concern in the former's life for the values that enter into the last judgment as Socrates described it to Callicles. The story which embodies or gives expression to these values, like the belief of Wisdom's child that his father in heaven sees all his actions and knows all his thoughts, is the measure of life for all those who accept it as the truth.

So when Socrates says, 'What I am going to tell you, I tell you as the truth', he is using the word 'true' to characterise a measure, his means of assessment rather than any assessment he has made. He is saying that no other form of assessment makes sense for him, that he cannot go along with and respond to it in the way he lives and acts—'that he cannot fill it with personal content'.[5] But there are others who can—those who do not share his beliefs. The truth of mathematical axioms, I said, is to be found in the way they are interlocked with so much of what we accept and judge by, so much of what we are agreed on. A man who has grown up in a community where mathematics is used in a variety of activities in which he participates and who, since childhood, has been able to calculate, will agree with others in saying that it is *true* that $2 + 2 = 4$. To deny it would exclude him from activities and ways of thinking which form part of the texture of the kind of life he lives. But when a religious man calls his beliefs *true* he means something more than this, since those who deny what he affirms can still carry on with much of the activities which make up the life they share with him—even if they cannot do so in the same spirit. The religious person who affirms the truth of his beliefs is *speaking for himself* in a way that he would not be doing when he affirms those mathematical truths which he takes for granted when he adds up his accounts or works out his holiday expenses. For accepting the truth of religious beliefs means more than participating intelligently in religious practices. It means finding their sense *in his own life*. A religious man who affirms the *truth* of his beliefs is saying something like: 'I find them indispensable for most of what I do; there is no part of my life that would make sense without them—I cannot go along with anything else.' Thus, what Socrates thinks 'personally' is not irrelevant to his claim that what he tells Callicles he tells him as the *truth*. To retort, 'I am not interested in what you think personally, all I want to know is whether what you think is true is really true', would be to misunderstand what 'truth' means in this connection.

This is not to say that whatever the believer says goes. Whether a person really believes the religious beliefs he subscribes to, whether he believes them to be true, is a matter of what they mean to him, what he makes of them in his own life. Whether he speaks them *as the truth* or merely *takes them on trust*[6] is to be seen in his life and in the way he speaks of earthly things—though the criteria of what his life shows about his relation to these beliefs are *religious* criteria. There are two questions it is possible to raise here: (i) Given his words as to what he believes, what do they amount to? How does he understand them? What is it he really believes? People who assent to the same words do not always hold the same beliefs—even though they believe whay they *say* they believe. Where religious beliefs are concerned it is notorious how much people who belong to the same religion nevertheless differ in what they believe. (ii) Given that we know what he says he believes, does he really believe it? Does he speak it, take it as the truth? Has he made it his own? Does it go deep with him? As I said, what he *says* on this matter is not our criterion of whether he speaks it as the truth.

Someone may ask: But supposing we appreciate that he does speak it as the truth, does this show that what he says is true? Obviously there are limits to what can count as a religious truth, to be found within religious traditions—and no individual can be the arbiter of those. Where there is no question whether such limits have been transgressed, the question 'Is what he believes true?' means: Can *I* accept it and make it my own? Can *I* find a new life in it? I cannot say 'it is true' unless and until I can. I cannot answer this question without bringing myself in. As Wittgenstein put it to Waismann: 'Here nothing more can be established, I can only appear as a person speaking for myself' (Wittgenstein, 1965, p. 16). This is *part* of what is meant by the saying that the Kingdom of God is *within* you.

I have suggested that when we speak of 'belief' in connection with religion we are not speaking of what becomes knowledge when justified and held with conviction. It is not something which we contrast with knowledge. We do, however, distinguish between different ways in which a person may be related to such a belief. In particular we attach importance to the distinction between the case where he has made the belief *his own* and the case where it is no more than a second-hand opinion. In this distinction we have a dimension in religious life and morality which is absent in the case of mathematics—a dimension of the personal. Thus believing in God is commitment to a certain way of looking at the world and hence of assessing and responding to the contingencies of life. The believer's response to what befalls him, his attitude to other people, is an expression of his attitude to God. It is this attitude that gives coherence to the way he responds to life in different situations. This attitude is part of his belief in God. You cannot say: 'Believing in God is one thing, trusting Him another.' For responding to God, in the different ways that this finds expression in a man's life, is part of what we *mean* by 'believing in God'. Where these expressions are absent, a man cannot be said to believe that God exists. Thus the atheist who rejects God, one who may be described by a believer as 'fighting against the spirit of God entering his life', is nearer the believer than an agnostic who says, 'Well, I'm not sure. Possibly.'[7]

Where a person has made a religious or moral belief his own he will *care* for certain values, show concern for certain things in life—which concern will find expression in various ways in particular situations. This is what Plato was thinking when he distinguished between knowledge and opinion in the sphere of moral and religious values. If we speak of 'knowledge' here, in contrast with 'opinion', what we mean involves *concern*, it involves what certain philosophers have characterised as an 'attitude of will'. Ignorance, on the other hand, would be equivalent to *indifference*.

There is another distinction, however, in the case of belief in the Christian God, which should not be confused with the above distinction between knowledge or belief and mere opinion. I am thinking of the distinction between genuinely believing in God and *coming to know Him* which, I think, is connected with the idea of God as a person. For even among those whose belief in God may be said to go deep only a few will claim to have come to *know* God. They refuse to talk of knowledge and direct experience of God because they wish to emphasise the *distance* that still separates them from God and the *difficulty* of bridging it—which distance is directly proportional to their love of themselves, their attachment to everything that is of this world. They know that they can only come to *know* God in God's response to them—but this response is determined by the quality of their own spirituality or 'inwardness'.

This is not to contradict what I said earlier about the indiscriminating character of God's love. God does not love and care for only those who deserve His love. Nevertheless He reveals Himself in the hearts of those few only who have ceased to expect anything for themselves. Thus at the pinnacle of his fame as a monk, when he lived for human praise, Tolstoy's Sergius felt that 'what was internal became external', while when he became a pilgrim and succeeded in helping people without even wanting to see their gratitude 'little by little God began to reveal Himself within him'. He had to die to his former ambitions and expectations before he felt 'the presence of God within him'. Sergius' part in this was to renounce everything in his life which had turned him away from God. When he finally did so and settled to the life which Tolstoy describes in the last two or three pages of his story[8] it was God who crossed the distance between them to come to him. Another instance of God's response, in the form of forgiveness, is to be found in Dostoyevsky's account of Raskolnikov's repentance—a repentance that involves an awareness of the enormity of his crime in the face of which everything which he had tried to possess and find sustenance in appears as nothing. Dostoyevsky describes such repentance as bringing him to the threshold of a 'new life'.

According to Christianity, then, it is in an awareness of his *nothingness* that the believer finds God's love, His mercy and forgiveness. He can come to such an awareness not only in repentance, but also in pity for the afflicted, in forgiveness of those who trespass against him, in the contemplation of beauty. It is in this sense that God may come to reveal Himself within the believer or non-believer.

IV Reason and Religious Conversion

In the latter case people speak of 'conversion'. At least this is one kind of conversion among others. Here people sometimes speak of having 'encountered' God and they may say that they *know* there is God *from personal experience*. What such a person encounters is something which he finds he can only identify as

God's response—His anger which rips him apart and crushes everything that gave him a sense of being somebody, or His love which makes him put everything he has considered important aside and transforms his whole life. It is *he* who identifies what he meets in this way, though the criteria which enable him to do so come from the religion with which he has been in contact through the culture it permeates—the culture in which he has his roots. When a man's life has been touched by God in this way the transformation is one that shatters him so that he is born to a new life.

Conversion does not, however, always mean this; it does not always come about through this kind of contact with God. It may come about as a result of reflecting on one's life or contemplating a natural scene. A person may, for instance, reflect on all his failures and come to think that they don't really matter. He may think of others who have made similar mistakes, even bigger ones, and it may strike him that he is not alone, that he has been too much concerned with himself. He may see that this concern, with its corresponding indifference to other people, has been the biggest trouble with him. This may lead him to see that there are other things in life, things of greater importance. This thought may bring him relief. It may suddenly strike him that he has a great deal for which to be thankful, and this may open his eyes to the simple everyday things around him. He may, for instance, watch the birds in his garden which he had been too busy to see. He may watch them with a friendship that comes from a realisation of their being 'travelling companions' which in their very transience invite attention. Words of thanks may then come to his mouth for being alive and nothing else, and even not for this, but because there is all this, the bird, the tree, the night sky, something bigger than his own personal life.

This way of thinking is in some ways very like the one sketched by Wisdom in his instance of the man who is trying to decide whether the world is a garden or a wilderness. But in the many examples Wisdom gives we have a mode of reasoning which leads to a conclusion which, if true, could have been false, and which it supports or justifies. The reasoning in which he is interested offers us a comparison between something too complex to be taken in at a glance, and a form of words, a conclusion, which aims to describe, sum up or represent it in a way which brings out its likeness to things familiar which we understand. It is in seeing this likeness that we arrive at an apprehension of it we did not have before. The question, 'Is the description correct or not? Do these things stand as the description says they stand? Do they stand, in the relevant respects, as in the cases with which the description compares them?' has an answer which the form of reasoning in question aims to establish. The answer may not be 'Yes' or 'No', 'They do or they do not stand exactly as in the cases with which they are compared'. It may be of the form: 'The way things stand here is *nearer* the way they stand there than the way they stand in such-and-such cases, and even *nearer* ... and so on.' It is this kind of answer which the form of reasoning which Wisdom is concerned to illuminate aims to establish or test. The answer, as he would say, is such that if it is true it could be false, and if false it still could have been true.

In the kind of reasoning I have sketched this is *not* so. The reasoning there certainly pays attention to details that could have been otherwise, connects them together in new ways or breaks connections we took for granted before, and it goes forward by comparison and contrast. It is also already permeated with certain moral categories. However it changes one's apprehension not merely by making or severing connections, but also by extending and transforming the moral categories in terms of which these connections are made or denied. It brings about in the reasoner a transition to certain values which engage with religious beliefs that have had no more than a merely verbal reality for him or, if they meant more than this to him, have since lost their sense. In this way it helps him to find or rediscover their *sense*—the sense of beliefs which constitute the framework of a particular perspective on life. This is like illuminating a mirror by throwing a light on the objects reflected in it. Thus the reasoner is led to see that it makes sense to look at life in this way.

This is not to say that he can look at life in this way or that he is *willing* to do so. For there is a difference between merely seeing sense in certain religious beliefs and making them one's own, resolving to live by them. Unless the reasoning in question is more than an intellectual process it cannot give the person engaged in it the will and the concern which, as I argued, is part of a belief in God. Where the reasoning is carried out in terms of moral categories which already have the reasoner's allegiance, their transformation by means of it will change not only his mind but also his heart. It will make a difference to what he cares for as well as to the character of his caring; it will redirect his will. The man in doubt, the man whose faith is in trial, is a man in conflict, one who is divided in his loyalties. The conflict is not confined to his intellect, but engages his heart and will; and the reasoning which helps him to sift out his reactions to life will resolve the conflict one way or the other. In another case the remorse which a non-believer feels for the evil things he has done and the desire to atone for this evil may get him to reflect on the kind of life he has known and lived. It is possible for such reflection to deepen his values or by extension to bring him to care for new values. Here too it may lead not merely to a new conception of life, but to a new attitude to life, a new concern; and this concern may open up the way to a belief in God.

The attitude or the concern is not something superimposed on the conception, an appendage as it were contingently connected with it, even though the conception can exist on its own. Let me illustrate this by means of a previous example. The man who, as a result of discussion with A, comes to see that it is possible to love someone like B in the way that A loves her, and that A is neither blind nor a fool for loving B in this way, and who further comes to admire A for the character of his devotion to B, may nevertheless not be capable of this kind of love and devotion himself. It is true that if he comes to admire it, this will at least change his attitude to himself and also to others. It will instill in him a new humility so that he sees himself as limited, and perhaps too he will be less prone to shun situations from which he may have turned away in some disdain. This is already a change in him, a difference wrought on his will, even if it is a relatively modest one. But the reasoning need not have taken him this far, even though it changed his conception of love and opened up a new possibility for his intellect. For he may have come to see that one can love someone like B in the way that A does without admiring anyone capable of it. Perhaps the change of conception is not the same then as it would be in a person who

admires what he comes to see in this new way; but this is not
to say that it is not a change of conception when it is
dissociated from a change of heart. This means that the fact
that you can have a change of conception in these cases
without a change of heart does not prove that when you have
both they are two different things contingently connected.

I cannot now go into the question of the relation between
the heart and the mind in these matters. What I wanted to
insist on is that unless the reasoning I have been considering
moves the heart as well as the mind it cannot bring one who
engages in it to a belief in God. I have tried to indicate that it
can do so by changing one's vision of the objects of one's
concern, objects to which one has given one's heart or been
unable to do so, and by changing one's values or moral
categories. One must not forget that the need for such
reflection arises from the emotions—the burden of religious
duties which previously had been a source of strength and joy;
remorse for one's past life; the revulsion one feels for the evil
in the activities going on around one; the urge to dedicate
one's life to the service of other men, particularly to the sick
and the needy; one's sense of joyous gratitude. Often the
reasoning or reflection in which a man in such circumstances
engages is itself an expression of what is working itself out
within him—the fight between good and evil in his own
breast. But this does not mean that it can move towards a
resolution which changes him as well as his apprehension of
life without the reasoning. When I used the metaphor of
'something that is working itself out within him' I was not
talking of something that goes on without his participation.
This participation, however, may take different forms, and
these may include *reflection* on the qualities of and relations
between the objects he cares for or despises, as well as on his
own desires to help others or hinder them, to make things
good or to destroy them.

Those philosophers who recently have wanted to deny that
there is room for reasoning in connection with religious belief
were thinking primarily of the justification of beliefs about
what is so, though it could be otherwise, in favour of adopting
an explanatory hypothesis, even of the justification of a policy
of action. They have, rightly, wanted to reject all of this, to
deny the 'reasonableness' of religious belief which either turns

it into something tame or prudent, divesting it of its spiritual character, or assimilates it to scientific belief. They have wanted to emphasise that when we speak of belief here we often refer to a mode or means of assessment which a man has made his own, rather than assessments which he has reached and for which he ought to be able to produce reasons. It is true that one can have reasons for adopting or accepting a means of assessment. But in these cases what is assessed will be something pretty confined, so that whether or not he assesses it in this way makes little difference elsewhere in his life. This is why he has a choice and it makes sense to talk of 'adopting' it. Besides, where this is so, what one accepts cannot bring any new dimension or orientation into one's life. In other words, even if a philosopher agrees that religious beliefs provide the believer with a new mode of assessment, the moment he speaks of 'reasons for adopting it' or of its 'justification' he cannot make sense of the kind of *necessity* which characterises the believer's conviction, nor of the way it changes him *inwardly*. In any case, as I pointed out, the kind of allegiance that is involved in religious belief is one that finds expression in those many situations in life which call for deep affective response. Allegiance, belief or conviction here involves a transformation in these responses, at least in the form of distress where his responses remain recalcitrant. The kind of reasoning which may guide a person towards a belief in God is one which in part helps him to sift out his reactions to life.

I have just pointed out where I think those philosophers are right who recently have wanted to deny that there is room for reasoning in connection with religious belief. This does not exclude what I have argued for in this section, namely that it is possible for a person to arrive at a religious belief or a deeper spirituality through reflection on the world or reasoning about his life. It is this possibility that Wisdom has in mind when he compares religious belief with beliefs that can be arrived at by means of the kind of reasoning he portrays in 'Gods'. He is right to bear this in mind. He is wrong, however, in his characterisation of the reasoning in question. To begin with, it does not have the symmetry which he attributes to it. In other words, we misapprehend its nature if we think that the reasoning which has guided one man to a belief in God ought to lead anyone else to that belief if he gives his heart and mind to it. This asymmetry is connected with the 'dimension of the personal' I spoke of earlier and the way religious belief engages the will. This is *one* reason why it will not do to say that the man who has been guided to a belief in God by means of such reasoning or reflection is *justified* in believing in God. I am inclined to say that the reasoning in question is *a way* to that belief—one way among others—but it does not provide a proof or verification of the belief. So although I agree with Wisdom that reflection and reasoning may play a role in renewing a man's religious beliefs or in helping him to accept new ones, I differ from him on what such reasoning amounts to.

V Summing Up: Wisdom and Wittgenstein

I began with a very brief statement of Wisdom's view of the nature of religious belief, its truth and the kind of reasoning to which it is amenable. I did not examine the kind of philosophical pressures against which he developed his views; I did not give an appreciation of the new possibilities he opened up and the contribution he made in the philosophy of religion. I simply said that in the views I briefly stated, truth and falsity are intermingled. I agreed with Wisdom that there is *more* to religion than 'commitment to a way of life' (Wisdom, 1965, pp. 53–4) and that the believer and non-believer differ in the way they *see* things even when there is no difference between them in what they expect by way of a life after death and no difference in what they infer about what lies beyond the reach of the senses.[9] I disagreed with him, however, on what this difference in vision and understanding amounts to. I argued that it may be characterised as *conceptual* and I described religious beliefs as 'concept forming'. They provide those who subscribe to them with a perspective on life, a fixed framework for their judgments and decisions. In that case can one intelligibly talk of religious beliefs as *true*? And is it possible for a person to reach a religious vision of the world through reflection on life?

I agreed with Wisdom in so far as my answer to these two questions was in the affirmative. But the philosophical difficulties we had to meet in reaching the same answers were different. My difficulties came from the view I take of the nature of religious belief—the close connection I make between belief and measure or criterion, and the reference I find in the notion of truth here to what I called a 'dimension of the personal' so that conviction involves a commitment of the will. If I am right on these points, all of which come from Wittgenstein, then how can there be a scope for reasoning in connection with religious belief? The question is the same as Wisdom's, but the context in which it arises is very different. It was against the background of Hume's philosophy and its later heirs that it arose for Wisdom. His contribution was to show that there are forms of reasoning excluded by Hume's dichotomy of inductive and deductive reasons. This helped him to make a break with the idea that if God's existence can be known at all it must be by means of an inference.

My question about the scope of reason in religion arises against the background of Wittgenstein's philosophy. Many have felt understandably, but I think wrongly, that Wittgenstein did not allow sufficient scope to reason in connection with religion. This is I think because of the universal connection *they* make between the notions of reason and justification.

My contribution here has been to disconnect these notions, to suggest that there is a sense of reason which is not connected with the idea of justification. It can guide a man in his apprehension and will so that what he comes to is not arbitrary, even though it does not have the kind of generality that cuts across personal boundaries so that we cannot say that he is justified in embracing what it leads him to. So I disagree with Wisdom about the kind of reasoning to which religious beliefs are amenable and the sense in which they are amenable to reasoning. But the nature of this reasoning and the way it guides the will need further examination.

7 Wisdom II: Metaphysical and Religious Transcendence*

I Wisdom's Position: the World Outside and the Soul Within

Professor Wisdom holds that the reference to be found in many religious beliefs to what lies beyond the world and *transcends* the senses is misleading. Religious beliefs speak and, indeed, can only speak about this world, the world we know by means of the senses. The religious believer is himself misled when he describes the God he believes in as transcendent. What gives content to his beliefs is how certain things stand in this world. To appreciate these and so to embrace the beliefs in question is for a person to change in himself, to come into contact with something that lies *within* him. Here lies the spiritual aspect of the content of religious beliefs.

Once more I want to argue that in these claims truth and falsehood are intermingled. In the earlier study I was at one with Wisdom in his stand against philosophers who are led to tamper with features of the language of religion which it is their business to try and understand. In that connection I spoke of what is obvious and important. In connection with God's transcendence Wisdom tends to depart from this path. In so far as he allows philosophy to interfere with the actual use of language in the scriptures[1] he goes wrong. This is not to reject his criticism of those epistemological theories, illustrated by his fable of the invisible gardener, which represent belief in God as based on an inference. I shall argue that one can accept these criticisms without denying the intelligibility of God's

* Originally published in the *Canadian Journal of Philosophy*, vol. V, no. 4 (December 1975).

transcendence. One must distinguish here between what belongs to philosophy and what belongs to theology, between metaphysical and religious transcendence. Secondly, while I agree with Wisdom in the connection he makes between the way the believer sees the world and what he finds in his own 'inner' life, I do not think that his account of what is meant by a person's inner life in the context of religious language is adequate. I shall argue that in this account he runs together the notions of psychological and spiritual truth. These are the two questions on which I want to take issue with him in this second paper.

II   God as 'Outside this World' and 'Timeless'

The idea of God as a gardener behind the scenes, beyond our senses, whose presence can be known only indirectly from the order discernible in the garden, reminds Wisdom of those epistemological theories which he has discussed elsewhere with illumination. I am thinking, for instance, of the temptation to think that the material objects around us, whose existence we are aware of through sense perception, are known to us in much the same way as a man may know that someone is standing behind him from his shadow. Here we could say that the shadow from which he knows the intruder's presence is one thing and the intruder himself is another thing. One can think of the one without thinking of the other. Wisdom would say that although one can know the intruder's presence from his shadow without actually seeing him, one can do so only because it makes sense to speak of seeing the intruder himself. One has a right to infer his presence from the shadow one sees, only because one has on other occasions seen besides the shadow the man who casts it and noted the connection between them. If we take all that we ever see as something other than the material objects around us and treat it as our evidence for their existence, if we think of a material object as something that *transcends* all that we ever see, we shall have made it impossible not only to know the existence of any material object but even to have such a conception. So Wisdom insists that if there is a God it must be possible to know there is, know this from considerations that start from what is in fact so, though not by means of an inference.

Since this idea of God as an invisible gardener, beyond the reach of our senses, is incoherent in much the same way that Locke's idea of a *substratum* was, and since Wisdom does not wish to dismiss the idea of God as an epistemological myth, he considers the possibility that this reference to an invisible gardener may be a way of talking about the garden itself. In that case the difference between someone who says that there is an invisible gardener and someone who denies this boils down to whether the garden in front of them is a well-cared-for garden or not. Its being one thing or the other, more nearly well-cared-for than not or more nearly a wilderness, is a matter of the garden's appearance. Yet it is something we may hesitate about or fail to discern even though no part of the garden is hidden by a haze or mist. So Wisdom argues that considerations which lead to a belief in God, whether or not they justify such a belief, are like those that start from the facts about a man's circumstances, thoughts and behaviour, and establish or support that he has been careful or negligent, kind or cruel. They are the kind that start with all the cards on the table, turned upwards, and help us to appreciate something we had not recognised. In Wisdom's words, 'they guide us in our apprehension of what is so'. Kindness, cruelty, negligence or nobility of character, are not things that lie beyond the appearances we consider, hidden behind them and to be known by inference. Though we may not see them in the appearances we are familiar with, they do not transcend these appearances in the way, for instance, that a man's secret thoughts may transcend the front he puts up for strangers.

In the previous paper I gave some reasons why I think this latter comparison is inadequate. Does this mean that we must embrace Wisdom's fable of the invisible gardener? Was not Wisdom's criticism of its logic impeccable? My answer is that Wisdom's criticism of this epistemological theory of God is impeccable, but that these two comparisons or epistemological theories do not exhaust the field.

I now wish to suggest that the Christian idea of God as a *transcendent* being, beyond time and our senses, his Kingdom outside the world, is *not* an epistemological theory. It is not a philosophical account of the kind of God Christians believe in, an account which may or may not be defective depending on whether or not it involves internal logical defects and, if not, matches the idea of God in the Christian religion. It is not a theory about what is meant by 'God' in the scriptures, but a direct statement about the kind of God Christians worship. So the philosopher's job is not to criticise it but to elucidate its logic. One can accept Wisdom's criticism of his fable of the invisible gardener without denying the intelligibility of God's transcendence. At best one can say, as I should, that if the idea of God as an invisible gardener is incoherent, this only shows that when Christians speak of God as a transcendent being this cannot be an adequate model of what they mean. The question remains: What is it they mean?

When I said 'this cannot be what they mean' I was assuming that they do mean something. A whole tradition of thought, one which has played a role in people's lives for centuries and enriched their life and literature cannot be inherently confused. To put it simply, if a form of words which people have uttered again and again is not an idle wheel, but has a use, then it cannot be logically defective. Any logical criterion which finds it so must itself be defective because formulated in abstraction from the contexts of speech in which the words it criticises have meaning.

The point I am making is one which I owe originally to Wisdom himself. No one I know has fought more vigorously what he calls 'the habit of abstract thinking'—what Wittgenstein once characterised as 'looking at language without looking at the language-game' (Wittgenstein, 1956, Pt V, §8). I am sure that if Wisdom had asked himself 'What is it that Christian theologians mean when they speak of God as a transcendent being, outside time and the world of the senses?' he would have treated such remarks with sympathy and imagination. What deflects him from doing so is, I think, his failure to distinguish the philosophical fable which he criticises from the theological statement which it duplicates verbally. The familiar ring he finds in the theological statement side-tracks him.

'Beyond our senses', 'transcendent', 'timeless', 'outside this world': these expressions do indeed have a ring familiar to the philosopher. However, even if it is true that they were originally coined in the context of philosophical speculation, this does not mean that they have no independent life of their own. Even in Plato's dialogues—for instance when he speaks of a timeless world of forms—we find him not only raising and discussing questions about the possibility of describing and understanding things that change, the kind of generality there must be in the words we use for the same word to apply to different things, but also contributing to a language in which certain forms of moral reflection are made possible. Why should we not say, then, that philosophers like Plato and Kierkegaard were at the same time *religious* thinkers and played a part in developing a certain kind of moral consciousness? If I am right, then such expressions as 'beyond the senses', 'transcendent' and 'timeless' have a life in a language and tradition of thought to which philosophers have contributed alongside with religious thinkers and also great literary writers and artists. If so, their sense is to be found in the use they have in such a language and in the role this language plays in the lives of those who speak it.

When the Christian God is described as 'beyond our senses' it is 'the world of the senses' that is in question. This latter expression has been often used in philosophy to focus on all those things that we may be said to perceive with the senses. What is the focus of attention is then contrasted with what is sometimes called 'the world of intelligible objects'—for instance, everything that pure mathematics is said to be about. The questions around which these distinctions revolve are epistemological; that is questions about what we can know, how we know those truths which none of us dispute and how we learn or acquire the many ideas in terms of which we think them. But the expression 'the world of the senses' is not used in this way in theology and religious discourse. What is in question when it is used there is a mode of life and a vision or conception of the world internal to it. This is the world in which we seek the satisfaction of sensual pleasures, bodily appetites and their derivatives—the desire for riches, power and fame. It is the world where concern for these pleasures and satisfactions overshadow all other concerns.

When God is described as 'beyond our senses' part of what is said is that He cannot be found in this world, that He has no reality there. If, in this connection, someone were to say that God is not visible to the senses he would not be making the epistemological point that you cannot see God through a telescope, but a different conceptual point, namely that God does not reveal Himself to one who is immersed in a life of the senses. A believer who gave in to the claims of such a life and began to be enslaved by it would inevitably start to doubt Him. Thus Tolstoy describes the claims of the flesh on Sergius' soul and the doubts that beset him when he gives in to them as one and the same foe. They are one and the same since in so far as a believer is claimed by the flesh he is necessarily turning away from God. This means that if these claims take root in his soul he can no longer look at things and respond to them from the perspective of the love of God. This antithesis is bound up with what it *means* to believe in a transcendent God; you cannot explain what kind of God Christians believe in without bringing it in. It is in this sense that the remark that God is not visible to the senses makes a conceptual point. In the *Phaedo* Socrates makes a similar point when he says that 'so long as we keep to the body and our soul is contaminated with this imperfection (infected with the nature of the body), there is no chance of our ever attaining satisfactorily to our object, which we assert to be Truth' (65c–66e). He means truth in spiritual matters, knowledge of which constitutes wisdom, a wisdom inseparable from virtue. So God is transcendent in the sense that turning towards Him means 'renouncing the amenities of the world' (Wittgenstein, 1961a, p. 81).

'He is not to be found in this world'—this does not mean that He is never present in human affairs, in transactions between human beings. As Simone Weil puts it, 'Whenever the afflicted are loved for themselves alone, it is God who is present' (Weil, 1959, p. 107). She gives the example of the good Samaritan who stops to attend to a dying stranger by the road-side (ibid., p. 105). She points out that such an act is extremely rare and goes against our nature. For it involves transporting oneself into the afflicted and partaking of his affliction; and this means consenting to one's own diminishment: 'It is to deny oneself' (ibid., p. 104). For this reason she calls it 'supernatural' or, in other words, other-worldly. One could say that when God is present in what takes place between human beings, the actions and relations in question do not belong to the natural order of things, they are not of this world.

Still His presence is not something that we can have in view when acting. For if we did, this would change the character of our actions, they would no longer involve self-renunciation. 'A man has all he can do,' she writes, 'to look at this small inert thing of flesh, lying stripped of clothing by the road-side. It is not the time to turn his thoughts towards God' (ibid., p. 107). Such a thought would necessarily separate him from God: 'Christ thanks those who do not know to whom they are giving food' (ibid., p. 108). The point is not only that a man who acts for the sake of a reward, religious or otherwise, is doing something for himself, but that the thought that he is giving bread for the love of God stands in the way of his partaking in the affliction of the famished sufferer. It glorifies the action and instead of diminishing the agent it enhances his sense of self. Even a martyr going to his death is supported by the bond which he feels unites him to God. He does not feel alone and abandoned. This is not to deny that his action may be completely selfless and disinterested. It may be so, but it does not diminish his sense of self. It does not replace it with a void. Christ felt no such support when he was nailed to the cross like a common criminal. He was on the cross because of his love of God, but he did not know that God was with him.

The Samaritan had no idea that the stranger by the road-side was Christ. Pashenka, in Tolstoy's story, did not have time to go to church and did not give much thought to God: 'The only thing is that I know how bad I am.' As he was dying Christ did not know that God was with him. The purity of their life and action, the spiritual stature of Christ on the cross, depends on that. In Simone Weil's words, 'God lives in secret.' This is what enables Him to exact from those who love Him the consent to be nothing: 'To consent to be nothing is to consent to the privation of all good. This consent constitutes the possession of the supreme good. Provided that one does not know it. If one knew, the good would disappear' (Weil, 1953, p. 194). 'To find God in a man convicted as an ordinary criminal, shamefully tortured and put to death—this is to vanquish the world. It is to renounce all temporal protection. It is to accept and love everything that happens, recognising that there is no reason why it should be so and not otherwise. But today who thinks of Christ as a man convicted like an ordinary criminal, except his enemies? Instead one worships the historical grandeur of the Church' (ibid., p. 95).

If one identifies God with anything wordly or temporal, if one turns the antithesis between what belongs to this world and what is supernatural into a contrast between what is here and what lies elsewhere, beneath, behind or beyond space, or into a contrast between what is now and what is to come later, then one will either deny God's transcendence or transform it into something that is logically incoherent. If one thinks of God's Kingdom as something that lies in the future one will have made it into something with which it is impossible to have any relation that is not worldly. Thus if a man endures suffering or acts with bravery because he hopes that his actions will help secure a better future for his children he may be heroic; but so far his heroism is of this world. It is possible that he will have suffered in vain. For his actions may not bring a better future. He knows this, but he has reason to think that there is some possibility that his actions will bring about the result which he hopes for. This hope sustains him now. If it is realised, the future will make up for the hardship he endures in the present. He has in view a certain objective. Its fulfilment would be the realisation of what he values. He has reason to believe that the sort of action he takes will help to bring it about. If he is lucky, he will enjoy seeing his children reap its benefits and he will feel that he has played some part in securing them for his children. I am thinking of a man whose actions we would praise and admire, a man whose actions are truly disinterested. The fact that he has his gaze fixed on the future does not diminish their moral worth. For he is not thinking of himself but of his children.

Imagine now that he is one among many who are engaged in this action, that the part he plays is a very small one, and that his services are not indispensable. His position in the whole operation is so undistinguished that no one notices him and no one will remember him. Perhaps his children die in the meantime so that his own future becomes dissociated from the future of the operation. His actions and sufferings continue to have a reference to the future via the objective of the operation. But he is now indifferent to his own future. Whether he survives or not no longer matters to him; the only thing that matters is that the operation should be a success. He wishes for this with all his heart; but he has nothing to gain from it. His personal grief and sorrow is too great for him to find any compensation in victory. In these new circumstances his courage, endurance and heroism assume a spiritual dimension. They are no longer of this world. This is brought about by the change in his relation to time, his indifference to his own future.

Before, it would not have mattered to him if he died, provided he could assure a better future for his children. He had made their future his own through his devotion to them. Hence his reward lay in the future. Even though he did not act in order to be rewarded the thought of it sustained him in his sufferings and difficulties. What he put out of himself was replenished; those sufferings did not diminish him. Besides this reward, in the future, was only contingently connected with his actions and sufferings. It could not be ruled out that in the end he would say 'It has all been in vain.' Now, however, although what he fights and suffers for lies in the future it does not belong to *his* future, and so he cannot thrive on it personally in anticipation. What goes out of him flows one way; nothing that he anticipates eases his burden. It is not in any thought about what lies in his own future that he finds heart since he has become indifferent to that. What gives him heart is his conviction of the justice of the cause he is serving. Whether or not he is serving justice does not depend on the outcome of his actions, though obviously he could not serve justice and not care to bring about one state of affairs as opposed to another. His love of justice makes his service its own reward. So long as he continues to love justice nothing that happens can make him say 'It has been in vain.' And just because what he gains from serving justice is not something he can himself contemplate, it cannot give him any sense of achievement.

What he served previously was in the future and his own future was bound up with it. Whether or not the world would be a better place for his children as a result of his actions is a contingent matter; and whether or not he served his children would depend on that. Whereas whether or not he serves justice does not depend on the outcome of his actions. It depends on his attitude of will. 'He tried to serve his children, but failed.' 'He tried to serve justice, but failed.' Failure means two different things here. In the first case he fails because, despite his intentions, things go wrong and his children do not flourish. In the second case he fails because his motives· and intentions are not all that they should be. Here, however hard he tries, if he fails he is always to blame. Because failure refers to his relation to justice; it characterises his state of soul. This does not mean, of course, that what he aims at is to achieve a certain state of soul. We have seen not only that this is not what he aims at, but also that it is not something he can contemplate under the aspect of an achievement. The only thing he can do is to examine his motives so that he can give himself to justice more fully and, ideally, without reservation. If he can do that then he necessarily serves justice no matter what happens. This is, I think, part of what is meant by saying that what he now serves is 'outside time', not in the same dimension as the one in which the self thrives.

Devotion to what transcends time or is eternal demands that one should be indifferent to one's own future, or at least that one should not put considerations regarding one's future before one's concern for it. But this is not to say that one should be indifferent to the outcome of one's actions. This is sometimes misunderstood. Rousseau, for instance, writes: 'The Christian homeland is not of this world. The Christian does his duty, it is true, but he does it with profound indifference towards the good or ill success of his deeds. Provided that he has nothing to reproach himself for, it does not matter to him whether all goes well or badly here on earth' (Rousseau, 1972, Bk IV, ch. 8). How near this description comes to that of a man whose main concern is to have a clear conscience. 'Suppose a foreign war breaks out. The citizens will march without reluctance to war; no one among them will think of flight; all will do their duty—but they will do it without passion for victory ... It does not matter to them whether they are victors or vanquished' (ibid.). Rousseau fails to distinguish here between a passion for the victory of the good and one for the victory of one's side. The latter always belongs to this world, even though it sometimes masquerades as a spiritual passion. Rousseau knows this, as his remarks on the crusaders show: 'Without disputing their valour, I shall say that they were far from being Christians. They were soldiers of the priests. They were citizens of the Church; they were fighting for its spiritual homeland, which it in some strange way made *temporal*' (italics mine). Simone Weil calls it 'idolatry'.

We see that when in the Christian religion God is characterised as 'transcendent' this in no way commits the believer to the kind of epistemological theory which Wisdom rightly criticises. Such characterisations are meant to provide the believer with a definition of the kind of God he is to worship and thus determine his attitude to life and death. They are *conceptual* not in the sense that they clarify concepts but in the sense that they fix concepts—in this case the Christian concept of God. They belong to theology[2] and not to philosophy. The philosopher's task is to bring this out and clarify their sense. What I said here goes only a little way in clarifying the concept of religious transcendence. But I shall be content if I have succeeded in indicating the direction in which we have to look if we are to make sense of it. There is a further problem, however, to which I should like to turn: namely, the relation between devotion to what is transcendent and inner life or spirituality.

III   Belief in the Transcendent and the Inner Life

Wisdom holds, I think rightly, that religions have something to say about spiritual matters. Certainly this is true of Christianity. He finds in many sayings of Jesus and in his actions a wisdom which may be described as knowledge of the human heart—a knowledge that cuts through appearances. He is thinking of the kind of knowledge which it is impossible to possess while one is ignorant of what lies in one's own heart. He thinks that although one can believe in God without possessing such knowledge, to know or to find God is necessarily to grow in this kind of wisdom. Hence the saying that the Kingdom of God is *within* you.

Wisdom understands the expression 'within' here to mean 'what lies in the depth of the soul'. Thus when he says that the Christian religion speaks about spiritual matters he means that it speaks about such relations as those that hold between joy and depression, envy and gratitude, guilt, remorse and repentance, and human life, about how happiness is to be attained and what it consists of, in the way that Freud, for instance, spoke about these matters. Joy, depression, hope, gratitude and remorse may be spoken of as 'states of soul' or as 'denizens of the spiritual world', and so Wisdom describes Dostoyevsky and Freud as 'explorers of the spiritual world' (Wisdom, 1963, p. 261). With them he includes Proust and Manet, St John, St Paul and Jesus Christ (Wisdom, 1953, p. 168; Wisdom, 1965, pp. 55–6).

One of the things that impress Wisdom most in great religious teachers is their emphasis on the good to be found in men and their dealings with each other. He finds it impressive because the good they emphasise is hidden and surrounded by its opposite, and because they make no attempt to conceal or deny this. They see this evil for what it is and are not daunted by it. What gives them hope and sustains them in the darkness is the good they manage to keep in sight when everything conspires to conceal it. Wisdom would say that in such vision of goodness there is profundity and courage. It takes courage to refuse to deny evil, not to paint a rosy picture of things; and it takes even greater courage 'not then to deny the good' (Wisdom, 1953, p. 261). We readily understand that men should deny the existence of evil in themselves and in others, especially those on whose support they depend. But we are far less alive to what it may cost a man to admit the good in himself and acknowledge its existence in those around him, a good that is not identical with those easy virtues and pleasantries familiar to us all: 'The paradox that you hated your sister needs to be balanced by the reassertion of the old truth that you loved her and the new truth that you loved her more than you knew when long ago you built houses in the trees and went pig-sticking in the orchard with her' (ibid., p. 263). This is the level of the soul from which spring those acts of deep generosity which may put at risk much that we have built in our lives, and also the kind of remorse which turns a single deed we ought never to have done into a knife which tears up the fabric of our life. It does indeed take courage to acknowledge its existence, to remain accessible to the level of soul in which such good is to be found.

There is no doubt that in the imaginative way in which Wisdom brings together the wisdom of great religious teachers with the vision to be found in the works of great artists, writers and psychologists, he is able to throw light on their teachings and enrich our appreciation of the words in which these are conveyed. But there is an ambiguity which runs through these comparisons, one that involves a confusion of psychological and spiritual truth. There is a long tradition in philosophy, dating back at least to Descartes, where the expression 'state of soul' is used to cover any state of mind in which a person may be, and the phrase 'inner' is meant to indicate anything that a person can keep to himself and need not reveal to others. The trouble is that this does not do justice to the sense in which people speak of the soul in religion—for instance in Christianity. Wisdom is influenced by this tradition.

The expressions 'state of soul' and 'inner life' or 'inwardness' are very closely linked together as these are used in religious discourse. *Inwardness* is the kind of orientation in which the life of the soul is to be found. It belongs to a man's relation to his moral and religious beliefs. A man's *inner life* is that aspect of his life in which these beliefs are active. Thus a man who is by and large indifferent to moral values and religious ideals, one who lives a life of moral routine or unrepentant wickedness or selfishness, has no inner life, however much he may fall in the grip of violent emotions, is eaten up by envy or jealousy, or driven by powerful ambitions. It is only when he is morally concerned about the kind of man he is that his inner life comes into being. A man's inner life appears in his struggles to relate himself to certain ideals, in the joy he meets with in such a life, the depression with which his failures fill him, and the remorse he feels for his bad deeds. The joy, depression and remorse in question are *states of soul* in the sense that they belong to his inner life. Thus the kind of happiness which Socrates speaks of in the *Gorgias* is a state of soul, whereas this is not true of the happiness which Polus attributes to Archelaus. When, thinking of the former, Wittgenstein said that there is no 'objective mark' of the happy life (Wittgenstein, 1961a, p. 78), he meant that not everybody would agree about the character of the life in question, however well informed, since the claim involves a moral judgment. If those who contemplate such a life differ in the values they believe in, none of its 'objective' features, including the thoughts and feelings of the man living it, could force them to agree on whether or not it is a happy life. When we speak of the soul, when we refer to and reflect on the state of soul a man is in, we are not using morally neutral language.[3] This is what Wisdom does not recognise sufficiently.

Now the religious remark that the Kingdom of God is *within* you is one that belongs to this language. I had suggested earlier that *part* of what it says is that one can find God only in one's own life, that how one lives is not irrelevant to one's relation to God, including one's belief in God. I am now suggesting that what is meant by 'the Kingdom of God is within you' is that one can find God only in a life of inwardness—that is, in a life of devotion to values one can make one's own only by becoming selfless. The phrase 'within you' means in an inner life, a life of inwardness, a life in which one turns away from worldliness. Such a life goes beyond the actions one does or refrains from doing, and the values or principles to which one's actions conform. The dimension in which it goes beyond one's individual actions is that of one's relation to the values and ideals one attaches importance to, the dimension of what they mean to one as an individual. I called it the dimension of the personal. Obviously one's actions are not irrelevant to the inwardness of one's life, but taken one at a time they will only lead those who consider these to what is outward there. If one's own concern in what one does comes to be confined to taking one's actions this way, then one's inner life will reach an ebb: it will be 'replaced by external life' (Tolstoy, 1960). In such a life there is no logical room for a belief in the Christian God—even if one pays lip service to it. One's whole life has to be different, not one's 'outer' behaviour but the spirit in which one acts, if one is to grow in inwardness and find a genuine belief in God: 'The Kingdom of God is *within* you.'

At first sight Wisdom *seems* to understand the sense of this saying in a radically different way: God is a power for good within us and when our actions are possessed by it we seem to be guided by a divine providence independent of us. Similarly for the devil, who is a power for evil in us. Wisdom is thinking here of what Freud wrote on 'unconscious determination' and the 'repetition-compulsion': 'Far more striking are those cases where the person seems to be experiencing something passively, without exerting any influence of his own, and yet always meets with the same fate over and over again. One may recall, for example, the story of the woman who married three men in succession, each of whom fell ill after a short time and whom she had to nurse till their death' (Freud, 1948, p. 23). Though 'such a life history is in a large measure self-imposed,' Freud writes, 'it gives the impression of a pursuing fate', a 'dæmonic trait' in the destiny of the person in question (ibid., p. 22). The passage Wisdom quotes from Freud's *New Introductory Lectures* goes with this: 'Dark, unfeeling and unloving powers determine human destiny' (Wisdom, 1965, pp. 16–17). Wisdom writes: 'One thing not sufficiently realised is that some of the things shut within us are not bad but good' (Wisdom, 1953, p. 166).

It is true that some of the things shut within us are good. I agree with Wisdom that this is not the same as the banal truth that there is some good in all of us. For the good which Wisdom is thinking of is buried, not normally accessible to the person in question, and it is a risky business for him to own it—although, of course, buried does not mean inoperative. Proust writes:

One should never hold men's bad deeds against them for good, never judge them on the basis of the memory of a malicious act, for we do not know all the good which at other times their souls have been able to will sincerely and realise. No doubt, the form of evil which one has observed in their actions will return; but the soul is much richer than this, it has in it many other forms which will also return in the lives of these men, forms which we refuse to admit on account of the bad deeds to which they have given themselves (Proust, 1954, 'La Prisonnière', Pt II, p. 153).

It is this kind of knowledge and courage which Wisdom finds in Christ when on the cross he said, 'Father forgive them for they know not what they do' (Wisdom, 1965, p. 141). His reading of the words, 'If you forgive men their trespasses your heavenly Father will also forgive you' goes with this. He takes these words to convey a *psychological* truth, though one that is far from trivial: If you can free yourself from the perspective of your anger for those who have wronged you, if you can see on the one hand that you are not so unlike them and on the other that there is more to them than what calls for your anger and indignation, you will have made room for what is good in you to emerge and heal the rift that exists not only between you, but also within you. This is what Wisdom seems to suggest 'your heavenly Father will forgive you' means: when you can allow the good you have shut within you to emerge, it will heal what separates you from your fellow men and also the division within yourself. See the Epilogue to *Crime and Punishment* where Dostoyevsky describes the transformation in Raskolnikov when he finally realises that he has violated more than the letter of the law, gives up his grudges against those to whom he owes a debt, and forgives them all that he held against them:

> They wanted to speak but could not; tears stood in their eyes. They were both pale and thin; but in those sick and pale faces the dawn of a new future, of a full resurrection to a new life, was already shining. It was love that brought them back to life: the heart of one held inexhaustible sources of life for the heart of the other.... That day it seemed to him that the convicts who had been his enemies looked at him differently; he had even begun talking to them himself, and they replied to him in a very friendly way.... He thought of her. He remembered how he used to torment her continually and lacerated her heart; he recalled her pale and thin little face, but he was scarcely troubled by these memories now: he knew with what infinite love he would atone for her sufferings now (pp. 557–8).

Wisdom's idea of what God's forgiveness comes to is important and putting it side by side with Dostoyevsky shows what there is in it. But it is still not the same as Christ's idea. For it does not do justice to the way in which God's forgiveness measures the spirituality one has attained. It does not sufficiently emphasise the transformation in one's scale of values implicit in the kind of forgiveness to which God responds in His forgiveness. We find this emphasis in Dostoyevsky and it is one reason why *Crime and Punishment* is more than a psychological novel.

Another doubt I have concerns the symmetry Wisdom finds between being possessed by evil and being possessed by good.

In the latter case, can one speak of anything like a 'repetition-compulsion' or 'an endless repetition of the same'? If there is any compulsion to repeat here, it lies not in the intermittent victory of what is good in a man, but in the way each time he subsequently manages to shut it out of his life. However at one a man may be with the evil that is in him, it rules him in a way in which the good in him does not. We may use the same words in both connections: being possessed, slavery, and so on. But they don't mean the same. Forms of the good, generosity, kindness, compassion, do not drive a man when he admits them into his life in the way in which forms of evil, greed, avarice, envy do. I shall not develop this point here, but if I am right then Wisdom is wrong in the symmetry he assigns to God and the devil in his treatment of them as powers within us. This, in any case, is in conflict with the teaching of Christianity which speaks *only* of the Kingdom of God as being within us. Hell or the devil is not within us in *this* sense at all. The claim that the Kingdom of God is *within* us goes with the claim that it lies *outside* this world. In other words, one can grow in inwardness by turning away from this world, by dying to its hopes and expectations. The devil, on the other hand, belongs to this world; his empire is to be found 'here below'.[4] To become subject to him is for one's life to lose its inwardness. It is certainly not in an inner life that one finds him—if one can speak of 'finding' him at all.

Having said that I find Wisdom's reading of Christ's teachings unacceptable I want to add that his reading is more subtle than I suggested and that his psychological interpretation has more spiritual content than meets the eye. 'The Kingdom of God is within you': he certainly understands this to mean that you will find God when you have the courage to keep in touch with the good that is in you and when you can see through the evil around you to the good which it does not exclude. This is still different from the reading I have offered of Christ's saying, but it is nearer. For a man who can keep in contact with the good that is in him is thereby changed by it and he can do this only by being prepared to give up certain pursuits and preoccupations which have a hold on him. Such a change is also a change in his scale of values, even if Wisdom does not sufficiently emphasise this.

However Wisdom does not like to think of such a change as a turning away from this world: 'Some of us would rather remain in the Lamb or the Elephant, where, as we know, they stop whimpering with another bitter and so far from sneering at all things, hang pictures of winners at Kempton and stars of the 'nineties. Something good we have for each other is freed there, and in some degree and for a while the miasma of time is rolled back without obliging us to deny the present' (Wisdom, 1963, p. 167). But is this not in some ways akin to the change in one's relation to time which I spoke of in the previous section? Does it not involve, in some degree, a detachment from what Kierkegaard calls 'the press of busyness'? This is not a form of aloofness to life, nor a 'sneering at all things', and those who choose to live a life of poverty do not look down on the simple pleasures of this life in which 'something good we have for each other is freed'.

Wisdom writes: 'Saints and cynics alike too readily assume it agreed that birds, beasts, flowers and fast cars have nothing to do with the case [i.e. with what makes life worth living or meaningful] or at any rate that they aren't good enough' (Wisdom, 1965, p. 37). There are two misunderstandings here. First, nobody would want to deny that a racing driver's interest in fast cars may be a genuine interest and add to the meaning of his life. When Simone Weil says that 'it is only necessary to be honest with oneself to realise that there is nothing in this world to live for' (Weil, 1968, p. 148) what she says does not imply that an interest in fast cars is never a genuine interest. She is saying that compared with a life dedicated to God these things are nothing. This is a value judgment from which Wisdom may want to dissociate himself. But we should be clear that in that case what he refuses to accept is a judgment of value. It isn't as if someone whose friend has discovered a treasure said, 'Don't kid yourself, there is no gold there, nor any diamonds; only cheap metal and glass' and Wisdom retorted: 'Some of it is cheap metal and glass; but you look close enough and you will discern some gold there and also diamonds.' We should also be clear about what it *says* as a judgment of value. It does not say that an interest in fast cars is evil, but that it cannot sustain our spiritual aspirations. It becomes evil when it comes to overshadow all other concerns in a man's life.

Secondly, birds, beasts and flowers do not belong with fast cars, and it is not true that saints have spurned them. 'There are some men for whom a tree has no reality until they think of cutting it down' (Merton, 1957, p. 248). Merton writes: 'Those who love their own noise are impatient of everything else. They constantly defile the silence of the forests and the mountains and the sea. ... The silence of the sky remains when the plane has gone. The tranquility of the clouds will remain when the plane has fallen apart. It is the silence of the world that is real. Our noise, our business, our purposes, and all our fatuous statements ...: these are the illusion' (pp. 247–8).

It is not the world, seen as God's creation, which saints have characterised as illusory, but a certain myopic absorption in schemes with which we identify ourselves, schemes which support our prestige and further our interests. It is these which Simone Weil says can never nourish our souls, these which make our lives 'external'.

'The vanity of this world'—this phrase is an expression of concern for human beings in *this* life. It is the *quality* of their lives, the kind of thing to which men give their hearts and allow to fill their lives, that is the subject of comment. Though Simone Weil says that 'there is nothing in this world to live for', she has never spurned the world: 'Let us love the country here below. It is real; it offers resistance to love. It is this country which God has given us to love. He has willed that it should be difficult yet possible to love it' (Weil, 1959, p. 132). These two remarks are not contradictory. Nor does Simone Weil think of earthly life as such as illusory. On the contrary, she takes it as the criterion of spiritual things: 'The value of a form of spiritual life is appreciated by the way it lights up things of this world.' 'A judge's faith does not appear in his attitude in church, but in his attitude in court' (Weil, 1953, pp. 97–8).

In a nutshell, then, a life of worldliness and earthly life are not the same thing. To turn away from the former is not to speak of the latter with contempt. In any case, contempt is very different from detachment; it may in fact be a form of attachment. Certainly it has no place in a life of inwardness. It is itself a worldly reponse; it partakes of that from which it turns away. Wisdom does not distinguish between contempt and detachment, nor between worldliness and life on earth.

Perhaps that is part of the reason why he doesn't like the idea of 'a timeless state not made of the stuff of this world', though it is a pity he should have turned to Aldous Huxley for an understanding of what it might mean (Wisdom, 1953, p. 167).

He is also suspicious of the idea of self-denial; he thinks of it as something which 'harms a man's power to give life to others' (Wisdom, 1965, p. 142). The gist of his reasoning is, I think, as follows: You cannot really think of others unless you can enjoy life; you cannot really care for other people if you think that all the pleasures of this world are vain. There are many relationships—friendship for instance, or the relation between husband and wife, parents and children—which would be impoverished if the give and take in them were not reciprocal. Very often to give pleasure to another person involves forgetting them and taking pleasure yourself in what you are doing. Even a saint's capacity to give of himself to those who are in need would be harmed if he never wanted anything for himself. Besides if you depreciate yourself then what you bring to a relationship with others will itself be suffused with this depreciation; it will lack sustenance.

It is not easy to sort out what is true here from what is not; the dialectic of self-renunciation is an intricate one. To begin with the last point, humility and spiritual poverty are very different from self-depreciation. It is, indeed, true that one who constantly depreciates himself is denying that he has received anything good. It is difficult to imagine that such a person should feel he has something good to give or be capable of genuine gratitude. As for the 'power to give life to others', one should not confuse 'spiritual poverty' with 'poverty of spirit'—what T. S. Eliot described as 'time-ridden faces, distracted from distraction by distraction ... men and bits of paper' (Eliot, 1955). Nor should one confuse selflessness with the 'objectivity' of Nietzsche's 'objective man' whose soul only reflects and 'no longer knows how to affirm, no longer how to deny' (Nietzsche, 1973). A selfless person is not one who is incapable of passion, one who finds no joy in life. He is one whose pleasures are not self-centred, not of the kind in which the 'ego' thrives. One can, for instance, enjoy music or painting with passion, and the purer one's enjoyment the less is one's pleasure shadowed by the self. One can share this pleasure with another, and just because the self is absent from it, one can kindle enthusiasm in the other and inspire him. As for the father in Wisdom's example, 'had there been in him still a love of locomotives, even toy locomotives' this would not prevent him from 'playing trains with his children entirely for their sake' (Wisdom, 1965, p. 142). It is true, of course, that if he did not enjoy the game himself he would not be able to give as much pleasure to his children. His enjoyment, far from turning him away from his children towards himself, becomes a means of contact with them. The fact that it is *his* does not mean that he is indifferent to whether they enjoy it or not. If they didn't enjoy it, then he would not enjoy it either. The enjoyment of each is sensitive to that of the other. This is not indifference towards the other; it is love.

Professor Winch has pointed out that such phrases as 'doing something entirely for someone else's sake' or 'acting for the sake of duty' in which one tries to capture the essence of concern or moral purity can never succeed in doing so. One can always find actions to which such phrases apply properly but which do not exemplify the essence in question—quite the reverse. This is true of the father in Wisdom's example, as Wisdom himself points out, in contrast with the father in Simone Weil's example who plays with his child 'not out of a sense of duty but out of pure joy and pleasure' (Winch, 1968, p. 13). Yet the latter is more selfless than the former; in the pleasure he shares with his child he has forgotten himself.

Perhaps the former father can only keep his 'ego' from intruding by not allowing himself any enjoyment. This is at least one possibility. Such a man keeps his 'ego' out at the expense of his 'power to give life to others' because he is unable to disentangle it from his passions and desires. He throws away the baby with the bath water. What he needs to do is not to give free reign to his ego, but to purge his actions and passions from its influence; and he will not achieve this by keeping at arm's length whatever has been contaminated by the ego. Wisdom is right in wanting to have none of this, but he is wrong in thinking that this is what self-renunciation means. Similarly, a man who wants nothing for himself *may* be a person who does not know how to want anything without being greedy. If he can stop acting out of greed only by rejecting all his desires, the guilt he feels about his greed will make him a moral cripple. Here his wanting nothing for himself is something of which we should be suspicious. Wisdom would say that *if* this is what dying to oneself means then it does not touch this man's spiritual problems. It is as false a solution of them as Mrs Solness' strict adherence to her duties was in Ibsen's play *The Master Builder*. Winch has pointed out how it stood in the way of 'genuine relationships between herself and her fellow-characters'.[5]

'You cannot really think of others unless you can enjoy life.' This is only true if 'enjoying life' means 'being behind what you do', 'finding sense in what you are doing'. But then this is in no way incompatible with self-renunciation. A life of self-denial need not exclude joy. Besides the man who wants nothing for himself is not one who wants nothing at all, since he may want much for others and fight for it with passion. As for the man who 'turns the other cheek', he is not necessarily one who feels that nothing is worth defending, one who enters into complicity with the insulting party. From where he stood Callicles could not see the courage in Socrates' attitude to life. We must not make the same mistake and identify courage and integrity with their 'visible', worldly forms. I don't believe you can defend God as you can defend your honour. He needs no defence. But you can remain true to Him by 'turning the other cheek', and this far from being a cringing attitude may take great courage.

A friend who wants nothing for himself is like the father in Wisdom's example who is 'playing trains with his children entirely for their sake'. But one should not confuse friendship and charity. There is an important sense in which charity is 'impersonal'; it is a response to the kind of deprivation or suffering in another human being which cuts through everything which differentiates him from other human beings, and it is a response which comes from that level of soul which has not been penetrated by the personality.[6] This, however, is not true of friendship. For friendship necessarily involves preference for one human being. Yet there is a friendship which is completely undemanding, even though it is rare.[7] This means respect for the other person's independent existence. It means an unwillingness to subordinate the friendship to what one wants for oneself. This is not to say though that one wants nothing for oneself, that one accepts the gift of friendship 'entirely for the friend's sake'.

I agree with Wisdom that a man who wants nothing for himself would make a poor friend. But I don't think that this is true of a saint's capacity to give of himself to those who are in need. This is a very different matter. The life of a saint is, of course, necessarily life here on earth, even though it is the antithesis of what I called a worldly life. Still, not every aspect of earthly life is open to a saint. Here, I think, one has to distinguish between serving God and wanting to do His will, and saintliness, or dedicating one's whole life to God. Of course, the former calls for selflessness. But this is not the same thing as taking up the cross. Perhaps friendship is still open to one who takes up the cross. I doubt, however, that such a person can enter into a earthly marriage or be a parent. Simone Weil writes: 'For the privilege of finding myself before dying in a similar state to that of Christ when, on the cross, he said, "My God, why have you abandoned me?"—for this privilege I would willingly renounce everything that is called Paradise' (Weil, 1953, p. 109). For a man or woman who sincerely speaks these words many of the goods of earthly life are impossible. But it is from the very few that God asks that they should take up the cross; it is to the very few that (in Simone Weil's language) He accords such a privilege. As I said before, believing in God is not the same thing as knowing Him.

We see that Wisdom is suspicious of the religious believer who 'picks this world into worthless pieces' because it seems to him, quite rightly, that a man who finds nothing good in this world cannot sing the praise of God—not with his heart in it. He is wrong, however, to think that the man who looks on worldliness as an illusion is one who belittles the small, simple things of life, or one who sneers at everything. Wisdom is also suspicious of a life of self-denial because he thinks that such a life is bound to be too negative and to exclude those things he considers good—love, friendship, praise of beauty, gratitude. I tried to point out that this is at best an over-narrow view of what self-denial means and that it goes wrong in identifying self-denial with its non-spiritual, impure varieties. But there is also the factor of temperament in Wisdom's dislike of a reading of Christ's words which puts too great an emphasis on self-denial and the renunciation of this world.

Being thankful for the good in life which might not have

been there, hidden amidst the forms of evil that surrounds it, is an attitude Wisdom can understand and respects. But he dislikes 'the only thing I can understand by "one who gives thanks for life no matter what" '. He is right this far: From the standpoint which sees the contingencies of life in their relation to our desires, intention and hopes some things will call for thanks, others not. Therefore, unless we can see the possibility of an alternative standpoint this thankfulness will strike us as foolish—as 'unamenable to reason', 'insensitive to what is so' (Wisdom, 1965, p. 51).

But the Christian faith provides just such a possibility. Simone Weil connects it with 'the beauty of the world' which she finds in its lack of finality: 'The essential truth to be known concerning this universe is that it is absolutely devoid of finality. Nothing in the way of finality can be ascribed to it except through a lie or a mistake.' (Weil, 1959, p. 130.) To this one's first reaction may be: So it is a delusion to think that even some things call for thanks and others not. Nothing calls for thanks except what takes place between human beings. One can only feel grateful for what someone *does*. This is a minimum requirement or necessary condition for what one meets to be an intelligible object of gratitude. But is this correct? Does this view not take an over-narrow view of gratitude? Have we not, some of us, felt gratitude before a really beautiful poem, for instance? And did this have anything to do with receiving something—something good that was meant for us? Was it not rather a response in which such considerations are transcended? If gratitude can be a form of transcendence initiated by contact with beauty, then nothing other than what can mar or make a difference to this beauty can make such gratitude misplaced. Now the gratitude of the believer presupposes that he sees and loves the world as a poem. If the beauty he sees in the world is inseparable from the contingency of life, then what makes his gratitude unconditional or invulnerable to what is so is the inevitability of this contingency which has also been called necessity: 'The absence of finality is the reign of necessity. ... If the soul is set in the direction of love, the more we contemplate the necessity, the more closely we press its metallic cold and hardness to our very flesh, the nearer we approach to the beauty of the world. That is what Job experienced. It was use

he was so honest in his suffering, because he would not
entertain any thought which might impair its truth, that God
came down to reveal the beauty of the world to him' (ibid.,
p. 131).

In one sentence, then, my suggestion is that if we can
remember the kind of gratitude which beauty sometimes
awakens in people, and also see that when religious people
speak of the beauty of the world they are thinking of
something that could not be otherwise, though it could be lost
sight of, then we might be better able to understand the
notion of giving thanks to God *no matter what*. The fact remains
that whether he makes sense of this or not Wisdom dislikes the
idea together with those of detachment and self-renunciation.
I have tried to show that a religion that gives prominence to
these ideas need not be a religion of mystery or unreason.
Reject them and what is meant in religious language by an
inner life will turn into what we normally mean by a life of the
emotions. For an inner life is a life of devotion to what
transcends the world of time and the senses. Wisdom rightly
emphasises that coming to believe in God necessarily involves
a change in the believer which puts him in touch with a deeper
level of the soul. But in so far as he rejects the idea of religious
transcendence his understanding of the kind of change which
a man undergoes in coming to believe in God assumes a
psychotherapeutic bias. I have examined the conceptual
aspect of what lies at the source of this rejection.

IV   Conclusion: Wisdom and 'the Logic of God'

I want to conclude with a few general remarks about 'the logic
of God'.

At the centre of Wisdom's contribution to this topic is a
clear recognition that God is not an object among or beyond
the objects we know and in interaction with them. This is not
to say that God is a myth or that He does not exist. The point is
a grammatical one about what it does not mean to believe in
God or to affirm His existence. As for what it does mean to do
so this can best be understood by turning to religious life and
language. But, of course, to understand this is not the same
thing as believing in God.

Thus if you wish to understand what God's existence amounts to ask yourself what it means to believe in God, to worship Him, to thank Him, fear Him, love Him, etc. Here you cannot take for granted the meaning of the verb 'believe' or any of the other verbs when they have God as their grammatical object. The grammar of God is determined in part by the use of these verbs in còntexts of religious worship, reflection, confession, discussion. Hence you have to consider the use of these verbs in religious discourse and what their use connects with in the individual lives of those who believe in, worship, love and fear God. In other words, there is the *word* to consider in its cultural background where it has sense and also those *personal lives* that are turned towards or away from God. This may seem an indirect and round-about route, but it is the only one possible. If one can follow it in all its by-ways, as these intersect one another at different points, then when one has covered sufficient ground what the idea of God amounts to in a particular religious tradition will begin to emerge. It is true, of course, that many direct remarks about God are to be found in a religion like Christianity which may be said to belong to its theology—such remarks as God is a *person*, He is a *transcendent being*, He is *timeless*. But these remarks cannot provide us with any short-cuts, since an elucidation of their sense would have to take the same line as I have indicated.

I believe that by and large Wisdom follows this kind of procedure in its double aspect. He wants to know (i) how the believer's *view of the world* differs from the way a non-believer looks at the world, and how this difference is tied up with the difference between belief and non-belief, and (ii) how the believer's *inner life* differs from that of the non-believer, and how this difference is tied up with the difference between belief and non-belief. He is also interested in (iii) how the believer's *inner life* is tied up with his *view of the world*. He doesn't think that these connections are contingent and he believes that they enter into what we *mean* when we say that he believes in God. This, as I understand it, is part of his rejection of the analogy of the invisible gardener in favour of a consideration of how the difference between one who still speaks of an invisible gardener and one who denies his existence may be bound up with the difference in their views of the garden when no part of it is closed to either of them. He turns to the second aspect of the matter when he asks: 'What are our feelings when we believe in God?' (Wisdom, 1953, p. 164). Perhaps the question is badly framed; perhaps the answer towards which it steers him is inadequate. But there is no doubt that Wisdom asks about the believer's feelings, his inner life, because he believes that these are logically relevant to the identity of his belief.

The strand I have singled out in Wisdom's exploration of 'the logic of God' needs to be underlined, I believe, because the comparative procedure which dominates the foreground of the discussion tends to push it to the background.

I should like to note, without discussion, that Wisdom has told me (May 1977) that he has grown dissatisfied with the account of religious belief he gives in his published writings, particularly in 'Gods'. He thinks now that it is an 'attenuated' account in that it does not do justice to what the ordinary Christian believes about God and the after-life and the consolation he finds in his beliefs. It fails to do justice to what he believes by reducing the claims made by a statement of these beliefs. The change in Wisdom's views, therefore, distance him further from the positive account I have developed in my criticism of his published views.

8 Wittgenstein: Meaning and Circumstances

I Words have Meaning 'in the Traffic of Human Life'

In the *Tractatus* Wittgenstein speaks of a proposition as something we can construct (4.026–4.03). What sense it has depends on what we have constructed. It is its truth-functional relation to the elementary propositions of which it is a truth-function that determines its sense. What Wittgenstein develops here finds the following echo in our hearts: The meaning of each word must be explained to us if we are to understand them. We have also to learn how to construct sentences with them—the syntactical or grammatical rules for constructing sentences. Once we have learnt this we can construct ever newer sentences and so say new things, and also understand sentences we have not come across before. What a sentence says thus depends on the meanings of its words and on the way these words are combined. It depends on nothing else. What we do with a sentence, when we utter the words that make it up, depends on its meaning and on what we want to say. But its meaning is logically prior to what we do with it. This meaning is written into the symbol and is independent of what we do with the symbol.

Similarly, what we do in response to the words spoken by someone else depends on our understanding them in their particular combination and on our particular interests and desires. Once more our understanding is our grasp of what is written into the symbol, the truth-conditions of the proposition expressed, and is independent of what we do in response to the symbol on the occasion in which it is used. What we do is determined by our understanding, given our interests, desires and fears.

Notice that here sense or meaning is the primary notion, while understanding is grasping the sense of the proposition.

From *The Blue Book* onwards Wittgenstein reverses this relation. The sense of a proposition is what we grasp when we can be said to have understood what it says. What we do on hearing what is said, under normal circumstances, is a criterion of our understanding it, not a consequence of it. But this is so only when it can be taken for granted that we speak the language in question. If a Chinaman shouted 'Jump' to me in Chinese and if, taking me unawares, it made me jump, this would not constitute a case of obeying an order, nor of course would we say that I understood what he said. If, on the other hand, I do speak and understand the language, then this is something that can be seen at other times and in other places. This is what lies behind my response to a command on a particular occasion. What lies behind it thus is not a mental process which constitutes my understanding and directs me in what I do. In brief, Wittgenstein also reverses the way we are inclined to relate our actions and our understanding: The actions are not a consequence of the understanding, they are what the understanding finds expression in, they constitute a criterion of the understanding. So if we want to get clear about what understanding a sentence or a formula consists in, we should not ask 'what goes on in us when we hear the words that make up the sentence uttered?', but instead 'in what circumstances do we say of someone that he understands what he has heard? and 'how is his understanding manifested in what he does?'

As a mnemonic one could say that in the *Tractatus* a proposition is something we can construct; in the *Investigations* it is something that we use. While there is still something to be said for the distinction between words and sentences, Wittgenstein no longer thinks it to be as important as he once thought. For one thing a single word can be used to express a proposition. Thus Sraffa's gesture to Wittgenstein: what is the logical multiplicity of what is expressed by it? On the other hand, a combination of words, a sentence too is something that has a use, a use that we can grasp: 'Someone who doesn't know English hears me say on certain occasions: "What a marvellous light!" He guesses the sense and now uses the exclamation himself, as I use it, but without understanding the three individual words. Does he understand the exclamation?' (Wittgenstein, 1967, §150.) 'Would it be equally easy to imagine the analogous case for this sentence: "If the train does not arrive punctually at five o'clock, he'll miss the connection"? What would guessing the sense mean in this case?' (ibid., §152.)

Certainly sentences which express propositions are constructed out of words in accordance with rules of syntax or grammar, and if we know the words and speak the language we shall understand new sentences, sentences we have not come across before. If we know the words and speak the language—but what does 'speak the language' mean, apart from knowing the vocabulary? We may think it means: knowing how to form sentences, knowing grammar or syntax. Wittgenstein thinks there is much more to it than that. This is part of what he has in mind when he insists that language is not a calculus. Rhees brings out the difference well in 'Wittgenstein's Builders' (Rhees, 1970).

To be sure there are rules for combining words into intelligible sentences. But that meaningful words are combined in accordance with such rules does not guarantee that we understand the words in that combination, or that they say anything. It is true that if someone were to write them down on a blank piece of paper to test our understanding of the language and ask, 'Do you understand what this sentence means?', we would say that we do—and may be truly so. But what does our understanding consist of? Surely, it consists of our ability to imagine numerous circumstances, situations in which someone could use those words, that sentence intelligibly. In most of these we could imagine a dialogue, a conversation, a clash, a quarrel in the course of which the words are used. Sentences are constructed out of words—all right. But they are also used, used in particular circumstances—just like words. And this is as important, perhaps more important, because it is something we tend to forget, especially when we do philosophy.

When we learn to speak, as children, we learn how to construct sentences and how variations in construction affect the sense and implications of what we say by means of them. We also learn how and when to use them. We learn to respond to them in various situations in which others utter them. What the words and the sentences mean is not independent of this. If you teach a child the meaning of new words—say 'knife', 'fork', 'spoon'—you would expect him to point to, fetch, etc., the right objects when you shout out these words, and you would also expect him to say the right word in response to the question 'what is this?' asked while you point to or hold up one of these things. This is obviously much more important than the ability to give definitions. The same considerations apply to sentences as well. If the child who had learned the meanings of many words was now able to construct many sentences with these words but was unable to use the sentences in appropriate circumstances we would not say that he understood them. We would say that although he had begun to learn the meanings of the words we taught him, his grasp of their meaning had remained stunted. For part of what shows that he understands the meanings of the words with which he constructs sentences is his ability to use these sentences in appropriate circumstances.

We were inclined to say: If someone understands the words of which a sentence is composed, and he is familiar with the rules of syntax governing its construction, he will understand the sentence. I did not deny this. But I drew attention to what we take for granted when we say this, namely that he has learned more than just how to construct sentences; for he has also learned how to use them. Unless he knows this, his understanding of the meanings of the words in those sentences will be incomplete. Our understanding of the meanings of individual words cannot be completely divorced from our knowledge of how to use the sentences out of which they are constructed. The sentences are what individual speakers use to say something in particular situations. The meaning which the sentences have independently of what each speaker says by means of them is not independent of the way they are capable of being used to say something on particular occasions. This, in turn, is not independent of how they are actually used by speakers of the language. This is an important part of what a person learns in learning to speak, namely how to use sentences meaningfully, when to use those sentences, in what situations it would be appropriate to use them, how to express sense with them. This is coming to have something to say himself.

If one says that he learns to express sense with words and sentences according to his aims and needs in particular situations, then one should remember that while these aims and needs are *his*, they come from the language he has learned to speak and speaks. Thus I may, on a particular occasion, want to tell someone off, or I may feel the need to communicate to someone with whom I have been working my thoughts about the problems we have met in the course of this work. I may wish to pledge my loyalty to someone at whose side I have been fighting, or to express my devotion to the woman I love. In each case I use certain words and sentences to tell them what I want to say in those situations. But I couldn't want to do so, have the need to tell them these things, have any interest in doing so, were it not for the language we speak and the culture in which it is embedded. The desire, the need, the interest, the aim is mine, but it is made possible by the language. What it is possible for the poet, the lover, the worshipper, the speaker to aim at saying in particular situations is determined by the language they speak—in the case of the poet, for instance, by the poetic tradition in which he writes. This does not exclude, of course, the possibility of individual speakers, poets, thinkers contributing to that language and literary, scientific, religious tradition, so that people are able to say new things and so come to want to say them.

Let me return, however, to the sentence as something we use in particular situations to say something—something it is appropriate to use in certain situations but not others. When we meet it in the abstract, when someone writes it on a piece of paper and asks whether we understand it, we shall normally say that we do, and truly so. But our understanding of it is our ability to imagine situations in which it can be used intelligibly, our ability to fill in a background against which it comes to life. Thus Wittgenstein gives the example of an ordinary sentence which may have been lifted out of a novel or narrative: 'After he had said this, he left her as he did the day before' (Wittgenstein, 1963, §525). He asks whether we understand this sentence: 'Do I understand it just as I should if I heard it in the course of a narrative?' He says: 'If it were set down in isolation I should say, I don't know what it's about. But all the same I should know how this sentence might perhaps be used; I could myself invent a context for it. (A multitude of familiar paths lead off from these words in every direction.)' He returns to the same question in a different connection:

'I was going to say …'—You remember various details. But not even all of them together shew your intention. It is as if a snapshot of a scene had been taken, but only a few scattered details of it were to be seen: here a hand, there a bit of a face, or a hat—the rest is dark. And now it is as if we know quite certainly what the whole picture represented. As if I could read the darkness (ibid., §635).

These 'details' are not irrelevant in the sense in which other circumstances which I can remember equally well are irrelevant. But if I tell someone 'For a moment I was going to say …' he does not learn those details from this, nor need he guess them. He need not know, for instance, that I had already opened my mouth to speak. But he *can* 'fill out the picture' in this way. (And this capacity is part of understanding what I tell him) (ibid., §636).

So if we meet such words in isolation our understanding them is in part at least our ability to fill out the picture, to invent a context in which it is appropriate to speak them. Where the context has not been supplied, we can supply it ourselves, invent it. This is what makes us say that we understand the words in question. Let us now block the possibility of doing so by putting the words in an inappropriate context. Would we still say that we understand them, that there is anything these words say? If not, do they still constitute an intelligible sentence? Wittgenstein gives many such examples:

If someone, in quite heterogeneous circumstances, called out with the most convincing mimicry: 'Down with him!', one might say of these words (and their tone) that they were a pattern that does indeed have familiar applications, but that in this case it was not even clear what *language* the man in question was speaking (Wittgenstein, 1969b §350).

He then gives a characteristic analogy to drive the point home:

I might make with my hand the movement I should make if I were holding a hand-saw and sawing through a plank; but would one have any right to call this movement *sawing*, out of all context? ... (It might be something quite different!) (ibid.).

In *Zettel* he imagines a man who *looked* and *acted* sad in all circumstances: 'If we taught such a one the expression "I am sad" and he kept on saying this with an expression of sadness, these words, like the other signs, would have lost their normal sense' (§526). This brings out what we take for granted and forget when we are doing philosophy, namely how much the varying background to the familiar words and sentences we say we understand contribute to their meaning. It is perfectly proper that we should take that for granted in speech; but not in philosophy when we are concerned to make clear what it is for words and sentences to have meaning. This is what Wittgenstein had neglected in the *Tractatus*. The unvarying look of the man Wittgenstein imagines cannot add up to a look of sadness except in the sense that if we took a photograph of him then the picture would depict a look of sadness. If we looked at it we would say: This man must have been sad when his picture was taken. What we do not know when we say this is that the man's look is fixed—just as much as it is in the photograph. Once we find this out we wouldn't know what to make of it. Similarly for his words 'I am sad'.

Wittgenstein compares the words and the expression to a fixed smile: ' "Smiling" is our name for an expression in a normal play of expressions' (Wittgenstein, 1967, §527). For instance, he says, I might not be able to react to a fixed smile as I do to the smile of someone who smiles at me in the ordinary course of affairs. He may be a stranger in the bus. He drops his ticket as he is fumbling with the parcels he is carrying. I pick it up and give it to him. He smiles as he says thank you. I smile back: 'No wonder we have this concept [of a smile] in *these* circumstances' (ibid.). The significance of the smile, indeed its very identity as a smile, is bound up with this background. Remove the background or alter it radically, freeze the smile (through the paralysis of the face) so that it no longer varies with the circumstances, and you no longer have a smile. This goes equally for linguistic expressions, including sentences. Thus compare with what Wittgenstein says about grief: ' "Grief" describes a pattern which recurs, with different variations, in the weave of our life. If a man's bodily expression of sorrow and joy alternated, say with the ticking of a clock, here we should not have the characteristic formation of the pattern of sorrow or of the pattern of joy' (Wittgenstein, 1963, p. 174). Sentences too are used in the course of, for example, a conversation, which itself takes place in the traffic of human life. Their significance, their being sentences, the meanings of the words in them, depends on this.

I spoke of the internal relation there is between the sense of a sentence and the circumstances in which it is appropriate to use it. Obviously I do not wish to deny that a sentence can be used to say something false. Thus a colour-blind man may point to a red object and say 'This is green.' A man may point to a china-egg and say 'This is an egg.' He is mistaken. Or he may introduce Jim to his friend as John. Perhaps he is mistaken about Jim's name or he has simply made a slip. An Englishman who has learned some Italian may systematically describe green things as 'giallo' thinking that this is the word for green, when in fact it means yellow. When he says 'Questa machina e giallo' we would say that *he* means 'This car is green', whereas the sentence means 'This car is yellow.' He is mistaken in his use of the Italian word, but he is not mistaken about the colour of the car. If you ask: Is what he says true or false? this needs a little bit of explaining. There is no one-word correct answer to this question. We could imagine a great variety of examples in which people use words intelligibly and what they say is false because they are mistaken, or they are lying, etc.

Take the case where a man is mistaken and says something intelligible but false. The fact that we describe him as *mistaken* means that we understand him, we understand what he says, that we find nothing strange in his use of the words he uses in the particular circumstances in question. We find it intelligible that he should not recognise the truth, that he should be mistaken in this way in these circumstances—for example he may be colour-blind, the light may be deceptive. And when we point this out to him, he reacts in the normal way—for example he looks at the thing more closely, probes, retracts his words. If all our attempts to get him to consider the possibility that he is mistaken failed, if regardless of our queries he repeated his words insistently, however correct his English we would no longer know what to make of them, we would not know what he was saying. We would also retract our claim that he was mistaken. We do not understand what he is saying to be able to say that he is wrong or mistaken: 'Whether a thing is a blunder or not—it is a blunder in a particular system. Just as something is a blunder in a particular game and not in another' (Wittgenstein, 1966, p. 59).

In *On Certainty* Wittgenstein has much more to say on this: 'When someone makes a mistake, this can be fitted into what he knows aright' (§74). For instance, he must be capable of making various kinds of judgment, which capacity will come into play when questioned about what he says and find expression in how he goes on in response to queries and criticism. As Wittgenstein puts it: 'In order to make a mistake, a man must already judge in conformity with mankind' (ibid., §156). If he did not, we could not read into his words the significance we would otherwise read. And then we could not say that what he says is 'false', or that he is 'mistaken': 'What we call "a mistake" plays quite a special part in our language-games' (ibid., §196). In the example I am imagining it doesn't seem that we are playing the same language-game. Wittgenstein gives a great many examples in *On Certainty*. To take any one at random: A man says he cannot remember whether he had always had five fingers or two hands (§157). What on earth is he saying? Do we understand? Is he simply mistaken? And if we were to say, 'Of course you remember; you have always had two hands and five fingers on each', would we have contradicted him?

Contrast with the following example. A man has always been what is nowadays called a 'sharp dresser'. He has a great many suits in his wardrobe and has always had. He counts them and finds he has twenty suits. He says: 'I have always had a great many suits, ever since I was twenty years of age. But I do not remember whether I had always twenty.' The point is that the number of suits a man has varies greatly from individual to individual, and also from one time of an individual's life to another. A man who has many suits and who discards them fairly regularly may easily lose track of the number of suits he has or had at any time. So it makes sense for him to ask himself, to wonder how many he has at any time. And if he hasn't asked, he may not himself be clear how many he had at a particular time in the past. He may have to remember and do a bit of deduction or calculation, and his memory and deductions may run into sand. He may then say: 'I do not remember how many suits I had when I was twenty-five.' There may be someone who could tell him.

The background I have indicated, or something like it, is necessary for the words 'I do not remember how many I had—or whether I always had as many as I now have' to make sense. Yet it is missing in the case of the man who says 'I cannot remember whether I always had two hands and five fingers on each.' Therefore we cannot know what he means; we cannot be sure that he means anything at all.

If we said, 'Of course you do; everyone remembers that he always had two hands', would we be saying something true, so obviously true that it hardly needs saying? The background without which Wittgenstein's man's words make no sense, also deprives *our* words of sense: 'Everyone remembers that he always had two hands.' To whom would we be saying this? And what sort of information would we be giving him? We wouldn't be saying it to the man in Wittgenstein's example, for it is not clear that he is saying something, that he is not demented. What such a man seems to have lost is not a particular memory, that he had two hands when he was young, or a piece of common knowledge that most people are born with two hands and five fingers on each, that they do not grow hands and fingers in later life. What he has lost is the capacity to make sense. He can still formulate correct English sentences, but they no longer have the connections they need to have in order to make sense. If we think we can contradict him and say, 'Of course you remember', or 'Everyone has two hands', we would show a failure to recognise what has gone wrong here. Besides we would be trying to state facts which are, in a way, presupposed by the intelligibility of the language we use. Wittgenstein would say: 'This fact is fused into the foundations of our language-game' (Wittgenstein, 1969b, §558). He asks: 'Indeed, doesn't it seem obvious that the possibility of a language-game is conditioned by certain facts?' (ibid., §617). That is why an attempt to state it cannot be a move in our language-game. For that to be a possible move, much else would have to be different in ways we would find difficult to follow or enter into. Anyway if that were the case, the language in which that were a move would be different from the familiar language in which we have been trying to say 'Everyone remembers that he has always had two hands.'

I asked: To whom would we be saying this? I answered: Not to Wittgenstein's man who may be demented, whose sentences no longer have any discernible connections with each other and with his actions. What about someone who says something equally odd, but whose sentences and actions do have a pattern of connections, only one not familiar to us? Wittgenstein considers such examples too in *On Certainty*. Of course, the man in question here is not an isolated individual, but one of a people who have a different world-view from ours, a different culture, and therefore also a different language. In one case he considers a man who believes that the world came into being with him at his birth. He writes: 'Men have believed that they could make rain; why should not a king be brought up in a belief that the world began with him? And if Moore and the king were to meet and discuss, could Moore really prove his belief to be the right one? I do not say that Moore could not convert the king to his view, but it would be a conversion of a special kind; the king would be brought to look at the world in a different way' (§92). He returns to this question more than once. In this last work certain *beliefs* are seen to be an indissoluble part of the language we speak. In §609 he considers people who are not guided in their actions by propositions of physics but who, instead, consult oracles:

> Is it wrong for them to consult an oracle and be guided by it?—If we call this 'wrong' aren't we using our language-game as a base from which to *combat* theirs?
>
> And are we right or wrong to combat it? Of course there are all sorts of slogans which will be used to support our proceedings (§610).
>
> Where two principles really do meet which cannot be reconciled with one another, then each man declares the other a fool and heretic (§611).

I said I would 'combat' the other man—but wouldn't I

give him *reasons*? Certainly; but how far do they go? At the
end of reasons comes *persuasion*. (Think what happens when
missionaries convert natives) (§612).

This is connected with what Wittgenstein says in his
'Lectures on Religious Belief' about the conflict between the
believer and the atheist. There he opposes the idea that
religious beliefs are *hypotheses* and, therefore, something for
which there can be *evidence*, something about which the
believer may be *mistaken*. His question is: What do they *mean*?
He does not take it for granted that someone who does not
share the believer's conviction always understands what the
believer says he believes. He does not take it for granted that
he, Wittgenstein, always understands it. He does not take it for
granted that the believer's words do not or cannot mean
anything—as many logical positivists have done. More recent
positivists have asked: 'Under what conditions would the
believer allow what he says he believes to be false?' Since they
could find no such conditions, they claimed that the believer's
words must be meaningless. Even in the *Tractatus* Wittgenstein
had not been dogmatic in this way. He thought of the words
used by the religious believer to represent attempts at saying
what cannot be said. In the 'Lectures on Religious Belief' he
took the fact that no evidence will induce the religious believer
to retract his words to highlight an important feature of their
use. He asked: What connections do these beliefs have in the
life of the believer? In what contexts does the believer use the
words in which he expresses his beliefs? It is here that the
meanings of these words are to be found.

This is the view of language that we have been considering.
Where you have a different pattern of connections you have a
different language. In the first case we considered the words in
question lacked the connections we expected them to have.
The man was demented, but not mistaken. In the second case
the words in question had radically different connections and
it was no good responding to them as if this was not so.
Otherwise we would simply be speaking at cross-purposes. So
we cannot address the words 'Everyone remembers he always
had two hands' to a man who would fall into our second
category—any more than Moore could address his words to
the king who, together with his subjects, believes that the

world began with him. The third candidate to whom we may think we could address these words, or others like them, as Moore thought he could, is the philosophical sceptic. But this will not do either, as Wittgenstein brings out well in *On Certainty*. To do so is to exhibit naïvity on two counts: first about what the philosophical sceptic is up to, and secondly about what the sentences we use in speech depend on for their meaning.

What the philosophical sceptic denies is not a truth or truths of which we are all cognizant. Therefore it is not something that can be reaffirmed or asserted, something we can claim to know. In *The Blue Book* Wittgenstein said: 'There is no common-sense answer to a philosophical problem. One can defend common sense against the attacks of philosophers only by solving their puzzles ... not by restating the views of common sense' (pp. 58–9). The point is not that you will not convince the philosophical sceptic in this way, get him to retract what he says; but that you will not succeed in stating anything. In trying to restate the so-called views of common sense you are labouring under the same misapprehensions as the philosophical sceptic is when he tries to deny them.

> To try to *state* or reaffirm what the philosophical sceptic denies.
> To claim that it is *true*.
> To insist that one *knows* it to be true.
> To try to *defend* it, or to *prove* it.

All this comes from confusion. I have discussed *some* of these confusions in *Matter and Mind*. The part that interests us now, and which was not at the centre of my interest in that book, has to do with the conditions for intelligible discourse. By this I do not mean anything that can be stated in general terms.

In *On Certainty* Wittgenstein thinks that there is something peculiar and interesting about Moore's 'truisms' (§137) and something important about his insistence that we 'know' them—even though Wittgenstein argues (i) that this insistence could not quell the sceptic's doubts and is the wrong way to go about doing so, and (ii) that it doesn't make sense to say that we know the things which Moore insists we know—for example, 'I know that this is a hand', 'I know that the earth has existed for a very long time', 'I know that every human being has forbears, that the sun is not a hole in the vault of heaven.' These are not instances of what we can claim to know. For if I know something then I could lack the knowledge I have. Also others may not know what I do know. Whereas what Moore prefaces with 'I know' belongs to the framework of our thought and language. Since it is something that is presupposed in the ordinary workings of our language, it is difficult to think of circumstances in which it can intelligibly be stated or affirmed; nor, for the same reason, can one claim to know it. Nevertheless Wittgenstein thinks that Moore's 'I know' expresses a *logical* insight (§59). Moore would have been much nearer the mark if instead of 'I know' he had said that it makes no sense to doubt what the sceptic says he doubts; if he had said: 'If what the sceptic denies is wrong, then I am crazy' (§155), 'If that were to fall then nothing could stand upright.'

What Moore calls 'common-sense view of the world' or 'the views of common sense' is an instance of what Wittgenstein refers to as a 'world picture', or features of one. Certainly Wittgenstein doesn't want to talk of it as 'true'—as Moore did—but as, something that enters the possibility of distinguishing between truth and falsity:

> But I did not get my picture of the world by satisfying myself of its correctness; nor do I have it because I am satisfied of its correctness. No: it is the inherited background against which I distinguish between true and false (§94—see also §95).

> I have a world-picture. Is it true or false? Above all it is the substratum of all my inquiring and asserting. The propositions describing it are not all equally subject to testing (§162).

> Think of chemical investigations. Lavoisier makes experiments with substances in his laboratory and now he concludes that this and that takes place when there is burning. He does not say that it might happen otherwise another time. He has got hold of a definite world-picture—not of course one that he invented: he learned it as a child. I say world-picture and not hypothesis, because it is the

matter-of-course foundation for his research and as such also goes unmentioned (§617).

But can it be mentioned? Can one express any part of it in words? I don't think that it is possible to answer this question *in general*. Let me quote Wittgenstein's remarks on a few of the examples he gives:

(a) Suppose I say of a friend: 'He isn't an automaton'.— What information is conveyed by this, and to whom would it be information? To a *human being* who meets him in ordinary circumstances? What information *could* it give him? (At the very most that this man always behaves like a human being, and not occasionally like a machine.) 'I believe that he is not an automaton', just like that, so far makes no sense (Wittgenstein, 1963, p. 178).

(b) 'Human beings have souls—or are made up of body and soul.' This may be part of the teaching of Christianity, and connected with such words as 'The soul can exist when the body has disintegrated.' Wittgenstein does not deny that one can understand what such words say, that they are intelligible. He speaks of the *service* which these words and the pictures that have been painted in connection with them do—e.g. Plato, Goethe, Dante. He says: 'And it is the service which is the point' (ibid., p. 178).

What about the philosopher who wishes to oppose materialism and says 'Human beings have souls' or 'Human beings have feelings'? In *Matter and Mind* (p. 119), I imagined special circumstances in which the words 'He has feelings' (said to someone who is treating him callously) have sense. I contrasted this with the philosopher's 'Human beings have feelings.' The philosopher may be *trying* to say something, even though what he comes up with does not make sense as it stands. What is in question is not so much a belief about human beings in general as a conception within the framework of which I may hold different beliefs—such as that my friend is in pain or angry. What, then, can the philosopher say here? Is there not something positive he can say, apart from resolving the difficulties which lead to the denials he wishes to oppose? Yes, there is. Wittgenstein talks of *description* here: not any general statement of what we all believe, but a description of what we all say and do and the circumstances in which we say and do these things. Thus on page 121 I describe how we react to people—for example, sometimes we resent what they say, we are insulted, hurt, angered or irritated by their words and deeds, we are sometimes grateful for what they do, we pity them, we feel embarrassed in their presence and so on. These reactions are a pretty basic feature of the life we live. They constitute what Wittgenstein calls our 'attitude towards a soul'—*N.B.* 'attitude towards' and not 'belief in the existence of'.[1]

(c) So when the philosopher utters the words 'Human beings have souls—or consciousness—or feelings' he is *trying* to say something, but what he comes up with does not make sense as it stands. Wittgenstein says something similar about the philosopher's 'There are physical objects': 'No such proposition as "There are physical objects" can be formulated. Yet we encounter unsuccessful shots at every turn' (Wittgenstein, 1969b, §36—see also Dilman, 1975, Pt I, chapter 2).

(d) 'I have consciousness' (See Wittgenstein, 1963, §416).

(e) 'I do not know how the sentence "I have a body" is to be used' (Wittgenstein, 1969b §258).

(f) About Moore's 'I know that I am a human being' Wittgenstein says: 'I do not know what it means. But I can imagine circumstances that turn it into a move in one of our language-games.' When I do so 'it loses everything that is philosophically astonishing' (ibid., §622).

Compare with the philosopher's: 'All human beings have feelings. They are not automata. Take me, for instance. Now I am a human being. You are not going to deny that I have feelings—are you? Surely, you will admit that I have feelings?' The philosopher, when he says this, believes that he is saying something *true*, something so obviously true that normally we have no reason for saying it—normally there would be no point in saying it. I shall return to this presently.

Now imagine circumstances in which there would be a point in saying something like this—for example, 'He has feelings too' said to someone who is treating him callously. We readily understand these words now, only they lose their connection with the earlier philosophical point. For its intelligibility takes for granted what the sceptic that the philosopher opposes denies.

But let me return to this philosopher's words and to his belief that what they say is *true*, though too obviously true to need saying normally. Presumably he thinks that here, in the context of philosophical discussion, it needs saying. But is this so? Does the sceptic to whom he is addressing these words need to be reminded of a truth which normally people need not be reminded of—because he has lost touch with it or his appreciation of what is in question? No, this is a distortion of what has gone wrong here and of what needs to be said.

So who needs to be told this 'truth'? Someone may answer: 'All right, no one. All the same it is a truth: what these words say is true all the same.'

Wittgenstein argues against this—and this is what we have been considering. He says: 'There is always the danger of wanting to find an expression's meaning by contemplating the expression itself, and the frame of mind in which one uses it, instead of always thinking of the practice' (Wittgenstein, 1969b, §601). He says that the expression has sense in the work it does and to understand its sense is to be able to imagine circumstances in which it does work or service. There a person may have reason to use it, to utter the sentence; there is a point in using the sentence there and a person may, therefore, have cause to say it. Where we cannot imagine any need to utter the sentence, any point in uttering it, where we cannot think of someone having a reason to utter the sentence, there the sentence has no sense either. It is not merely redundant or superfluous because it says something that is too obviously true.

We may be inclined to resist Wittgenstein here: 'The fact that we do not say something does not mean that it is not true.' 'The fact that we have no reason to say something does not mean that we cannot say it intelligibly.' 'The fact there is no point in saying something does not mean that it would be senseless to say it.'

Let us consider these remarks one by one. Of course, there may be circumstances in which, for one reason or another, we do not say something. Nevertheless what we do not say remains true. Think of the story of the Emperor's clothes which only intelligent men were supposed to see. Nobody said that the emperor had no clothes on, for fear of being thought stupid; it remained true nevertheless that he was naked. We could think of many other examples. Of course, the truth of a statement is independent of its being asserted. Wittgenstein most certainly does not deny this. Nor, when his opponent insists that it is true that he is a human being or that he has a body, does Wittgenstein say 'It is not true', meaning that it is false. He is saying (i) that he does not understand what this man is saying, that he may be saying nothing at all, and (ii) that his idea that he is saying something too obviously true to need saying comes from confusion, from a confused theory of meaning.

'The fact that we do not say something': Wittgenstein means the fact that normally, apart from exceptional circumstances, speakers of the language do not use such-and-such a sentence. He means this as a comment on a fact about the language, or on the behaviour of speakers of that language—which comes to the same thing. He is saying something like: 'That is not a move in the language-game.' Or: 'Even if the rules of the language permit the formation of such a sentence, normally its utterance would be like an empty gesture. It is like the turning of a cogwheel that is not in mesh and so does not engage or move anything.'

'Whether we say it or not, the fact remains that I am a human being.' My response is: 'I have not denied that you are a human being.' You protest: 'But you have not affirmed it either.' I reply: 'Indeed I have not. I said that I do not know what it would mean to affirm it here and now. I know, in contrast, what it would mean for you to say it to your torturers. That is one instance where the cogwheel is in mesh. In those circumstances your sentence does work and so has sense.'

'But I am a human being. This is independent of language, of whether we say it or not.' You say 'this is independent ...', but what does 'this' refer to? That you are a human being. But that is what is under discussion: whether you can say it here and now, in ordinary circumstances. On the other hand, if what you wish to say is that there may have been human beings on this earth before there was any language which they spoke, again this is not something I have denied—although there are some special difficulties here outside the scope of this paper.

Let me take the other two remarks together: 'The fact that we may have no reason to say something, the fact that there may be no point in saying it, does not mean that we cannot say it intelligibly.' Again, I am not confusing 'reasons that people may have for saying something' with 'what it means to say it'—any more than I confused sense and truth. 'Unless a form of words can be used to say something true, it cannot have sense.' This is what Wittgenstein holds in the *Tractatus*—that is, the symbol of a significant proposition 'TFFF (p,q) must have at least one T and at least one F in the row of Ts and Fs that are part of the symbol. There was no contradiction when in the same work he insisted that the sense of a proposition is independent of its truth. Now, similarly, the *sense* of a proposition is independent of anyone's *reasons* for asserting it. Yet unless there are circumstances in which people can have reason for asserting it, it has no sense. And if there are special circumstances where people may have reason for asserting it, then it is in those circumstances that it has sense: its sense lies in the point it has in asserting it in those circumstances, in the service it does there. As Wittgenstein puts it: it is in conversation that words have their meaning (Wittgenstein, 1967, §135), 'it is only in use that the proposition has its sense' (Wittgenstein, 1969b, §10).

Again, it is perfectly true that I can say to someone: 'I understand *what* you are saying, but I do not know *why* you say it—I do not know the *point* you wish to make.' I have never suggested that there is any contradiction involved here. If I understand *what* he is saying, then I know why one *may* be saying it in such circumstances, what point one *may* wish to make. But I may not know what *his* reasons are, what point *he* is trying to make. I may not know, for instance, whether he is saying it in order to shock me. But in understanding what he says I know that in such circumstances it could be a shocking thing to say. That it can be used to shock people is internal to what it means.

II   Meaning and Experience: Understanding and Imagination

Wittgenstein says: 'How a sentence is *meant* can be expressed by an expansion of it and may therefore be made part of it' (ibid., §349). The expansion of such a sentence—the words and sentences that follow it—may be part of a conversation, and they throw light on what I meant by it; they provide an elucidation of the sentence's meaning on this occasion. The sentence has meaning in these circumstances, in the course of this conversation. What comes before it and what comes after is relevant to what it means. As we have seen, if we are inclined to say that it has meaning when presented in isolation, this is because we can imagine such contexts.

There may be a great variety of such contexts. While we focus on the contribution the sentence makes to what we are doing in such contexts, to the conversation we may carry on there, we shall speak of its meaning as being *the same*. The contribution, however, is a two-way one. The context contributes to its meaning equally, different contexts making different contributions. If we think of this we shall be inclined to say that the sentence means something somewhat *different* in different contexts. I have already mentioned the following example which Wittgenstein gives: 'After he had said this, he left her as he did the day before.' He asks: 'Do I understand this sentence? Do I understand it just as I should if I heard it in the course of a narrative?' (Wittgenstein, 1963, §525). There it is full of meaning, a meaning which it lacks in isolation—even though in isolation it is not devoid of meaning. So Wittgenstein compares understanding it when heard in the course of a narrative to understanding a theme in music (ibid., §527). The significance of the theme, the way we hear it, depends on the whole tune in which it recurs. There we *hear* it differently, we *experience* it differently, and its significance cannot be separated from the way we experience it.

Wittgenstein emphasises how much what we have here is part of our concepts of meaning and understanding—which he would have characterised as 'widely ramified' (Wittgenstein, 1967, §110). He reminds us of the way, as we say, music speaks. He writes in *Zettel*: 'Do not forget that a poem, even though it is composed in the language of information, is not used in the language-game of giving information' (§160). Yet, of course, we say that a poem *tells* us something and we speak of its *truth*. We also speak of *understanding* what it says.

Wittgenstein asks: Can we explain what it means? He does not deny that we can, but he wants us to notice the form which this takes. Someone may ask: 'What is it all about?' meaning 'What does is speak about? What does it say?' I may answer: 'I know what it is about, I know what it says, but I don't know how to convey it to you.' That I am unable to explain its meaning by giving a paraphrase of it doesn't mean that I don't understand it. My understanding can be seen in the way I read it, in the kind of comment I make about it, about other poems, and about other things. If, on the other hand, I didn't see certain connections both with the poem and also between it and things outside, you should not say that I understood. If I did appreciate the various connections that the poet makes, sees and draws on in his poetry, I might be able to convey this appreciation to you by drawing your attention to them, by making comparisons that will help you to see them. In that case, this is at least part of what explaining the meaning of a sentence or line in a poem amounts to; this is what understanding is like here (Wittgenstein, 1963, §527). Wittgenstein says:

> We speak of understanding a sentence in the sense in which it can be replaced by another which says the same; but also in the sense in which it cannot be replaced by any other. (Any more than one musical theme can be replaced by another.)
>
> In the one case the thought in the sentence is something common to different sentences; in the other, something that is expressed only by these words in these positions. (Understanding a poem) (ibid., §531).

He denies that this means that 'understanding' means two different things. He says that these kinds of use make up its meaning, make up the concept of *understanding* (ibid., §532).

When you read the line of a poem without comprehension, you may understand the meanings of all the words in it. When you come to understand it, you hear it differently, it strikes you differently. The way you experience the line changes. It *may* be part of that experience that you enjoy it, or that you feel the horror of what it says, or the sadness in it. This feeling is part of the meaning of the line, it resides in what the line means (ibid., §§543–6). But even apart from this, isn't the way the line strikes you, the impression it makes on you when you understand it, the way you hear it, a new experience, one that is a part of your understanding? Wittgenstein describes this as a 'change of aspect' and compares it with the way the aspect under which you see a face may change, though the face doesn't change (ibid., §§536–9, and Wittgenstein, 1969a, p. 179), and he discusses the question whether the dawning of a new aspect is a new experience in the *Investigations*, Pt II, section xi—especially page 208. He also compares it with the difference in the way we hear a musical phrase or even a chord when we hear it on its own and when we hear it in the course of a musical piece where it recurs, is taken up into the melody, varied and so on. The phrase or the chord is the same, but we hear it quite differently. We say: 'How rich, how full of meaning, or what a lot it has got in it.' Wittgenstein's point is that what it has got in it, it has *by virtue of what surrounds it*—what comes before it and what comes after: 'I think of a quite short phrase, consisting of only two bars. You say 'What a lot that's got in it!' But it is only, so to speak, an optical illusion if you think that what is there goes on as we hear it' (Wittgenstein, 1967, §173). He then adds: 'Only in the stream of thought and life do words have meaning' (ibid.). It is because what is there is not what goes on as we hear it that he speaks of 'a different though related concept' of experience here (Wittgenstein, 1963, p. 208). And that is why, of course, one sentence here cannot be replaced by another—any more than one musical theme can be replaced by another—and why the thought in it is not something that is common to other sentences or phrases and so cannot be conveyed or explained by producing an equivalent sentence or phrase. He writes in *The Brown Book*:

> In certain cases I can justify, explain the particular expression with which I play it by a comparison, as when I say 'At this point of the theme, there is, as it were, a colon', or 'This is, as it were, the answer to what came before', etc. (This, by the way, shows what a 'justification' and an 'explanation' in aesthetics is like.)

He goes on a little further down:

> This doesn't mean that suddenly understanding a musical theme may not consist in finding a form of verbal expression which I conceive as the verbal counterpoint of the theme. And in the same way I may say 'Now I understand the expression of this face', and what happened when the understanding came was that I found the word which seemed to sum it up (pp. 166–7).

Wittgenstein asks what we mean by 'meaning' in connection with a musical phrase or a line in a poem (Wittgenstein, 1967, §177; and 1969a, pp. 166–7, 178–9). Take first a sentence that purports to give a piece of information. We ask what it says and we want to say that it points to something outside itself—something with which we compare it to ascertain whether what it says is true or false. It is not like that with a musical phrase. Wittgenstein points out that when it makes its full impression on us we say 'this tune says *something*' (Wittgenstein, 1969a, p. 166). Yet if we asked ' *what* does it say?' this would show that we had misunderstood the grammar of the expression 'this tune says something'. He counteracts that misunderstanding by saying: 'It expresses itself.' We could say, 'It expresses a musical thought'; but we must not forget that the thought belongs to music, to the language of music, and that it is even more impossible to render it in spoken language than it is to render what a poem says in the language of information. Of course, this is not to say that we may not find a simile that will help us to see the musical thought expressed. But the simile is a simile for what is *in* the music, even though it could not have this in it, have the significance we find in it, make this impression on us, but for its connection with what lies *outside* music. So when in *Zettel*, section 175, Wittgenstein asks: 'Doesn't the theme point to anything outside itself?', he answers: 'Yes, it does! But that means:—it makes an impression on me which is connected with things in its surroundings—e.g. with our language and its intonations; and hence with the whole field of our language-games.' He mentions one example: 'If I say: Here it's as if a conclusion were being drawn, here as if something were being confirmed, *this* is like an answer to what was said before—then my understanding presupposes a familiarity with inferences, with confirmation, with answers.' Similarly, if in the Jastrow figure Wittgenstein uses in the *Investigations*, Pt II, section xi, I can see now a duck, now a rabbit, that is because I am acquainted with ducks and rabbits. Thus Wittgenstein points out that what I perceive in the dawning of an aspect has an internal relation to other objects (p. 212).

But if music, and more obviously poetry, has this relation to what is outside it, the dependence is a two-way one. Both poetry and music can change the aspect under which we see and experience things outside, deepen our understanding of life. And so we speak of the *truth* each contains. The opposite of 'true' here is 'shallow', 'sentimental', etc. Instead of deepening our contact with life, making us feel the horror and the beauty to be found there, it dulls and deadens it. This is a subject I cannot explore here. Notice, however, that in so far as we find a poem shallow or sentimental we are less inclined to speak of its meaning. We may say: 'It doesn't *say* much.' Here the concepts of *meaning* and *truth* are much closer together in their sense, and even merge together—as they also do in mathematics: 'When longing makes me cry "Oh, if only he would come!" the feeling gives the words "meaning" ... But here one could say that the feeling gave the words *truth*. And from this you can see how the concepts merge here. (This recalls the question: what is the *meaning* of a mathematical proposition?)' (Wittgenstein, 1963, §544). The truth of mathematical propositions is not anything over and above their meaning, and a mathematical proposition that isn't true would be meaningless—hence '2 + 2 = 5'.[2] But, of course, unless mathematical propositions were related to things outside mathematics there would be neither sense nor truth in mathematics. This is Wittgenstein's criticism of the formalistic view of mathematics—that mathematics are games played with marks on paper. What he says about whether a musical theme points to anything outside itself in *Zettel*, section 175, is a criticism of Schopenhauer's view that 'music is a world in itself' and parallels his criticism of the formalistic view of mathematics—although Wittgenstein also shows what truth there is in Schopenhauer: 'The tune expresses itself', 'Music conveys to us *itself*.'

In *The Brown Book*, page 178, Wittgenstein gives the example of his friend's reaction to beds of pansies: 'Each bed showed a different kind. We were impressed by each in turn. Speaking about them my friend said: "What a variety of colour patterns, and each says something." And this was just what I myself wished to say.... If one had asked what the colour pattern of the pansy said, the right answer would have seemed to be that it said itself. Hence we could have used an intransitive form of expression, say "Each of these colour patterns impresses one".' He comments on the next page: 'We are distinguishing between meaningless patterns and patterns which have meaning; but there is no such expression in our game as "This pattern has the meaning so-and-so". Nor even the expression "These two patterns have different meanings", unless this is to say: "These are two different patterns and both have meaning".' Wittgenstein goes on to point out that nevertheless it is not an accident that we use the transitive form of expression. He gives the example of our saying 'This face says something': 'We should perhaps follow up such a remark by saying, "Look at the line of these eyebrows" or "The *dark* eyes and the *pale* face!", these expressions would draw attention to certain features. We should in the same connection use comparisons, as, for instance, "The nose is like a beak"—but also such expressions as "The whole face expresses bewilderment", and here we have used "expressing" transitively' (p. 179).

Facial expressions are, of course, the expressions of a sentient being who reacts to various things, sees them in various ways and takes up various attitudes towards them. We take an interest in these expressions both in an aesthetic sort of way and also as expressions of the feelings and attitudes of the people whose faces they characterise. We are interested in the *look* of certain faces and also in the *feelings* of people as they are revealed in their faces. We then characterise the look in terms of descriptions of the feelings which the looks reveal, even when we are only interested in the look, that is when our interest is purely aesthetic and not psychological. When we use the transitive verb 'to express', this is related to the psychological interest—hence 'His face expresses bewilderment'. We speak similarly in connection with music too. We say that it conveys joyfulness, melancholy or triumph; and no doubt this is because of the connection with facial expressions. But we do not mean this as a comment on the composer's feelings, nor as a comment on the feelings it evokes in us. The connection we make with human feelings is a kind of simile used to describe the character of the music. Thus if you say, 'This phrase expresses triumph—or sadness', this is like saying 'The two voices here are like an argument', or 'This is like a conclusion being drawn'. In the one case the comparison is with human emotions, in the other with logic. With these comparisons you focus on and contemplate the *aspect* that struck you, the aspect under which you hear the phrase as it recurs in the song. The contemplation is purely aesthetic. You can contemplate a face in this way too; artists do. When they do, they are interested in it as something unique, rather than as an instance of a kind. The comparisons are meant to bring out what is unique in it—this involves no paradox.

Just as the case of music is different from the case of facial expressions—though they are connected—so is it also different from the case of natural scenes. For music is something human beings compose and these compositions belong to a musical tradition, they are in a musical language. This is certainly not true of natural scenes. I cannot now discuss this question of the difference between art and nature, the way art can hold a mirror to nature, and the way art can embody ideas. Rush Rhees discusses these questions in a really excellent piece called 'Art and Philosophy' in *Without Answers*.

Wittgenstein uses these analogies to throw light on an aspect of language and of what meaning and understanding amount to in connection with it, an aspect which comes into prominence in the use of language in literature, and particularly in poetry. But this aspect is not absent in the use of language outside literature. It is an aspect of language which is important to recognise and which logicians are apt to ignore or forget, especially when they are carried away with their talk of rules for the use of words and the construction of sentences, laws of logic and principles of inference and reasoning. In 'Wittgenstein's Builders' Rhees brings out how much more there is to both speaking and learning to speak than constructing sentences and learning to use them in accordance with rules.

Where words and sentences cannot be replaced by others

which say the same thing their appropriacy cannot be recognised by rules. This is where we say that such-and-such words are the right ones and that no others will do. Finding the right words here calls for imagination. We are dealing with a creative use of language. Here the search for the right words is at the same time a search for the truth, a search for a grasp or better understanding of what one is using the words to talk about. Unless someone can appreciate the words, see why exactly these words are used and no others, he will not see what they say. Hence their saying something, their meaning or truth, depends on the rest of the poem. It depends too on there being a language in which very much more is done than writing poetry—as in the case of mathematics too. In 'Wittgenstein's Builders' Rhees points out that language is something that can have a literature. For language to have a literature it must have a great deal more besides literature. Here Wittgenstein talks of *culture* (see Wittgenstein, 1967, §164). He says that to imagine a use of language you have to imagine a culture (Wittgenstein, 1969a, p. 134). That the musical phrase makes an impression on me, then, depends (i) on its immediate surroundings, the musical piece in which it recurs, and also (ii) on its less immediate surroundings—for example 'our language and its intonations' and 'the whole field of our language-games' (Wittgenstein, 1967, §175). Wittgenstein's comparisons of language with music is an attempt to show how much this is true of the use of language not only in literature, but also to a lesser extent outside literature. It is, therefore, a continuation of the discussion I have tried to bring into relief in the first part of this paper.

9 Bambrough: 'Universals and Family Resemblances'

I Preliminary Statement

The following is a study of *one* aspect of what Wittgenstein was getting at in §66 of *Philosophical Investigations* in the light of Bambrough's comments in his paper 'Universals and Family Resemblances' (Bambrough, 1960–1).

In section II I ask what Wittgenstein was *rejecting* when he said: 'Don't say "There *must* be something common, or they would not be called 'games' "'—but *look and see* whether there is anything common to all.' What kind of misunderstanding was he concerned to combat—misunderstanding about what?

In section III I try to evaluate his positive contention: 'They are related by a complicated network of similarities overlapping and criss-crossing: sometimes overall similarities, sometimes similarities of detail.' What was Wittgenstein getting at here? What is the philosophical significance of this claim? What contribution does his emphasis on 'family resemblances' make to the problem of universals?

In section IV I examine what Bambrough reads into Wittgenstein's positive claim about 'family resemblances' in the last two pages of his paper, namely that *in the end* all classification rests on 'objective similarities and differences'— that is, similarities and differences with which nature presents us independently of our systems of classification. I argue that Wittgenstein did not hold this view and that, in any case, it is open to criticisms that come from Wittgenstein himself.

In the final very short section I suggest certain comparisons between Wittgenstein and Plato. These are no more than suggestions for further thought.

II   Rejection of 'Essentialism'

What is 'the problem of universals' to the discussion of which Bambrough claims Wittgenstein to have made a lasting contribution? It asks: How is it that we can apply a general noun like 'cat' to many individual cats? We are inclined to answer: Because the individuals in question *are* all cats. But this leads to another question: What makes them cats? By virtue of what about them do we group them together? What is it that justifies us in doing so? Whatever it is must be the same thing as what justifies us in applying the word 'cat' to many cats—instance after instance. This has obviously something to do with the word's *meaning*, and it gives it the kind of *generality* it has. But which comes first, the word's meaning or its application in particular cases?

Bambrough points out in a footnote (fn. 3, p. 214), rightly, that even proper names have a certain generality. He says that Professor Wisdom pointed this out to him in discussion. What he means, I take it, is this: There are many situations in which one has occasion to use a particular proper name, say 'John'. Confining ourselves to the use of the name to refer to the man, in his presence, we could still ask, as in the case of general nouns, what is it that justifies us in calling the man before us on these different occasions by the same name. As above, the truistic answer is that what justifies us is the fact that the man before us on these different occasions is the same man. But what is it that makes us say it is the same man? Just as the use of general nouns presupposes principles of classification, or criteria for the identity of kinds, so likewise the use of proper names presupposes criteria for the identity of individuals.

There is, I think, a close connection between problems connected with the identity of individuals and those connected with the identity of kinds, although the problem of universals has traditionally revolved around the notion of the identity of kinds. The problem, in any case, can be given a broader perspective. One can talk of the occasions on which a particular word is intelligibly used, occasions on which it is correct to use it. What is it that binds these together? Here the notion of criteria for the identity of a kind is broadened into rules governing the word's use. As Wittgenstein puts it in the

Investigations: 'The use of the word "rule" and the use of the word "same" are interwoven' (§225).

A connection is thus established between our concern to understand the relation between a word and the various instances of its application and our concern to understand the relation between a rule and the steps that accord with it—a question to which Wittgenstein returns many times in the *Investigations* and in his other writings. One of the big questions that exercised him in this connection was this: What is the *basis* of our use of words—of our using the same word on different occasions? Is there some reality that corresponds to the rules governing our use of words and to the principles in accordance with which we reason? I am suggesting that the traditional problem of universals is connected with this broader question, that it is a part of this broader issue. In his paper Bambrough is well aware of this connection.

To revert to the traditional perspective: Is the identity between the members of a class, between individuals we call by the same name, one which exists independently of language, so that the language we use simply mirrors it, or is it something which is, at least in part, conferred on the individuals by the language we speak? In their answer to this question philosophers have lined themselves up, broadly speaking, into two opposite camps: Realism and Nominalism. I think that Bambrough is right in claiming that Wittgenstein cut through this philosophical conflict without embracing either position. Just as, I should add, he cut through the philosophical conflict between Realism and Conventionalism in connection with logical necessity and mathematical truth without embracing either position. And just as, equally, he cut through the philosophical conflict between Cartesianism and Behaviourism in connection with 'the nature of the mind' without embracing either position. I further agree with Bambrough that he cut through these opposing positions by bringing out to daylight and rejecting assumptions shared by the opposing parties. I do not think that this means that he embraced some third 'philosophical theory' about universals, or logical necessity, or mathematical truth, or the nature of the mind. But I don't want to make an issue of this.

How does Bambrough think Wittgenstein cut through the conflict between the Realist and the Nominalist?

The Realist claims that all games, for instance, must have something in common, a set of properties, which *makes* them games and so *justifies* us in calling them by the same name.

The Nominalist denies this, over-reacts to it, and claims that they have nothing in common except that they are *called* games.

Wittgenstein argues against the Realist—it is not *this* that makes them games: 'Don't say: "There *must* be something common, or they would not be called 'games' "—but *look and see* whether there is anything common to all' (Wittgenstein, 1963, §66).

He does not accept the Nominalist's position either. It is not for nothing that we call the many things we call 'games' 'games'. They are related to each other by 'a complicated network of similarities overlapping and criss-crossing: sometimes overall similarities, sometimes similarities of detail' (ibid.).

In other words, though they do not in fact share any set of common properties, yet it is not for nothing that we call them 'games'. We are justified in calling them by the same name by the 'complicated network of similarities' that relate them to each other in the way Wittgenstein describes.

So far so good—I agree with Bambrough. But what is the philosophical significance of what I have summarised? Let me consider this afresh.

'They must have something in common, otherwise they would not be called by the same name—something that *makes* them, for example, games.' This is a very persistent idea. Thus, to give one example, in the *Meno* Socrates asks Meno to tell him what virtue is. He says: 'Even if they are many and various, yet at least they all have some common character which makes them virtues.' He is convinced that if they did not have a 'common character' they would not be virtues and we would be wrong to call them by the same name. In other words, if we are right to call them by the same name, they *must* have something in common.

Wittgenstein's claim is that there is no *must* about it, that the idea that Socrates gives expression to *misrepresents* what it takes to use a general noun. There is no *necessity* for things to have a certain set of properties for us to be justified in calling them by the same name. 'What makes you say that this is a game, that

that is a case of negligence, that t'other is an instance of expectation?' We think that what we must mention in substantiating or justifying our claim has to be something *necessary* to the thing's being of the kind in question, otherwise it cannot have anything to do with what we *mean* by the words in question—'game', 'negligence', 'expectation'. I examine below Wittgenstein's rejection of this idea, and one of the sources of its attraction, namely some of the reasons behind the temptation to link meaning and necessity in this way.[1]

'They *must* have something in common.' Wittgenstein rejects this, and its contradictory is, 'They *need not* have anything in common.' This is, of course, compatible with 'They do have something in common.' Wittgenstein is not saying that we can never refer to a thing's properties in justifying our claim that it is a thing of a certain kind; nor is he saying that the properties we refer to may not be necessary to its being of that kind. Clearly this is sometimes the case. What Wittgenstein is saying is that it is not necessary for the properties to which we refer to be necessary, and that even when they are necessary they do not provide what we expect of them.

Take the case where a set of properties is *necessary* to a thing being of kind K and, therefore, *common* to all things of that kind: 'If it is a triangle then it must be a three-sided plane figure with straight edges; and if it is such a figure then it necessarily is a triangle—and therefore correct to describe it as such.' Similar definitions are possible and can be given of the terms used in the definition of 'triangle'. 'A straight line is the shortest path between two points' and '$3 = 2 + 1$', and similarly for the terms used in these definitions. Thus one word is defined in terms of other words and those in terms of others still. But so far nothing has been said about how any of them is to be applied in a particular case—how, for instance, we are to establish that a given line is the shortest path between two points in a particular case. It is a triangle *if* its sides are straight; and its sides are straight *if* they constitute the shortest path between the corners. These 'ifs' must be removed if we are to know when to say that a figure before us is a triangle; and they cannot be removed by further definitions. What I have in mind is sometimes referred to as 'giving an application to a calculus' or 'interpreting a calculus'.

Wittgenstein argued that it is this application that gives meaning to the terms of the calculus—in this case to the terms 'triangle', 'straight line', etc.: 'It is essential to mathematics that its signs are also employed in civil life' (Wittgenstein, 1956, Pt IV, §2). In his paper on 'Universals', Mr David Pears puts this point as follows: '*Ultimately* there must be some exit from the maze of words, and, wherever this exit is made, it will be impossible to give an informative reason except by pointing' (Pears, 1953, p. 53).

This is precisely what bothers us. For at this point we can only say: 'This is an instance of the kind of thing in question.' 'This illustrates what we mean by a K.' 'This *and similar things* are called "games"' (Wittgenstein, 1963, §69). We are bothered because we feel that this does not tell us *enough*. We think that where we *are* given the meaning of a word we are given a blue-print which guarantees its application in case after case after case, and that nothing that falls short of this could have given us the word's meaning. We think that a definition such as that of 'triangle' in geometry satisfies this condition. Wittgenstein argues that it does not, and that *nothing* can satisfy it—that is, nothing can provide a blue-print which guarantees the application of a word in case after case. We wrongly think that a strict definition does provide such a blue-print and consequently imagine that if anyone *means* or understands a word, then 'he is operating a calculus according to definite rules' (ibid., §81). So where we are unable to formulate such a strict definition, we imagine that we don't understand the term in question, that we don't really know the thing it names—what a game is, what constitutes negligence, what it is for a man to be in a state of expectation. Thus in the *Theaetetus* Socrates seeks for such a definition of 'knowledge', one that will capture the 'essential nature' of the different things that we call 'knowledge'—'the thing itself— knowledge—is'. He says: 'You do not suppose a man can understand the name of a thing, when he does not know what the thing is' (147b).

This is the misunderstanding that Wittgenstein is concerned to straighten: 'Do you want to say I don't know what I am talking about until I can give a definition of a plant?' (Wittgenstein, 1963, §70). The tendency to think that a blurred concept is no concept at all is part of the same misunderstanding (ibid., §71). Is Wittgenstein saying that concepts that are blurred cannot be made more definite? Of course not. For instance he says that the concept of a game does not have a sharp boundary. But, he goes on, 'we can draw such a boundary—for a special purpose. Does it take that to make the concept usable?' (ibid., §§68–9). Notice that if we can sharpen the boundary of a concept in a particular direction we do so for a special practical purpose. What this involves is removing some of the vagueness in the *application* of the term or concept. For instance, we may say, 'It is not domestic oil until it meets certain stringent requirements, passes certain tests; and anyone who calls it so and sells it as such will be prosecuted.' The tests are perhaps specified in a leaflet or manual, and some general description is given of how they are to be carried out. Perhaps certain instruments, gauges, chemicals are to be used. How accurate are the instruments supposed to be? Will such-and-such a gauge be acceptable? There are thousands of questions that could be raised which the instructions never anticipated and so do not answer. If any of them were to become important for practical purposes, the need would arise to formulate an answer to these. Doing so would be drawing a boundary, or making the existing boundary tighter. But for every such question answered a great many new ones could be asked—asked intelligibly, but not necessarily taken seriously. 'That is not to say that we are in doubt [Wittgenstein says] because it is possible for us to *imagine* a doubt' (ibid., §84). And: 'An explanation serves to remove or to avert a misunderstanding—one, that is, that would occur but for the explanation; not every one that I can imagine' (ibid., §87).

It is the same with giving a concept sharp boundaries in a certain range of its applications. It is not the concept itself that requires it in order to have meaning; *we* require it for specific practical purposes. Wittgenstein argues that we cannot 'stop up all the cracks', as he puts it, and so remove all possible doubts as to whether a term is applicable in a particular case. He imagines the case where I say 'There is a chair', go up to fetch it and it disappears from sight. But in a few moments we are able to touch it and so on, though a little later it disappears again. 'What are we to say' he asks. 'Have we rules ready for such cases? And if not, do we miss them when we use the word "chair"?' (ibid., §80). In *Zettel* he asks: 'How should we have to imagine a complete list of rules for the employment of a word? What do we mean by a complete list of rules for the employment of a piece in chess? Couldn't we always construct doubtful cases, in which the normal list of rules does not decide?' He goes on: 'The regulation of traffic in the streets permits and forbids certain actions on the part of drivers and pedestrians; but it does not attempt to guide the totality of their movements by prescription. And it would be senseless to talk of an "ideal" ordering of traffic which should do that ... If someone wants to make traffic regulations stricter on some point or other, that does not mean that he wants to approximate to such an ideal' (§440).

We think that such an ideal is realised in logic and mathematics, and that in so far as our language deviates from it, as it undoubtedly does, it must be defective. And so when someone, explaining what a game is, perhaps to a child, says 'This *and similar things* are called "games" ', we think this is not a proper explanation, only a second-best. We think that *ideally* we should be able to do better, that *ideally* the concept must have sharp boundaries, that the possibility of proof and explanation, inference and justification depends on that. I am suggesting that the idea of universals as common properties, properties essential for a thing to be of a certain kind, is the same as the idea that concepts must have sharp boundaries and that their meaningfulness depends on that. There is no doubt that Wittgenstein thought so—any careful reading of §§65–89 in the *Investigations* should be enough to convince one. So when he says, 'Don't say: "There *must* be something common, or they would not be called 'games' "—but *look and see* whether there is anything common to all', this is the idea he is combatting. He is concerned with certain deep-going misunderstandings about logic and mathematics which distort the philosopher's understanding of how words have sense in a language—and that means generality in their application. He is not contrasting one kind of concept with another. On this point I agree with Bambrough completely.

In the first chapter of his book, *Thinking and Experience*, entitled 'Universals and Resemblances', Professor H. H. Price examines carefully and refreshingly the merits and demerits of the 'common properties' thesis and its rival, the theory of resemblances (what Pears calls 'moderate nominalism'). He says at the end of that chapter: 'The danger of the terminology of Universals has been pointed out already. If we can only do our philosophising in this terminology, we may be led to regard universals as *things* or *entities*' (p. 31). Earlier he had said: 'One danger is ... we shall be liable to suppose that redness is in the tomato somewhat as juice is in it' (p. 11). This is the idea of universals as *ingredients*. Price goes on: 'Perhaps there is another danger as well. The Philosophy of Universals may tend to make us think that the world is a more neat and tidy place than it is ... The Philosophy of Resemblances delivers us from this danger, by reminding us that most of the resemblances we think and talk of are by no means exact ones. It restores to human thought and language that fuzziness or haziness, that absence of hard and fast boundaries, which do belong to them, and even in a way to the world itself' (pp. 31–2). Professor Wisdom who discussed the book on the Third Programme of the BBC (I think it was in 1957 or 1958— this is now included in his collection *Paradox and Discovery*) quoted this sentence '... it may tend to make us think that the world is a more neat and tidy place than it is' and said that it is 'a pregnant statement' but commiserated that Price does not develop it.

Price says that both of the opposing philosophical positions here involve *ontological* claims—the kind of claim he, himself, makes right at the outset of the book:

> When we consider the world around us, we cannot help noticing that there is a great deal of recurrence or repetition in it ... The same old features keep turning up again and again. The best they can do is to present themselves occasionally in new combinations, as in the black swan or the duck-billed platypus. There is a certain *monotony* about the world ... Nevertheless, this perceptual repetition, this dullness or staleness, is also immensely important, because it is what makes conceptual cognition possible. In a world of incessant novelty ... no concepts could ever be acquired; and thinking, even of the crudest and most primitive kind, could never begin (pp. 7–8).

I take it (and I stand open to correction) that an *ontological* claim is a claim about a *reality* independent of language, one against which language is measured. Price is saying: The world is a tidy place, full of repetitions, otherwise we could not think and speak at all. I ask, in passing, how does Price think the world would have to be, in contrast with the way he thinks it is, in order for it to be thinkable—or, for thinking to be possible? However Price does not think it is as tidy as the 'common property' philosopher imagines. Plato, by the way, did not imagine the world to be a tidy place. But because he too thought that speech and thought requires tidiness in its object—not 'some' tidiness as Price thought, but absolute or perfect tidiness—he postulated a changeless, timeless world where tidiness reigns supreme.

According to Price, the Philosopher of Resemblances claims that the world is not as tidy a place as the Common-property Philosopher imagines. In Socrates' words from the *Phaedo*: 'No two logs are perfectly equal.' But as an *ontological* claim this is just as confused. I have argued that 'the danger of thinking of the world to be a neat and tidy place' is no other than the danger of thinking of language as formal logicians sometimes think of it, namely as free of 'all slag and impurities', not at first sight but in the final analysis. This was Wittgenstein's own view in the *Tractatus*. The misunderstandings behind this idea of language as an exact calculus are not misunderstandings about what the world is like. Just as if there is any truth in Socrates' claim that no two logs are perfectly equal, this is not that the world is like the back-yard of an incompetent lumberjack. No—Socrates' remark draws attention to the contrast between the concepts of physical and mathematical equality. But how are they related? This is one of the big questions at issue.

My contention is that what is wrong with the common-properties thesis is not that it misrepresents the world we live in, claims it to be a tidier place than it is. It misrepresents what it takes for words to be usable, so that they have meaning and generality. It does so by thinking that there must be a blue-print which guarantees a word's application in case after case, and that it is in this that its generality lies—namely, in something that anticipates its application in particular cases, the very thing that we put into words in a strict definition such as we find in mathematics. This, Wittgenstein argues, is a misrepresentation of the relation between logic and language, and also between mathematics and physics—the sense in which logic regulates our use of words and the transitions in our reasonings from one formation of words to another, and also the sense in which mathematics enters into the various measurements we carry out.

III General Rules and Particular Cases

Now I believe that Wittgenstein's remark that what we call 'games' are related to each other by 'a complicated network of similarities' sheds light on this. This is something which Wisdom has illuminated for both Bambrough and myself. But here I go along with Bambrough for only part of the way. I think that he goes too far in what he says, and attributes to Wittgenstein a view which I believe he would have rejected. First, very briefly, what contribution does Wittgenstein's emphasis on 'family resemblances' make to the problems he was concerned with? He says that the cases in which we use the same word, the things we call by the same name, are not all *directly* related. This means that there is no way of grasping or presenting the application of a word at one go. We have to turn our attention to particular cases. *In the end* instances are what we have to turn to and compare with each other. *In the end* the meaning of any word can only be gathered from the particular cases in which it is applicable—whether or not the word is definable in terms of necessary and sufficient conditions for its application. So Wisdom speaks of the *ultimate* proof that a word is applicable in a particular case as a 'proof by parallel cases': 'With every name we apply we compare one thing with another, with many others' (Wisdom, 1953, p. 274). In thus comparing one thing with many others we see what sort of thing it is. For its being this kind of thing is a matter of how it stands with regard to other things. Wisdom says: 'A person's understanding grows as his ability to carry out comparisons grows' (Wisdom, 1957). He argues that we can carry out other forms of reasoning, including deductive reasoning, in this way—that is by a comparison of cases. But the reverse is not true. There are many areas of reflection, for instance a kind of reasoning carried out in law courts, of which Wisdom has discussed examples, in which there is no substitute for it.

This emphasis is in Wittgenstein too. I am thinking particularly of his discussion of the way we learn to continue mathematical series, to match objects to samples, to pick out a certain kind of object from among miscellaneous groups. Thus soon after his comments on the example of games he writes: 'One gives examples and intends them to be taken in a particular way. I do not, however, mean by this that he is supposed to see in those examples the common thing which I—for some reason—was unable to express; but that he is now to *employ* those examples in a particular way. Here giving examples is not an *indirect* means of explaining—in default of a better one' (Wittgenstein, 1963, §71). In other words, he is saying that we shouldn't think there is anything more fundamental than the giving of examples—something beneath or behind them which, if only we could get to it, would enable us to dispense with the examples, to by-pass them. In *Zettel* he says: 'The *like this* (in "go on like this") is signified by a number, a value. For at *this* level [what may be called "the ground level"] the expression of the rule is explained by the value, not the value by the rule' (§301). 'For just where one says "But don't you *see* ...?" the rule is no use, it is what is explained, not what does the explaining' (ibid., §302). By 'ground level' I mean the level at which learning takes the form of what Wittgenstein calls 'training'. Here there is as yet nothing on which an explanation or definition can get a grip, and 'training' is a building of just that. 'Not only rules but also examples are needed for establishing a practice. Our rules leave loopholes open, and the practice has to speak for itself' (Wittgenstein, 1969b, §139).

So I am suggesting that when Wittgenstein says that if we look at the different things we call by the same name we shall *not* see 'something common', as we had imagined, but instead 'a complicated network of similarities', he is saying that if we wish to understand what gives a term its generality, what makes it applicable in many instances, we should look at the *instances* themselves, and not look for anything that stands apart from them, anything that can be distilled from them—so to speak. There is nothing here which we can examine in separation from the examples. Anything which at first sight seems to stand apart in this way (a rule, a definition, a sample of pure green) has itself to be understood, and the attempt to understand it inevitably brings us down to examples.

This philosophical lesson which is directed to the non-philosophical question 'What is a game?', is equally directed to the philosophical question 'What is it to use a general term, and what gives it its generality?' Thus while considering that latter philosophical question in the *Brown Book*, Part II, Wittgenstein himself observes this very lesson and on pages 145–6 he asks us to consider what we are guided by when we describe a face as 'friendly', what gives it a friendly expression, what justifies us in characterising it as friendly. This is *one* example of the use of a general term completely familiar to us, *one* example of seeing the particular under a certain aspect. Yet it is just the sort of example we forget when we ask, 'What is it to use a general term?', 'What is it to see or refer to the general in the particular?', and that is why it is important to consider it. Wittgenstein considers it as an artist, that is as someone who is looking at it afresh, unblinkered by any general notions that have been ossified into prejudices. And here I am reminded of the words, quoted by Wisdom, of a Mr Flood, once a keeper of lions at the Dublin Zoo, 'Every lion is different', and of Wisdom's comment on those words: 'It is not to be thought that Mr Flood, in seeking to understand an individual lion, did not bring to bear his great experience with other lions. Only he remained free to see each lion for itself' (Wisdom, 1965, p. 138). This is just what Wittgenstein does with the individual examples he considers, in this case that of seeing a facial expression. What he makes us see in that example contrasts shatteringly with the philosophical preconception he is concerned to combat. We are strongly inclined to think that what we see when we see the general in the particular is something which the latter shares with all individuals we call by the same name. We think that it is *this* that enables the word to latch on to the individual. Looking afresh to an example which gives the lie to this idea is a powerful way of combatting it.

There is also an 'object lesson' in philosophy to be learnt here, one that concerns how questions like 'What is knowledge?', 'What is an inductive reason?' are best investigated. With this in mind Wittgenstein once thought of prefacing the *Investigations* with the words 'I'll teach you differences'. He hoped that his students would learn this lesson in practice, what they learned thus being something that would show itself in their treatment of a wide range of questions within as well as outside philosophy. But, in the specific case of the philosophical question 'What gives a word generality?', the general lesson amounts to this, namely that what gives a word its generality, what justifies us in using it in many different cases, can *in the end* be gathered only from *instances*—instances of the word's use, of the occasions of its use, and of the surrounding circumstances—and there is *nothing more fundamental* than the instances themselves. I said that this is a general lesson we are meant to learn; but I did not mean that we can learn it from the general words in which I have stated it.

IV   'The Ultimate Basis of all Classifications'

Up to this point I take it that Bambrough and I are in complete agreement. I part company with him in the ontological superstructure with which he tries to underpin this lesson. The difference between us may be put like this. I said:

> A word's generality can *in the end* be gathered only from instances, and there is nothing more fundamental than the instances themselves.

He says:

> *In the end* all classification rests on the similarities and differences with which nature presents us *independently* of our systems of classification. He calls them 'objective similarities and differences' (p. 221). *Ultimately*, he says, 'there are only similarities and differences from which we may choose according to our purposes and interests' (p. 222).

What is the difference between these two claims? I said: 'There is nothing more fundamental than the instances themselves' and implied that *how they are to be taken* can only be gathered from the instances and the context in which they are given. It can only be gathered by someone who has successfully received a certain training—and that means someone who has been initiated into a particular culture and shares certain natural inclinations with others belonging to it. Of course Bambrough knows all this. Yet in the way he talks about 'objective similarities and differences' and in the role he assigns to them in the 'solution' he attributes to Wittgenstein regarding the problem of universals he ignores it. He could not have taken the line that he takes in the last two pages of his paper if he had not done so. For what he is saying, in effect, is this—namely that though there may be more than one way of taking the examples in question, there is a basis in nature for each of these different possible ways of taking the examples; a basis which exists independently of the culture to which the person considering the examples belongs. He puts this unequivocally as follows: 'We may if we like say that there is one complete system of classification which marks all the similarities and all the differences' (ibid., p. 222). The classifications which human beings formulate and are guided by may vary according to the culture to which they belong; but the similarities and differences which underlie the different systems of classification do not. They are absolute, as opposed to relative—as absolute as Plato's 'forms', except that Plato's 'forms' were described as 'outside the world of the senses', whereas Bambrough's 'objective similarities and differences' are part of nature. In this respect the real Wittgenstein was nearer Plato than Aristotle, whereas Bambrough's Wittgenstein is nearer Aristotle. I shall return to this point in my concluding remarks.

Now I am *not* saying that genuine classifications do not have a basis—a basis in nature. Of course they do. And this basis is what we refer to when we are called upon to justify a claim that something is of a certain kind. While it is philosophy's job to point out *where* this justification comes to an end, this is not the end of what philosophy has to say on this point. It cannot stop there if it is to shed light on the generality of language and thought with which the traditional problem of universals is concerned. The reason for this is that reference to similarities and differences involves generality and necessarily brings in language. In which case the similarities and differences on which a classification is based will themselves be relative to the language in which the classification is carried out and the culture in which the need for it arises. This does not mean, of course, that the similarities and differences are *man-made* or *subjective*.

If my judgment of similarity is *objective* then there are criteria independent of my thought to which it is responsible. Independent of my thought, but not of the language I speak. They come from that language and belong to it. They cannot, therefore, give foundation to our use of words. Thus the source of the objectivity of our judgments is language itself; not anything independent of language. Objectivity goes with the possibility of a court of appeal independent of any one person, one we can appeal to when our judgments are doubted or contradicted. But as Wittgenstein puts it in *On Certainty*: 'All testing, all confirmation and disconfirmation of an hypothesis [and, let me add, all comparison aimed at establishing a judgment of similarity or difference] takes place already within a system. And this system is not a more or less arbitrary and doubtful point of departure for all our arguments: no, it belongs to the essence of what we call an argument. The system is ... the element in which arguments have their life' (§105).

Professor Wisdom has often spoken of 'likenesses and differences concealed by ordinary language' (Wisdom, 1953, p. 41) or 'not marked by language at all'. He said that metaphysical statements can bring to our notice 'what all the structure of our language conspires to conceal' (ibid., p. 245). They may do so by stretching the use of certain concepts to mark 'unspoken connections' (ibid., p. 162). Such stretching of concepts often issues from 'reflective thought not within the bounds of ordinary convention' (ibid., p. 266). I want to make quite clear that there is no incompatibility between such talk of 'likenesses and differences not marked by language' and what I have argued and attributed to Wittgenstein, namely that the very reality of any form of similarity and difference presupposes the logical space that belongs to a particular grammar. Given that grammar and so the various respects in which it is possible to compare things that have a reality within the language, comparisons can *discover* affinities that are new to the speakers of that language and force them to revise some of their classifications. But since the space within which the revision takes place is already provided for by this grammar, we cannot say that these affinities are new to the language.

And so we can speak of them as 'unspoken affinities'. Here we have one kind of case; but it is not the only kind. At the other extreme we have the case of a people who do not see similarities and differences that are important to us, and whose life and reactions are so different from ours that some of these do not exist in their world at all. They have no reality within their language to so much as go unmarked by it.

In *The Brown Book* Wittgenstein imagines people who differ from us in certain ways in their culture and education and so in their habits of reacting to colours. They assimilate colours we distinguish between, and distinguish between colours and shades we classify together (pp. 134–5). We can take parts of such an example and develop it in certain ways: These people don't see transitions from one colour or shade to another and so never speak of shades of the same colour for instance. Perhaps they even lack this concept altogether. They take no interest in nature, never paint or contemplate natural scenes. Their talk of colour lacks some of the connections it has in our lives, etc. Will it not be the case that a whole range of affinities and differences between colours, as we see them, will simply not exist for them? They simply will not see these. If *we* say that they are *blind* to these, we can mean no more than that *they* do not see what *we* see. There is nothing more ultimate, neutral between our different languages to enable us to mean more than this. In *Zettel*, discussing the relation between grammar and reality, at one point Wittgenstein considers the question of the basis of our way of grouping colours around four primary ones: Does this reflect something about 'the world as it actually is'? 'Doesn't one put the primary colours together because there is a similarity among them?' These words echo Bambrough. Wittgenstein responds: 'If I say "there is a particular similarity among the primary colours"— whence do I derive the idea of this similarity? Just as the idea "primary colour" is nothing else but "blue or red or green or yellow"—is not the idea of that similarity too given simply by the four colours? Indeed, aren't they the same?' We resist the suggestion because it seems to make our grouping of colours and therefore our concept of primary colours *arbitrary*: 'Then might one also take red, green and circular together?' Once more Wittgenstein's interlocuter expresses the same unease which Bambrough feels and wishes to dispel. But

Wittgenstein's response is: 'Why not?'

No doubt such a grouping (red, green and circular) strikes us as *arbitrary*. Just like that it would be arbitrary—as arbitrary as Bambrough's class of 'alphas'. But is it not possible to imagine a particular cultural background against which it no longer strikes us as arbitrary—much in the way that Wittgenstein does in *The Brown Book* in his example of a people who have a common name for red and green and another common name for yellow and blue? My point is that what makes such a classification not arbitrary is not its basis in any similarities and differences. I repeat: Of course there are many similarities and differences which we do not note and could have noted. And it may be revealing, as Wisdom brings out so well, to note them and mark them in our language by an alteration of the boundaries of some of our concepts. But there is not a common pool of similarities and differences from which different cultures make different selections. As Wittgenstein puts it in *The Brown Book*: 'We use the word "similar" in a huge family of cases' (p. 133). And let me add that people belonging to alien cultures may well use the word 'similar' in ways different from any of the ways with which we are familiar. In any case, within our own culture, Wittgenstein points out: 'There is something remarkable about saying that we use the word "strain" for both mental and physical strain because there is a similarity between them. Should we say we use the word "blue" both for light blue and dark blue because there is a similarity between them? If you were asked "Why do you call this 'blue' also?", you would say "Because this *is* blue too" ' (ibid., pp. 133–4).

It is indeed remarkable that we use the word 'strain' in these two cases, remarkable that we use the word 'deep' to describe a man's sorrow, a singer's voice, and the well in his garden, remarkable that we use the word 'high' to describe the note that a man sings as well as the position where he stands, remarkable that we call a note and its seventh 'the same note', and no less remarkable that we use the word 'blue' to describe the colour of the sky, one of the colours of the French flag, and that of the litmus paper when dipped in an alkaline solution. To say that we do so because in each case we see certain similarities explains nothing. It is just a restatement of what should strike us as remarkable. Our calling them by the same name, 'blue', and our finding them similar, are on the same level. Neither is deeper or more fundamental, neither supports the other; they are just two sides of the same coin. We may wonder: But are we not right to call them 'blue'? Are we not saying something true when we say that they are similar? The answer is: It depends what we are asking. In one kind of case we could say: Of course he is right; take the materials into the daylight and you will see he is right. As if to say: Indeed they are the same colour. In another case, where these questions are an expression of philosophical unease, we could say: Of course, we see a similarity between these things: 'That is how our concepts take it' (Wittgenstein, 1967, §568). Of course we are right, for that is the way we speak, that is how we use the word 'blue'. But are we right to use it that way? I am suggesting that this last question comes from confusion, as does the answer to it: 'We are right if there is really a similarity between these things.' In saying this we seem to be basing our use of the word on something more fundamental, something that we think justifies it. I don't mean something that we think justifies it in this particular case, but in any of the cases in which it is correct to use it. In the former case we take the use of the word for granted; in the latter we only succeed in going round in a circle.

I said that this does not mean that there is nothing further that philosophy can say here. It can. But what it says should enhance what is remarkable, not explain it. It should kindle wonder, not smother it. Thus about the claim that there is no colour that is both like red and green, Wittgenstein's alter-ego asks: Has nature nothing to say here? Wittgenstein answers: 'Indeed she has—but she makes herself audible in another way' (ibid., §364). She makes herself audible through the kind of reactions we exhibit naturally when we have received a certain kind of training, or through more primitive reactions, or through what we find memorable, etc. I do not have the time to develop this further now: I touch on it very briefly in my paper to the Aristotelian Society (1978–9), in the two paragraphs that follow the question 'Does this leave language suspended in mid-air?' on page 52, and discuss it in greater detail in *Induction and Deduction*. But in any case Wittgenstein discusses it in great detail in *Zettel* and also in his other writings.

I want to make a brief comment about Bambrough's example of the South Sea islanders who differ from us in their classification of trees—because it is pertinent to what I have been saying. We and they differ in the way we classify trees, but we both agree on what we call a tree. It is *trees* that we both classify, though we classify them differently. Our names for trees and theirs draw on similarities and differences *between trees*, albeit different ones. Classification necessarily presupposes objects, or situations, or whatever, that we can refer to, name and characterise prior to and, therefore, independently of the classification. The similarities and differences that it draws on goes with that; they belong with our name for or characterisation of what we classify. We do not, as it were, classify bare particulars; we do not start in a grammatical vacuum. And where we have objects to classify, we have already names for them, and so a whole range of similarities and differences which we can select from in classifying them in different ways. That is we must already have come a long way before we can classify things; we must already have things to classify. So the similarities and differences that hold between what we already call by a certain name cannot give us the basis for our use of that name. Consequently, neither can they give us the *ultimate* basis for our use of any word which presupposes its use. The reason for this is the same as the one Bambrough gives as to why common properties cannot give us the ultimate basis for our use of any word: 'Even a concept which can be explained in terms of necessary and sufficient conditions cannot be *ultimately* explained in such terms' (p. 214). And Bambrough underlines 'ultimately'. For, he says, 'to satisfy the craving for an ultimate explanation of "brother" in such terms it would be necessary to define "male" and "sibling", and the words in which "male" and "sibling" were defined, and so on *ad infinitum* and *ad impossibile*.' Similarly, if we are to explain what we mean by, say, 'elm tree', we shall point to similarities and differences between trees we call by that name and others we call by other names—as Bambrough suggests. But then we would have to go on to explain what makes a plant a tree as opposed to, say, a shrub, and so on. And what we shall come down to *ultimately* will not be, as it were, bare particulars which we call by the same name because of the way they resemble each other, but the *grammar* in which we carry out the comparisons in question.

So what we come down to *in the end* are not similarities and differences exhibited by nature. It is just at this point that Wittgenstein raised the question whether nature has nothing to say about the ways in which we go on in our use of words, about what we call 'the same', 'similar' and 'different' in various connections of our lives. That is he took a very different view from Bambrough's with regard to what is *ultimate* as far as the meaning and generality of our words are concerned. He took a very different view with regard to what underlies the way we take the examples we are given when learning to speak.

V Concluding Remarks: Wittgenstein and Plato

Certainly Wittgenstein was not a nominalist, and neither was he a realist. But he was even less of a realist than Bambrough makes him out to be. He criticised Plato's 'essentialism', the kind of essentialism he had himself embraced in the *Tractatus*. But there was something important in Plato's 'transcendentalism' which had appealed to him in the *Tractatus* and continued to do so later. I should like to conclude by making some general remarks about this because Bambrough, himself a scholar of Plato, ignores this side of Wittgenstein in his contribution to the problem of universals.

Bambrough puts the Platonic position of *universalia ante res* as the view that all games (for instance) must have a common relation to something that is not a game, namely a form (p. 218). But this is no longer the idea of a common property, as that of a common relation to a norm, measure or paradigm. Such norms or forms are *transcendental* in the sense that they are not among the things we talk about; they are among the things that enable us to talk in the ways we do about the things that we use language to talk about. We could say, as Wittgenstein said of samples or standards, that they are part of our language, paradigms in our language-games, something with which comparison is made (see Wittgenstein, 1963, §50). Certainly Wittgenstein regarded mathematics, including geometry, where the concepts used are sharply de-

fined, as a 'network of norms'. It is not in this that he differed
from Plato for whom too mathematics was a model for the
Forms—the most important. He agreed with Plato that
mathematical truths are timeless; but he thought that it does
not follow from this that mathematics itself is timeless. For he
thought that if, with Plato, we are to say that mathematical
truths are contained in the forms of mathematics, we should
not forget that these forms (Wittgenstein talks of 'concept-
formation' here) are in turn an expression of what we accept
as incontrovertibly true in mathematics and of what we regard
as the correct way of carrying out mathematical operations.
He would have said that the forms are not, as Plato thought,
something over and above what we actually do in carrying out
these operations. This is, of course, the same idea as the one I
have considered in connection with our use of words and their
generality; and it is just this part of Plato's 'essentialism' which
Wittgenstein rejected. He rejected the Platonic idea that
mathematical practice flows from the forms. He thought that
momentous discoveries in mathematics constitute *extentions* of
mathematics. Plato's view was that nothing that is new to us in
mathematics can be new to mathematics itself, and he took
the discovery that Meno's slave-boy makes as a paradigm of
mathematical discovery. Wittgenstein, on the other hand,
argued that developing a new proof in mathematics is more
like 'saying something new' than like 'making explicit the
implications of what has already been said'.

However Plato's view of the forms as distinct from sensible
objects is part of his critique of empiricism, though it is more
than that, and Wittgenstein would have gone along with this
critique a good part of the way and, in fact, did. Thus in the
Phaedo Socrates argues that we could not have acquired the
idea of equality from a perception of sticks and stones of
approximately equal length lying side by side. We would see
them lying side by side, but we wouldn't think of them as
equal unless we had the idea of equality. That idea cannot thus
be derived from sense experience. More generally Plato's view
is that we cannot derive our conception of what he calls the
forms from what is given to us in sense experience.
Wittgenstein expresses this same idea in the following remark:
'Do not believe that you have the concept of colour within you
because you look at a coloured object—however you look'

(Wittgenstein, 1967, §332). In other words, just because a creature can see coloured objects, it doesn't follow that he knows what a colour is, or has the concept of colour. In learning the meanings of words from 'ostensive definitions' we are pointed out things which we can see, hear or otherwise experience. But this doesn't mean that we can learn or acquire all the concepts that enter our judgments in this way. Wittgenstein points out that 'we must already be master of a language in order to understand an ostensive definition'. This does not mean, as Plato thought, that if a child is to learn from experience he must be in possession of certain concepts which he could not have acquired in his present life. It is here that Wittgenstein talks of 'training'. It makes it possible for the child to come to ask questions, among them questions about the meanings of words, and to understand explanations and definitions. Thus he learns some of the important concepts which belong with Plato's forms *indirectly*. For instance, he acquires the concept of number, among other things, in learning to count. He acquires these concepts in learning to act. What is true and important in Plato's view here is that we cannot acquire *all* our concepts *directly*, through abstraction from experience and generalisation, since all abstraction and generalisation presupposes a grasp of certain concepts and operations. And neither, for the same reason, can we acquire them by comparing one thing with many others, noticing similarities and differences between them. Here Wittgenstein speaks of 'the limits of empiricism'. It is here that justification by experience, with reference to similarities and differences, comes to an end.

I have suggested that there is a fairly close analogy between Plato's forms and what Wittgenstein called measures, norms, paradigms and exemplars. They lie outside the class of things we talk about and describe; they measure the members of the class. Hence those things that we describe as blue, for instance, may be said to be more or less blue, nearer to or further away from a standard sample of pure blue. In this way we are enabled to compare the members of the class with one another. Pure blue, as defined by the sample, is not something we can abstract or distil from blue things; it is what blue things 'approximate' to (in Plato's language)—some more, some less. It is itself an *ideal* in the sense of measure. But this term 'ideal' may mislead us. Its absolute purity, its undiluted character, its one-hundred per cent blueness, is not an extraordinary property which no actual object possesses. It is a matter of its role as an instrument of language (Wittgenstein, 1963, §50). It is a character of the phraseology we use in describing and comparing colours. In a sense it is perfectly true that it can only be realised in a world of pure intellect, such as we find in mathematics—an ideal world, a world of limits and parameters, a world in which all thought is absolutely sharp and perfectly determinate. But if we think of it as another place (and it is not at all obvious that Plato did— just as when he talked of a day when we would be judged naked by judges that are themselves naked it is not at all obvious that he was talking of another place and another time)—at any rate if we are ourselves inclined to do so, Wittgenstein's rejoinder is: 'Are you not confusing the hardness of a rule with the hardness of a material?' (Wittgenstein, 1956, Pt II, §87). Much further down he says: '... mathematics is *normative*. But "norm" does not mean the same thing as "ideal" ' (Pt V, §40).

Both Plato and Wittgenstein were concerned to get clear about the relation between forms or norms and the things we think and talk about in terms of them. I suppose that one of the differences between them was that while Plato thought of the world of physics as a shadow cast by the world of mathematics, and as such as having less reality, Wittgenstein thought that mathematics derives its reality as much from its use in 'civil life' as he called it—that is, its application in physics, engineering, accountancy, shopping, etc.—as these activities, in the form in which we practice them, are dependent on mathematics. That is, for Wittgenstein the dependency is a two-way one. In this he differs from Plato on one side and from Bambrough on the opposite side, for both of whom the dependency seems to go one way.

This is relevant to the central question about where we are to find the foundations of our forms of thought and speech without which they would be arbitrary. Plato and Wittgenstein in the *Tractatus* thought that they are to be found in a logic underlying the use of our language, itself authenticated by its very purity and absolute character. Bambrough is right in thinking that what Wittgenstein tries to bring out in his consideration of the example of games is that such an idea of the basis of our forms of thought and speech involves a deep-going misunderstanding. I have suggested that in so far as Wittgenstein did make a contribution to the traditional problem of universals, as I agree with Bambrough he did, this is part of a larger mosaic which embraces his whole philosophy of logic and mathematics. But I have also suggested that the line he took in turning away from his own early, quasi-Platonic ideas about the non-arbitrary character of our thought and language did not take him where Bambrough puts him.

When philosophers, like Plato, asked for a definition of 'knowledge' or 'virtue', the most serious of their difficulties came from the peculiarity of the situation in which we are when we do philosophy—'the tail catching' character of this enterprise as Professor Wisdom once called it. For it is the very ground on which philosophers stand with everyone else which they subject to inquiry. Here, not surprisingly, the greatest of them—Plato, Kant and Wittgenstein—though they moved in different directions, agreed at least on this much: that if scepticism is to be met, the 'basis' of our modes of speech and thought cannot be found among the things we speak and think about. It is, I think, precisely on this point that Bambrough misunderstands Wittgenstein. I find his attempt to follow Wittgenstein through in his 'relativism' half-hearted, and while he is absolutely right to make much of Wittgenstein's emphasis on instances and particular cases, he is wrong to make little of what Wittgenstein had to say on norms and paradigms. These are the two poles of Wittgenstein's treatment of the *generality* inherent in all forms of thought and speech, of which the traditional problem of universals is only a part.

10 Identity and Self-Knowledge

Of late sociologists and social psychologists have rightly wished to emphasise how much 'one's identity and self-evaluation seem importantly wedded to social circumstances'. These words come from a paper by the American psychologist Kenneth Gergen, read to a conference at the Centre for Psychological Studies in Chicago in December 1975 and later published in a book edited by Theodore Mischel entitled *The Self, Psychological and Philosophical Issues*. I take my start from that paper, and what interests me is how this right emphasis on 'social circumstances' leads the writer in the wrong direction.

Gergen has some perception of our nature as social beings and of the way we find our individuality in the life we share with other people. But he is led astray by confusing this with the contingent truth that we are influenced in the way we think of ourselves by the way others think of us. This latter is a matter of degree and varies from person to person. Whether and to what extent we are so influenced depends on how secure we are in our identity and how independent we are in our thinking. The fact that everybody has a breaking point and that once this point is reached one can become like putty in the hands of those who try to manipulate one, does not prove that one's identity is given to one by others. There are different possibilities here and they need to be distinguished from each other: (i) A person may change radically and come to a new identity. (ii) He may take on a false identity. (iii) He may shed a false identity and find himself. But on Gergen's view the notion of a false identity makes no sense. Hence the title of his paper: 'The Social Construction of Self-Knowledge'.

'One's identity and self-evaluation seem importantly wedded to social circumstances' (p. 147). This is right if it means that it is in the social environment into which one was born and in which one grows up that one finds one's identity and becomes oneself. It is wrong if it means to compare an individual's identity to the colour of a chameleon. For a chameleon has no true colour; only the one which its background gives it. But it is the latter view which Gergen supports. Individual identities are 'virtually interchangeable' and 'the notion of "true" knowledge of self' is a chimera. In any case, on Gergen's view, one does not find one's identity.

Once more, if this means that it does not come to one ready-made, that it is not something that awaits discovery and exists independently of what one gives oneself to and makes of oneself in the giving, then it is right. As Jean-Paul Sartre argues in *L'Etre et le Néant*, personal characteristics that define an individual's identity are not simply *given*; they do not exist 'en soi', or in themselves, as the properties that define a stone as granite do. The individual 'transcends' them through his power to make decisions and embark on new projects. However, this is not the line which Gergen takes. His view is that one does not find one's identity, since it is given to one by others. This is the opposite of Sartre's view, according to which we have the power to fight and reject the identity which others attempt to foist on us. Accepting it is sinking into 'bad faith'. Thus see Sartre's play *Huis Clos*.

There is an important sense in which what one can make of oneself is both made possible and given limits by the language and culture of the society to which one belongs, and also a sense in which the exceptional individual can transcend and innovate these limits. This needs discussion. But there is a big difference between the forms of apprehension and existence which one's culture and language make available to one and what other people actually think of one, the aspect under which they see one. Gergen runs these together and wrongly suggests that the aspect under which others see one determines one's identity. Such an aspect is certainly made possible by the concepts which one shares with others, and these concepts enter into the way one thinks of oneself. Thus the evaluative concept of cowardice may enter into one's soul-searchings when one asks whether one has been cowardly. In the very asking of this question one is taking a certain attitude towards something one has done. This attitude is personal; it defines an aspect of one's personality. But it is made possible by the public concept in question and the minimum of agreement in reactions and attitudes which underlies its sense. All that follows from this is that other people too can raise the question as to whether one has acted in a cowardly manner and condemn one's actions if they reach the conclusion that one's actions were cowardly. But from this much it does not even follow that one accepts other people's values and so shares their condemnation in a particular case. The relation between the individual and other people who share the concepts that enter into his thinking is much more complicated than Gergen appreciates.

There is another confusion. To say that 'the socially mediated constructions of ourselves are vitually interchangeable' (p. 150) is one thing, to say that it is 'possible for the individual to confirm virtually any concept of self at any time' because human behaviour is many-faced (p. 151) is quite another thing. On the first view there is no anchorage for what we think of ourselves; it is at the mercy of what others think of us. This, in turn, is determined by arbitrary social conventions. Such a view is incoherent, although it contains a distortion of something important, namely the social character of human beings and the dependence of individual identity on the language and culture of the individual. On the second view, there is an anchorage for what we think of ourselves in what we are like, only it is built on shifting sands—too shifting to provide an adequate mooring for our ideas. This too contains the exaggeration of an important truth: 'A person does not stand motionless and clear before our eyes ... like a garden at which ... we gaze through a railing, but a shadow ... behind which we can alternately imagine, with equal justification, that there burns the flame of hatred and of love' (Proust).

In his paper Gergen is avowedly opposing an empiricist view of the self of the kind to be found in the writings of Hume and Russell. On that view self-knowledge is to be characterised in terms of the possession of true beliefs about oneself. But in turning away from that view one needs to be careful not to fall into the kind of relativism which Gergen embraces. One reason why one must reject that view is because it entirely fails to do justice to the role of decision in what we normally mean by 'self-knowledge'. In fact one of the distinctive features of this is the way in which it straddles between the notions of belief and decision. Obviously a person who fails to recognise the truth in what could truly be said about him cannot be described as having self-knowledge. But recognising this is not enough, because a person may know a great deal about himself and still manage to make little of his life. He may know what he is like and yet not know his own mind where this is most crucial to him. And this is fundamental to what we mean by self-knowledge.

If I were pressed to make a brief statement, I would say that self-knowledge is knowing who one is and where one stands. Knowing who one is *is* being true to oneself—*authenticity*. A person who does not know where he stands does not know his own mind in the sense that he has not made up his mind, committed himself to a line of action. This is not a matter of not knowing what is in his mind in the sense of what he secretly yearns for, though he will not admit it to himself. It may involve that. But if it does, the failure does not consist merely in not recognising it. It consists primarily in not facing up to it, thus evading taking responsibility for it and making up his mind whether to endorse or to reject it. To endorse it would mean throwing his weight behind it, committing himself to pursuing it in certain circumstances. To do so or to give it up he must already stand somewhere, he must have other desires and concerns, regard certain things as important.

He may not know his own mind and still move in this direction or that under the pressure of certain needs—the need to please others, or to think well of himself, or to avoid passivity. Such a man has either not found himself, hasn't got a centre from which he acts, or he is false to himself. If we say that he is false to himself, we should remember that it is the self that is false, not his beliefs about himself—although, of course, these too may be false. But if so, he will have to see what is false in these beliefs before he can come to self-knowledge. He will have to stop running away. For only then will he be in a position to realise that it is up to him what he does with his life. To make anything of his life he must, of course, care for certain things, have independent interests, be related to people. If he has been running away from himself, then he must have found certain things painful, thought of some things as shameful. It cannot be that he is altogether indifferent. If he has been too dependent on other people to show initiative, then this is itself a form of relatedness to people which can provide a leverage for movement towards greater independence. Still there is also a certain kind of protective indifference which, given sufficient time, can smother all possibility of initiative. There are certain forms of evasion of autonomy where people reach a point of no return.

I said that self-knowledge is knowing who one is and where one stands. Knowing where one stands is taking responsibility for one's deepest and most fundamental beliefs. It is to think for oneself and act on one's own behalf—not because anybody else says so or expects it of one, not because it is the done thing, not because one has always done so. This is what is meant by *autonomy*. It involves the idea of being accountable for what one thinks and says. The former brings in criteria of truth, accuracy and reasonableness, and the latter the idea of taking responsibility for what one does. A person who is thus accountable is prepared to justify what he says or does, he stands by it, and will not shirk blame and punishment where it goes wrong.

In short, the two central ideas in our notion of self-knowledge are authenticity, or being true to oneself, and autonomy, or acting on one's own behalf. The idea of true beliefs about oneself is relevant in so far as false beliefs about oneself are normally maintained by a division of the self which frustrates autonomy and runs counter to authenticity. Here we should not forget that authenticity and autonomy are forms of knowledge—the former 'knowledge of who one is' and the latter 'knowledge of what one wants'.

When I say that false beliefs about oneself are normally maintained by a division of the self I am thinking of one common form of self-deception. Here a person is drawn into doing something in order to keep an unwelcome truth at bay, or to keep up certain appearances for self-consumption. The show of enthusiasm, concern or indifference by which he is taken in is not genuine; it is a put-up job. To keep it up he embarks on courses of action which he would otherwise have no cause to pursue, or refrains from embarking on projects which would otherwise interest him. Or, again, he may grow insensitive to his own reactions to certain situations, muffle them to the point of unrecognisability. That is, he is drawn into forms of action and behaviour which are protective or defensive in character and run counter to the development and pursuit of concerns and interests which would give substance to his life. This is the very opposite of the kind of wholeheartedness which is the mark of self-knowledge. Such wholeheartedness involves (i) knowing what one wants and having the courage of one's convictions, and (ii) being in touch with one's feelings, allowing them to inform one's intentions and actions.

When I speak of allowing one's feelings to inform one's intentions and actions I mean pusuing what one wants and what one can make sense of in what one goes for. This, of course, does not exclude doing things that are asked of one. By no means. One could say: If you are going to do what is asked of you, then be sure that you really want to do it. If you are going to do something in order to please someone, then be sure that you want to please him. In other words, don't do it out of anxiety or submissiveness. If you care for the other person, then in doing something to please him you will be acting on your own behalf. And if, by any chance, this involves displeasing others who do not hold him in favour, you would not be deterred. This is what it means to be autonomous and independent; and a person can hardly be that if he is not in touch with his feelings, if he is not behind his actions.

'But, on this view, if he is submissive, if that is the way he feels, should he not act that way?' Here one needs to distinguish between submitting to another's will and submitting to discipline or authority which may, in particular circumstances, be invested in another person, say, as a teacher. One can will to submit to discipline or authority, which may involve unquestioning obedience to another person in the role of spiritual teacher. Here one is behind the act of submission as an autonomous person with certain values and beliefs. Doing so may be something that does not come easily and requires a considerable degree of self-mastery. In such a case submitting, obeying and in the extreme case making oneself an instrument to, let us say, God, is not the expression of a submissive character, the character of a man who cannot stand opposition, withstand domination. For a person who cannot do so cannot serve God, since he cannot serve God unless he can do so on his own behalf. Besides if he is to serve

God he will have to oppose evil, in whatever form, and do so for no other reason than that it is evil. My point is that submissiveness is a mark of dependence, and a person who submits to another for the sake of a reward or in order to avoid incurring his displeasure resents what he gives up even when it serves the purpose for which he does so. He is thus not wholeheartedly behind his actions and behaviour.

I said that 'self-knowledge' straddles between the notions of belief and decision. The kind of decision that is in question here is the kind that enters into one's most basic beliefs— beliefs about what is important and valuable. The attitude of will that is at the heart of these beliefs is not something which the agent chooses, although it is subject to reflection and revision.[1] It involves his responsibility: it is *he* who endorses the values in question or evades doing so. And until he endorses them he is not a moral agent in the full sense—which doesn't mean that he is not responsible for what he does. There are, of course, degrees of evasion; but one who evades making his moral beliefs his own is a man who has no bearings and who may be said not to know what he wants. He plays at the things he does in life, or he does things for the sake of appearances, or merely to please others, to gain their approval, to keep their good opinion. Or he throws himself into projects to avoid facing the void in him. The latter is Kafka's 'complete citizen' who 'travels over the sea in a ship with foam before him and wake behind, that is, with much effect round about'. But, as Kafka points out, different though he may seem from 'the man in the waves on a few planks of wood that even bump against and submerge each other', they are nevertheless alike. 'For he and his property are not one, but two, and whoever destroys the connection destroys him at the same time' (Kafka, 1948). It is at such extremes that the question 'What do I want?' shades into the question 'Who am I?' The search to which it may be a precursor involves decision—at least it involves the will. Negatively this consists of giving up pursuits and attitudes to which one clings defensively, and positively it involves entering into commitments which give direction and sustenance to one's life. The man in question may thus be described as 'having found himself' or as 'having come to self-knowledge'. The two expressions are equivalent.

If we say that he has *found* himself, this does not mean that there was something there waiting to be discovered—as Freud misled himself into thinking with Leonardo da Vinci's analogy of the sculpture in the block of marble. Although even here there is this truth, namely that the analyst does not impose what he sees or believes he sees on the patient, but enables him to shed what he clings to defensively so that he can himself face what he has been avoiding. Analysis does not work 'per via di porre', that is by adding or appending something, but 'per via di levare', that is by discarding something. This is what I referred to as the negative aspect of self-discovery—what Freud calls 'making the unconscious conscious'. Here there *is* something waiting to be discovered. But that discovery is not the end of the road to self-knowledge, it is the beginning. For now the person in question has the freedom and the opportunity to look for a way in life. It is here that 'finding' what one wants *is* 'making' something of oneself.

I think it is important to distinguish between this sense of 'coming to know what one wants' and 'coming to recognise one's desires and appetites' which, in Freud's terminology, one has 'repressed'. Consider a man in whom the politeness and consideration he shows to others is a 'reaction-formation'. We may say: 'Under this kind exterior he really wants to hurt the people who come closest to him, although he doesn't know this and won't acknowledge it.' If we are right, then that he wants to hurt those who are close to him is a fact about him and it is this that he deceives himself about. Now contrast this case with the man who 'doesn't know what he wants'. He may be a drifter or he may be a man faced with a dilemma and not knowing which way to go. Here not knowing where one is going, or which way one should take, is what we *mean* by 'not knowing what one wants'. What it calls for is a decision. But deciding here *is* finding a resolution to the dilemma that faces one. Such a decision, as Professor Winch puts it, is 'itself a sort of finding out what is the right thing to do' (Winch, 1972, p. 165). More than this, it is a finding out where one stands as a person. So Winch says that what such a person finds out is something about himself (p. 168). In the case of the drifter this amounts to finding something he can make sense of, something to which he can give himself. This would be a change in him we characterise by saying: 'He has stopped drifting; he has at last found himself.'

The difficulty lies in seeing how commitment or decision can amount to a discovery. A decision that resolves a dilemma is obviously not 'irresponsible' or 'arbitrary', since we do distinguish between a right decision and a wrong one. Yet it has to be 'creative',[2] it has to lay down a path as opposed to find one that is already there. All the same, this path must be one which the subject finds acceptable. Further, others must be able to recognise that when he says 'it is acceptable' he is not fooling himself. We can compare it, in some ways, to a judge's verdict which, though informed by a consideration of past verdicts in parallel cases, nevertheless creates a precedent and innovates the law. It innovates the law because it hits the right chord and is accepted by jurists. In the moral case what the decision innovates is the person who resolves the dilemma that faces him; and it can only do so if it is right. Otherwise he would be deceiving himself; he would be opting for a line of action he cannot fully support and stand behind. So if it is right (i) it must be *intelligible* to those who share the agent's values (though it need not be what they, themselves, would decide to do in his place), and (ii) it must be *accepted* by the agent, there must not be any part of him which opposes or remains aloof from it. This is what makes it a discovery.

So there are two different kinds of case in which a person may be said not to know what he wants—though we do not use the same expression to talk about the two cases: (i) 'He wants to do such-and-such, but he doesn't himself know *that* he wants to do so.' (ii) 'He doesn't know *what* he wants.' Correspondingly, there are, broadly speaking, two different forms of self-deception.[3] (i) In the one case, a person avoids facing or acknowledging some truth which he finds unpalatable. This may be a truth about himself. Consequently, he will have false *beliefs* about what is in question, beliefs for which he is responsible in the sense, at least, that he clings to them and is unwilling to give them up. (ii) In the other case, the deception consists not in the person having a false belief about himself, but in being *false in himself* or *false to himself*. So in the former case the person is deceived *about* something—it may be about himself, about what he feels or about what he is like. In the latter case he is deceived *in* himself. This often means that he is other than he *ought* to be and so involves a judgment of value.

Where a person is deceived in his beliefs he need not, of course, be self-deceived. To be self-deceived he must actively avoid recognising his error. But where he is deceived *in* himself he is *necessarily* self-deceived. For he is as he is because of the way he lives and the ends he pursues. His activity is confined to the pursuit of certain positive ends and the evasion that flows from this has to do with the nature of these ends. It stamps the self with duplicity in one kind of case and with falsity in another kind of case—where the person has himself no moral reservations about the ends he pursues: pleasure, power, prestige. (I have studied these two kinds of case in *Sense and Delusion* in examples from Tolstoy's stories and novels—Kitty Scherbatsky and Father Sergius as examples of the former kind, and Ivan Ilytch as an example of the latter kind.)

The terms 'duplicity', 'falsity' and 'unreality' which are used in cases of these kinds characterise the self. When a person to whom one of these epithets is applicable changes in such a way that the epithet no longer applies to him, we could say that 'he has stopped deceiving himself', 'he has found himself', 'he has come to know himself'. This involves coming to recognise certain things *about* himself, but is not the same thing as gaining this recognition. Thus self-knowledge is the antithesis of the kind of deception in which a person is deceived *in* himself—not merely about himself.

In a paper entitled 'Self-Knowledge' (in the volume where the paper I mentioned by Gergen was published) Professor Hamlyn largely agrees with my analysis.[4] Partly for this reason he thinks that self-knowledge is not the primary goal of psycho-analytic therapy (p. 185). While I can see why he says this, it seems to me that this claim takes a narrow view of analytic therapy. I would say, on the contrary, that analysis is concerned to get the analysand to face unpalatable facts about himself so that he is free to find himself—free because he is no longer engaged in fighting off their recognition. Doing so absorbs a person's energies and interests and so prevents the kind of exploration and outward movement necessary to finding and, therefore, coming to know oneself. To Hamlyn this 'outward movement' seems the opposite of what one would expect an analysis to encourage: 'Too much attention to facts about oneself may lead, not to self-knowledge ... but to self-consciousness' (p. 174). I would say that this depends on the spirit in which one attends to facts about oneself. Is one doing so defensively, or out of narcissism? If it involves pleasure, if it is infected with self-love, then indeed the movement will be an 'inward' one and the analysand will turn in on himself. This may be so even when the facts he keeps his gaze fixed on are themselves painful. For there is such a thing as feeling sorry for oneself or wallowing in one's misery. But such a movement of the soul constitutes a 'resistance' to analysis and its hold on the analysand will have to be loosened by analysis if the analysis is to move forward. In contrast, a discipline which demands the kind of attention that leads to facing up to what one finds unpalatable goes against the grain and is liberating. It does not lead to self-consciousness. Thus, unlike Hamlyn, I think of psycho-analysis as offering the possibility of a true spiritual exploration.

When describing the goal of psycho-analysis Freud said that its aim was 'to make what is unconscious conscious'. He believed that insight calls for some change so that it can be received and that it, in turn, opens up the possibility for further change. He was particularly sensitive to the charge that the analyst imposes his own views and values on the patient and so he insisted on the analyst's passivity and neutrality: He should be like a mirror. The patient must be provided with the opportunity to assume responsibility for the course the analysis takes and for his life. Later, when formulating the aim of analysis, Freud said: To ensure that 'where id is there ego shall be'. He meant that analysis should provide the opportunity for the growth of the self towards autonomy. Obviously this needs discussion.

11 Rhees: 'The Tree of Nebuchadnezzar'—some Questions

In 'The Tree of Nebuchadnezzar' (Rhees, 1971) Rush Rhees writes about what stands in the way of discussing with others one's difficulties and perplexities about sex. This has to do with the nature of these difficulties. He contrasts them with difficulties in learning arithmetic for instance: 'You can describe the difficulties which children generally have in learning arithmetic, and you may discuss methods for meeting them.' Sexual difficulties are not like that. Rhees brings out their differences by comparing them with other kinds of difficulty. He contrasted elsewhere[1] philosophical difficulties with difficulties which an engineer may encounter in building a bridge. It were better if the engineer hadn't met any difficulties and he will do his best to overcome or remove them. Those after him who learn from his contribution may manage to avoid them. This would be a gain. In philosophy it is not like that; the difficulties are not external to the subject. But with sex we cannot speak of a 'subject' and the difficulties cannot be separated from the person who has them. In that case what does overcoming them, learning or coming to terms with them amount to?

Rhees compares them with moral and religious difficulties—perhaps someone whose child has died. He needs time, patience, attention (to collect himself) and solitude. He needs to work things out for himself. One could even say that things must have time to work themselves out in him—two sides of the same coin. Still he can talk with a friend or priest—not just any friend or priest—and find help. In a chapter in *The Brothers Karamazov* entitled 'Peasant Women Who Have Faith' (Bk II ch. 3) Dostoyevsky illustrates what this may amount to.[2]

But Rhees wants to emphasise where perplexities and

difficulties about sex differ from these difficulties and why a man should not even wish to discuss them with *anyone*. In a later contribution (Rhees, 1972) he puts the whole emphasis on this point: 'There are two topics I wish I could have brought out; the rest does not matter.' In 'The Tree of Nebuchadnezzar' he connects this point ('the two topics') with the fact that 'sex is something between people; a form of communication (if the word has any shape left). Awakening and bewilderment are both connected with this.'

He criticises the psycho-analyst for failing to appreciate this. He is thinking of the analyst, I think, as someone who thinks of the bewilderment as a symptom of something having gone wrong which needs to be put right. The difficulty is perhaps regarded as something in the nature of an inhibition which stands in the way of satisfaction. In this way of thinking the fact that 'sex is something between people' is lost sight of. Wilhelm Reich at his worst provides a good example of what Rhees has in mind. We can find examples of it in Freud's thought too; only we find there also what pulls in the opposite direction. But more than this Rhees thinks that the psycho-analyst, by the very nature of his trade, cannot understand and respect his patient's need for privacy as far as his treatment goes, and with *some* justification. No part of the patient's life, thoughts and feelings must be kept out of analysis. If the patient does so this is an expression of his resistances to being analysed and so to becoming different. He doesn't want to speak because what is in question is painful, or he feels ashamed of it, or because speaking about it will make it impossible for him to continue to live as he has always done: 'A man told a Freudian psycho-analyst that he did not mind speaking of his sexual aberrations ...—although he was ashamed of these and would not speak of them in public; but he was not willing to speak of his deeper feelings for his wife, nor of hers for him, though *shame* didn't enter here. The psycho-analyst was irritated and could not see why, "when there's no earthly reason why you should *not*" ' (Rhees, 1971, p. 24).

Why on earth should he not want to speak about these things if he is not ashamed or find doing so painful! I suppose many psycho-analysts would not understand. Perhaps their very way of looking at things, the psycho-analytic framework of thought, would prevent them from doing so. I am not so sure. But let us turn to the 'two topics' which Rhees wishes he could have brought out in his earlier contribution. These have to do with what it means to 'surrender what is innermost in one'. Rhees considers Thomas Mann's story 'Mario and the Magician'.

He distinguishes between not wishing to speak about something shameful in one's past, something one is ashamed of, and not wishing to speak of something intimate, something that is not for display or even for other people's ears—something that is part and parcel of one's very soul, what is 'innermost'.[3] In the latter—for example Mario's feelings for Sylvestra—we have something that one can only expose oneself. Someone else, for instance Giovanotto, may know something about Mario's feelings and tell others what he knows. But that would not be the same—it would not be 'surrendering' what is innermost. Only Mario *can* do that.[4] That is the second topic. The first one is this: If what Mario exposed of himself had been something disgraceful it would not have been 'what was innermost in him'. So the first topic concerns the matter or character of what is exposed ('what is innermost') and the second the manner in which this is done ('surrendered'). Both bring in the self. The first brings it in as the object of surrender and the second as the agent. Hence the two topics are inseparable: 'no one else *could* have exposed Mario's innermost feelings and so degraded them' (Rhees, 1972, p. 51).

'Suppose a man did something ugly and disgraceful in the past, and he's terrified now lest it come to light ... Suppose I discover and expose this. He may be broken and may kill himself.' There is something apparently paradoxical here. Why should his being broken wait upon his being exposed? If what he did is something terrible and he himself thinks so, then it seems that whether or not the world knows of it must be irrelevant—it cannot make what he did more terrible than it already is. On the other hand, if it is other people's knowledge of it and their condemnation of him that leads him to kill himself, then what distresses him is not what he did and the terribleness of it, but public disgrace. And the pain caused by public disgrace is not as deep a pain as the one that belongs with the realisation of having done something terrible and ugly. Even if they are often intertwined they are distinct.

Still a man who tries to keep what he did a secret for fear of public disgrace may be fearing that public knowledge and disgrace, painful as this is in itself, may turn into a vehicle of self-knowledge. Once exposed he may no longer keep his thoughts in check; public knowledge may give the character of what he did an independent life which destroys his equanimity. There is here food for thought on the nature of *shame* which, it seems, logically requires an onlooker, even though it is possible to feel shame for something one has done which nobody knows about.

It is important to distinguish, as Rhees does, between (i) those things which a man may be reluctant to speak about because of an overpowering sense of shame or guilt, and (ii) those things of which he would not speak although he feels no shame or guilt. There are things, for instance, a man would not speak of out of modesty or 'pudeur'. For instance, an act of bravery he has done. If it were absolutely essential he would speak of it in a matter of fact way (not affected) and when it is over and done with wish that everyone should forget it.

With Mario's passion for Sylvestra it is I think somewhat different. It is not something Mario could bring himself to talk about. It is too 'private' or 'intimate' a thing. But can the horribleness of what takes place at the end of 'Mario and the Magician' be confined to this? There Mario is brought, through trickery and manipulation, to expose (not merely talk about) an emotion which is intimate. This takes place in front of an audience, contact with whom (even if it were compassionate) wounds and bruises it. Mario, then, surrenders what is innermost in him. But in different circumstances would it have amounted to this? Are the circumstances relatively unimportant? Does it make little difference who receives Mario's words? Is a confession of what is innermost always a surrendering of it in the sense in question? (Surely one can confess one's love and one's faith as well as one's guilt.)

I do not know whether Rhees thinks these matters are relatively unimportant. He thinks, for instance, and I agree, that Giovanotto whose will Cipolla manipulates is not degraded in the way that Mario is. The latter is degraded because of what he has surrendered and he could not have emerged with his self-respect and dignity intact:

A devotion like Mario's is nothing that a hypnotist or politician can heal or bend or govern ... Cipolla ... may never have imagined that there could be any devotion into which his 'division' could not be forced—in which it is 'the whole man' or nothing. Devotion cannot be organised ... No more than courage can. A devotion like Mario's can only come from him ...[5] The further we take this, the better we see how it is something of which he cannot speak (Rhees, 1972, p. 53).

I find it difficult to follow the logic of the last sentence I have quoted. I am not saying that Rhees is wrong or illogical; but simply that I am unable to follow him in the transition to that last sentence. The idea is that to speak about it, given what it is—that is, what is innermost in him—is to *betray* it and therefore *oneself*.

Is this why Cordelia cannot speak her love for her father like her sisters? They had no real love and so they could be eloquent. Their words came to them easily: it was just a question of uttering the right words, of arranging them in the appropriate manner—words did not have to be pulled out of their soul. What Cordelia felt was not something that could be shown at will, given on demand. It could at best be snatched from her heart—for it was something real and deep. It could not be exhibited in public, lend itself to the flattery or gratification[6] of the person loved. But here again are special circumstances: the occasion is a public one and what Lear wants to hear is for self-consumption. This is manipulation, exploitation and the kind of devotion which Cordelia had for her father cannot be pushed or manipulated thus—not even by her father. My point its: She cannot speak about it because of what speaking amounts to in *these* circumstances—for here she cannot speak without being manipulated; speaking here *is* 'surrender'.

But is it always? If, for instance, Tolstoy's Anna, troubled for loving someone other than her husband, were to speak about it to a priest, would she have degraded her feelings? Would her confession be a 'surrender'? Would speaking to a psycho-analyst about what is innermost in one be necessarily a 'surrender'? I do not know the answer to these questions; I am merely asking them.

To return to Mann's story. There is, then, the nature of
what Cipolla draws out of Mario. There is the fact that Mario
does not merely talk about it—which would have been bad
enough under the circumstances—but lives it through. What
is revealed is not something related, something the audience
come to know second-hand; it is the real thing. This is one
aspect of what takes place which Rhees draws attention to,
namely that Mario himself does the giving away—as no one
else could—and so betrays what is innermost in him. If what
he revealed or displayed had been something else it might not
have mattered in the same way. If he had revealed his feelings
for some advantage or personal gain he would have done
something base of which he might later feel deeply ashamed,
and it might have broken him. If he had revealed his feelings
to a friend or psycho-analyst it *might* not have been the same.
Mario would not have done so, but that is another matter. I
say 'might' since there would have been a conflict of loyalties:
Could I be helped to try to come to terms with what I feel
without cheapening, debasing or betraying it? The question is
a moral one and the answer to it would depend on who I am
and what it is I feel. Rhees' claim, I think, is that there are
certain things I cannot share, communicate or reveal to
another without degrading it and so lowering myself, and that
if I must come to terms with it I must do so alone. Here no one
can help me—neither friend nor analyst. Talking about it to a
psycho-analyst, taking it to psycho-analysis, is itself endowed
with a moral significance to which a psycho-analyst's whole
training tends to blind him.

Returning to Mario, there is, I think, another aspect of the
matter of which I thought at first Rhees made little. I mean the
kiss, meant for Sylvestra, which Mario implants on the
deformed Cipolla. This is not incidental to what takes place on
the fated evening and Thomas Mann could not have left it out
without diminishing the impact of what happens. Earlier I
distinguished between exposing one's feelings and merely
talking about them, between letting someone know what one
feels about some matter and letting him witness it directly—
and one cannot do the latter passively, without putting oneself
into action, without coming alive to the feelings and thoughts
in question. That is why where there is betrayal here it is
necessarily self-betrayal—one betrays oneself. Now the kiss is

part of that. It is meant for Sylvestra; it carries or embodies what Mario wants to give her—her and no one else. Yet he is tricked and deluded and he gives it to Cipolla. This is surely part of what makes what is happening so horrible—a horror which is built up gradually, step by step, in Mann's narrative of the evening's performance, even of the earlier events related in the story.

If Mario had been able to give this kiss to Sylvestra in the privacy of his room all would have been well. If he had given it to her and she had rejected it and ridiculed it this would have been wounding to Mario. It would have hurt him deeply, but he would not have been degraded. If he had kissed her in public, or worse in front of an audience, knowingly and deliberately, he would have been doing something foul to her; but then the kiss itself would not have been what it is in the story. It would not have been the whole souled thing it is, capable of withering in the wrong hands and the wrong place. If Mario thought he was giving her the kiss in private and suddenly realised he was being watched by a thousand eyes this would come much nearer to what we have in the story. But not quite. For not only does the kiss bear Mario's soul and what it is alive with is not for other people's eyes, but it must find the light of Sylvestra's response. Otherwise it would bruise and perish. In Thomas Mann's story it is made into an object of public spectacle and it does not find the light of Sylvestra's response. But more than this, it lights upon Cipolla's flesh and hurts itself against its response. There is something grotesque here which adds to the sinisterness of what takes place.

Giovanotto, the cheeky youth, who at a word from Cipolla bends forward in pain, the defiant Roman whose limbs at first merely twitch (like an engine which won't start straight away but gives a sign that it is in working order) and who later joins the crowd of somnambulistic dancers, and finally Mario—these blend to weave a sinister pattern. The pattern is, as Rhees points out, part of a larger whole. But each part of it is different and has its own peculiar character.

The character of Mario's kiss is complex and what it is makes it fit for the climax of the story. Rhees was not, of course, primarily concerned with its position in the story, though this cannot be entirely separated from the questions he discusses. On first reading Rhees' letter I disagreed with him on several points until reflection brought me to understand him better. I think that what he tries to bring out is important, namely that there are certain matters concerning a person which he cannot communicate or discuss with another, not because these involve something of which he feels ashamed. Certain matters concerning love and sex are among these.

But is there no need for qualification? I ask and I do not know. Which way one goes would have serious implications for how one regards psycho-analytic therapy.

Notes

CHAPTER 1

1. Here Wittgenstein speaks of 'the limits of empiricism'.
2. This is not always true in philosophy. There are times when I have to enter into and appreciate a part of language and the kind of activities in the weave of which it is used which, in one sense, I may be familiar with (and even this may not be the case) although my understanding of the language is external or perfunctory.
3. What I come to in this kind of philosophical reflection is contained in what I already know. This is not the same point as the one made in saying that I must ask the question for myself and so come to the 'answer' on my own. If one says that the 'answer' must come from myself one runs the risk of confusing these two points, namely that (i) the 'answer' is already possessed by me and (ii) that it cannot be an 'answer' for me if it is second-hand. Both these points apply to the discovery which Meno's boy makes. In the case of coming to moral knowledge it is only the second point that is relevant and important.

CHAPTER 2

1. Wittgenstein's characterisation of logic and ethics in the *Tractatus*.
2. Equivalent to the sense in which Simone Weil uses the term 'supernatural'.
3. What is in question is the same as what Simone Weil calls 'la pesanteur' or 'moral gravity'. She discusses its manifold vicissitudes in her book *La Pesanteur et la Grâce* (*Gravity and Grace*).
4. Even Christ knew temptation and experienced the void which remaining true to the highest good generates.
5. This idea raises difficulties which I shall not consider now.
6. These come to the same thing.
7. Both Kierkegaard and Simone Weil characterise this attitude of will as 'patience'.

CHAPTER 3

1. See Chapter 6, section II below.
2. I use the expression 'eternal life' to mean something that is opposed to and, therefore, something that excludes what is meant by 'eternal damnation'.

3. Remember Socrates' equation between virtue and knowledge.
4. The unity of the virtues.
5. See Weil, 1953, esp. pp. 95–9.

CHAPTER 5

1. I do not think I need to argue this point now. See Phillips 1964–5.
2. It is, of course, true that in coming to know and love someone I may discover new values and so acquire a new disposition of will. But my point is that there is no necessity about this.

CHAPTER 6

1. He wrote 'Gods' (1944) against the background of the influence of logical positivism in the philosophy of religion. 'Religious Belief' (1955–6) is a discussion of the philosophical views in Professor Braithwaite's lecture *An Empiricist's View of the Nature of Religious Belief* and in a collection of papers edited by Professors Flew and MacIntyre under the title *New Essays in Philosophical Theology*, papers in a positivist tradition.
2. I am not saying that *any* view of the world as a whole is religious, nor that the right kind of view of the world is all there is to a religious belief.
3. Dostoyevsky meant it to be a portrait of Christ's love for the afflicted.
4. For a detailed discussion of this point see Dilman, 1973a, chapter 11, 'Logical Necessity' and Wittgenstein, 1956.
5. These are words which Wittgenstein used in elucidating the notion of logical truth. See Wittgenstein, 1956, Pt I, §116.
6. Here 'taking them on trust' does *not* mean 'believing them without grounds or reasons'.
7. 'Suppose someone were a believer and said: "I believe in a Last Judgement", and I said: "Well, I'm not sure. Possibly." You would say that there is an enormous gulf between us. If he said, "There is a German aeroplane overhead", and I said, "Possibly, I'm not sure", you'd say we were fairly near.'—Wittgenstein, 1966, p. 53.
8. He walked from village to village, begged for his bread, took some scolding and reviling, until he was arrested, classed as a tramp and sent to Siberia for having no passport, where he became a hired-man to a well-to-do peasant, working in the kitchen garden, teaching children and attending to the sick.
9. There are some further questions here which I take up in the following study—see pp. 109–35.

CHAPTER 7

1. Reference to a world beyond this one, one that transcends time and the senses, can be found in the language of other religions as well.

2. Wittgenstein speaks of theology as 'grammar' and says that 'grammar tells what kind of object anything is' (Wittgenstein, 1963, §373). He might have said that such theological remarks as 'God is a transcendent being' are deposited in the archives of Christian language.

3. For a more detailed treatment of this topic see Dilman, 1972.

4. 'Below' here is an evaluative term.

5. Winch, 1968, pp. 12–13. For a fuller discussion of this point see Dilman, 1973b, §1V, pp. 28–32.

6. See Weil, 1963.

7. Simone Weil says of it that although it is 'personal' it 'enshrines an intimation of divine love'—Weil, 1959, p. 152.

CHAPTER 8

1. I do the same in connection with the so-called 'principle of induction' or 'belief in the uniformity of nature' which Russell was disturbed at being unable to justify—see Dilman, 1973a pt I, ch. 3.

2. One could say that what shows a mathematical proposition to be false also shows it to be senseless—its sense and truth collapse together (see Wittgenstein, 1967, §131). This is also related to Wittgenstein's argument that in mathematics *proof* gives *sense* to mathematical symbols.

CHAPTER 9

1. See also Dilman (1978–9), sections I and II.

CHAPTER 10

1. See my discussion of this in Chapter 5 above.

2. This is intimately connected with what Winch says about its 'non-universalisability'.

3. This is one of the central themes of Dilman and Phillips, 1971.

4. I should like to acknowledge a debt to Hamlyn. What I say here partly grew from reflecting on what he says in his paper.

CHAPTER 11

1. Rhees, 1969, see 'The Study of Philosophy'.

2. I think these examples throw light on some aspects of psycho-analytic therapy. This needs developing; but I shall not do so here.

3. Why is love a deeper feeling than envy, for instance, or hatred? Why does it belong to a deeper level of the soul?

4. This is a grammatical remark and has to do with what 'surrendering' means in this context.

5. It cannot be put into him—i.e. induced by hypnosis—or pushed around. If you try to push it around you break the man: ' "the whole man" or nothing'.

6. I mean self-gratification.

Bibliography

Bambrough, Renford (1960–1), 'Universals and Family Resemblances', *Arist. Soc. Proc.*

Braithwaite, R. B. (1955), *An Empiricist's View of the Nature of Religious Belief* (Cambridge University Press).

Dilman, İlham (1972), 'Wittgenstein on the Soul', *Understanding Wittgenstein*, edited by Godfrey Vesey (Macmillan).

—— (1973a), *Induction and Deduction, A Study in Wittgenstein* (Blackwell).

—— (1973b), 'Freud and Psychological Determinism', *The Human World*.

—— (1975), *Matter and Mind, Two Essays in Epistemology* (Macmillan).

—— (1978–9), 'Universals: Bambrough on Wittgenstein', *Arist. Soc. Proc.*

Dilman, İlham and Phillips, D. Z. (1971), *Sense and Delusion* (Routledge & Kegan Paul).

Dostoyevsky, Fyodor (1957), *The Brothers Karamozov*, translated by Constance Garnett (Everyman's Library).

—— (1956), *Crime and Punishment*, translated by David Magarshack (Penguin Classics).

Drury, M. O'C., *Letters to a Student of Philosophy* (unpublished).

Eliot, T. S. (1955), 'Burnt Norton', *Four Quartets* (Faber and Faber).

Flew, Antony and MacIntyre, Alasdair (1955), *New Essays in Philosophical Theology* (SCM Press).

Foot, Philippa (1958), 'Moral Beliefs', *Arist. Soc. Proc.*

Freud, Sigmund (1933), *New Introductory Lectures on Psycho-Analysis*, translated by W. J. H. Sprott (New York: W. W. Norton).

—— (1948), *Beyond the Pleasure Principle*, translated by C. J. H. Hubback (The Hogarth Press).

Gergen, Kenneth J. (1977), 'The Social Construction of Self-Knowledge', *The Self, Psychological and Philosophical Issues*, edited by Theodore Mischel (Blackwell).

Hamlyn, David W. (1977), 'Self-Knowledge', *The Self, Psychological and Philosophical Issues*, edited by Theodore Mischel (Blackwell).

Hume, David (1957), *An Inquiry Concerning the Principles of Morals* (The Liberal Arts Press).

—— (1967), *A Treatise of Human Nature*, edited by L. A. Selby-Bigge (Oxford University Press).

Ibsen, Henrik (1971), 'The Master Builder', *The Master Builder and Other Plays* (Penguin Classics).

Kafka, Franz (1948), *The Diaries*, vol. I (1910–13), edited by Max Brod (London).

Kant, Immanuel (1961), *Critique of Pure Reason*, translated by Norman Kemp Smith (Macmillan).

Kierkegaard, Søren (1961), *Purity of Heart*, translated by Douglas Steere (Fontana).

Mann, Thomas (1956), 'Mario and the Magician', *Death in Venice and Seven Other Stories* (New York: Vintage Books).

Merton, Thomas (1957), *No Man is an Island* (Dell Paperback).

Nietzsche, Friedrich (1973), *Beyond Good and Evil* (Penguin Classics).

Pears, D. F. (1953), 'Universals', *Language and Logic*, vol. II, edited by A. G. N. Flew (Blackwell).

Phillips, D. Z. (1964–5), 'Does it Pay to be Good?', *Arist. Soc. Proc.*

Plato (1952), *Symposium* (Penguin Classics).

—— (1957), 'Theaetetus', *Plato's Theory of Knowledge*, translated by Francis Cornford (The Liberal Arts Press).

—— (1961), 'Meno', *Protagoras and Meno* (Penguin Classics).

—— (1973), 'Phaedo', *The Last Days of Socrates* (Penguin Classics).

—— (1973), *Gorgias* (Penguin Classics).

Price, H. H. (1953), *Thinking and Experience* (Hutchinson's University Library).

Proust, Marcel (1952), *In Remembrance of Things Past*, translated by C. K. Scott Moncrieff (London).

—— (1952), *A La Recherche du Temps Perdu* (Gallimard).

Rhess, Rush (1969), *Without Answers* (Routledge & Kegan Paul).

—— (1970), *Discussions of Wittgenstein* (Routledge & Kegan Paul).

—— (1971), 'The Tree of Nebuchadnezzar', *The Human World* (August).

—— (1972), 'Correspondence and Comments', *The Human World* (February).

Rousseau, Jean-Jacques (1972), *The Social Contract* (Penguin Classics).

Sartre, Jean-Paul (1939), *Esquisse d'une Théorie des Émotions* (Paris: Hermann).

—— (1945), *Huis-Clos* (Gallimard).

—— (1953), *L'Être et le Néant* (Gallimard).

Tolstoy, Leo (1960), 'Father Sergius', *The Kreutzer Sonata and Other Stories*, translated by Aylmer Maude (Oxford University Press).

Weil, Simone (1948), *La Pesanteur et la Grâce* (Librairie Plon).

—— (1953), *La Connaissance Surnaturelle* (Gallimard).

—— (1959), *Waiting on God*, translated by Emma Craufurd (Fontana Books).

—— (1963), 'Human Personality', *Selected Essays 1934–43*, translated by Richard Rees (Oxford University Press).

—— (1968), 'Some Thoughts on the Love of God', *On Science, Necessity and the Love of God*, edited and translated by Richard Rees (Oxford University Press).

Winch, Peter (1968, 1972), *Moral Integrity* (Blackwell), reprinted in *Ethics and Action* (Routledge & Kegan Paul).

—— (1972), 'The Universalizability of Moral Judgments', *Ethics and Action* (Routledge & Kegan Paul).

Wisdom, John (1953), *Philosophy and Psycho-Analysis* (Blackwell).

—— (1957), 'Proof and Explanation', Virginia Lectures (unpublished).

—— (1965), *Paradox and Discovery* (Blackwell).

Wittgenstein, Ludwig (1956), *Remarks on the Foundations of Mathematics* (Blackwell).

—— (1961a), *Note-Books 1914–16* (Blackwell).

—— (1961b), *Tractatus Logico-Philosophicus*, translated by Pears and McGuinness (Routledge & Kegan Paul).

—— (1963), *Philosophical Investigations* (Blackwell).

—— (1965), 'Notes on Talks with Wittgenstein', taken by Friedrich Waismann, *Phil. Rev.* (January).

—— (1966), *Lectures and Conversations on Aesthetics, Psychology and Religious Belief*, edited by Cyril Barrett (Blackwell).

—— (1967), *Zettel* (Blackwell).

—— (1969a), *The Blue and Brown Books* (Blackwell).

—— (1969b), *On Certainty* (Blackwell).

Index